Sex Tips for Pandas

Sex Tips for Pandas

Brian Luff
& Georgina Sowerby

Fit2Fill Limited

Sex Tips for Pandas

First edition published 2009 by Mam Tor Books

This second edition published 2011 by Fit2Fill Limited, 7 Bourne Court, Southend Road, Woodford Green, IG8 8HD

© Copyright Brian Luff & Georgina Sowerby 2009-2011

All rights reserved. No parts of this publication may be produced, stored in or introduced into a retrieval system, or transmitted in any form or by any means such as electronic, mechanical, or otherwise without the prior permission of the author and publisher.

Cover design: Liam Sharp

ISBN 978-1-4478-6098-3

Acknowledgements

We would like to send a million thanks to the following people, without whom our podcasts and radio shows, and this book, would not have been possible. Barbara and Malcolm Sowerby, Ralph and Olive West, Richard Cray, Alan Benns, Julie Church-Benns, David Kibble, Emily Gordon, Lawrence Staden, John Florey, Joey Robinson, Peter Buckley Hill, Peter Grahame, Steve Simms, Nathan Hill, Peter Buckman Timothy Blahout and Liam Sharp. Also, huge thanks to all the artists and writers who have contributed to both Comedy 365 and Sketch Club, and to the thousands of listeners who have downloaded our podcasts, listened to our radio shows and sent in content for our programmes. Please note that one or two of the names in this book have been changed to far more amusing ones.

Kalashnikov Vodka sponsored The Sowerby and Luff Show, and Sowerby and Luff in Edinburgh in 2007-2008.

Introduction

Much has been written about Giant Pandas. But not many people know that when you stroke a Giant Panda, it feels unpleasantly rough and spiky, not soft and cuddly like the fake fur on the panda toys we're more used to cuddling. Georgina and I know a lot of unusual stuff about Giant Pandas. These fragile and endangered animals are undoubtedly the favourite creatures of we sentimental and sensitive human beings, but few of us have ever found our lives entangled emotionally with a panda. Fewer still have felt the need to get involved with a panda's sex life.

In order to understand how a couple of writers from London became unexpectedly concerned with the mating habits of two young pandas in a zoo in Hong Kong, we must first learn more about something called "podcasting". For those who are unfamiliar with this relatively new entertainment phenomenon, we should quickly explain that a "podcast" is a radio programme which people download from the internet and then listen to on their computer, or on a portable MP3 player, such as an iPod.
"But what has this got to do with pandas?" we hear you ask.
"Fuck all," would be the most honest and, frankly, accurate reply. But in the case of this book there is a connection. A slim connection admittedly, but a connection which will take us on an extraordinary adventure.

Just as a good deal has been written about pandas, rather a lot has been written about podcasting, and very little of it is terribly interesting. In fact most of it is little more than technical gobbledygook. The "RSS feed" was originally invented by pimply technical geeks, and was used exclusively by those exact same geeks in order to syndicate nerdy information about string theory, CSI Miami and DC comics.

Then some internet boffin suggested the idea of using an RSS feed to deliver radio shows and the rest is history. RSS feeds were now unexpectedly cool and the medium of podcasting was born. This new communication tool was destined to make the world of broadcasting a much smaller place and almost overnight change the face of radio for ever. But more significantly, it was to become the most intimate form of communication ever invented. In downloading radio shows onto their personal audio players and listening to them in their own solitary, private space, listeners were going to feel a closer connection with podcasters than they had ever felt with traditional broadcasters. They weren't just going to *listen* to radio programmes anymore. They were going to *own* them.

For this reason, the early pioneers of podcasts developed a surprisingly close relationship with their audience. An unprecedented phenomenon that is explored for the first time in this book and which will eventually lead us back to the subject of pandas. We promise.

The first people to find fame through podcasting were probably Dawn and Drew, a pair of "ex-gutter punks" who charmed the world by simply getting stoned and mumbling junk into a microphone in their living room. Meanwhile, on the other side of the Atlantic, Georgina Sowerby and I were sitting in an Irish pub, listening to Dawn and Drew on our brand new iPod, and wondering if we might do something similar. We'd already made a modest name for ourselves in London by presenting Sketch Club - a weekly showcase gig on the comedy circuit - and we'd helped to develop the careers of many up-and-coming comedians, including that brilliant double act Colin and Fergus, if.comedy nominees Fat Tongue and the last Perrier Award winner, Laura Solon. Even comedy superstar Russell Brand had used our show to test out his new act after coming out of rehab.

Maybe, like Dawn and Drew in America, we'd be able to use this exciting new technology to reach out to a worldwide audience and give our careers a bit of a kickstart.

Georgina and I were to discover that podcasting was much more than just a technical innovation. It was and still is an incredibly emotive new medium for connecting people. More importantly in our case it was highly addictive - an obsessive shared interest, that at times may actually have helped to hold our relationship together.

When Georgina and I started recording our podcasts, in a spare bedroom in Crouch End, we had no way of knowing that our voices would touch the lives of so many people, or that ultimately it would be the love we received by email from others, that would help us to overcome many of the challenges we had in our own lives.

We received emails by the thousand, many from people who had become hopelessly addicted to our daft little podcast. Georgina even received a proposal of marriage. But it was one email in particular that became the catalyst for this book. If you haven't guessed already, it was an email about a Giant Panda…

Chapter 1
Step Away from the Computer

The sparkling, high rise apartments of Hong Kong flashed past us in the taxi, as we headed for the Giant Panda Habitat at Ocean Park.
"Are you sure we've got everything, Brian?" Georgina said.
"MP3 recorder and spare batteries?"
"Check."
"Digital camera?"
"Check".

Georgina Sowerby and I had just travelled two thirds of the way around the world. From London, via New York City, to Hong Kong and we were about to present a lucky fertility statue to a couple of young pandas, which, let's face it, is not something you do every day. And we were going to record the whole thing, in glorious stereo, for our comedy podcast The Sowerby and Luff Show.

Georgina suddenly let out a nervous laugh.
"What on earth are we doing here?" she said.
"I have absolutely no idea!" I replied. But of course, that's not strictly true. We both knew exactly how we'd arrived at this moment. It's just that it was rather an odd story.

As the taxi sped past the towering Bank of China building towards our official breakfast meeting with the pandas, our minds flashed back to the very beginning of our podcasting adventure and the first thing that popped into our heads was something that happened at the end of November 2005. Comedian Ricky Gervais had appeared on News At Ten, and said that he was going to start doing something called a "podcast". Everyone got terribly excited, but no-one quite knew what Ricky was talking about.

A few days later, a freelance journalist from the *Ham and High* telephoned us at our little flat in the leafy North London suburb of Crouch End. He said he'd heard our podcast The Big Squeeze on iTunes, and asked if we'd got the idea from Ricky Gervais. We probably should have told him to "sod off", but instead we politely explained that we'd been podcasting since July 2005, and that it was Mr Gervais who had more than likely got the idea from us – or at the very least, podcasters like us. The journalist laughed, but we didn't. We politely answered his questions, then quietly put down the phone.

So, how did fate take us from that phone call in 2005 to the other side of the world for such a strange rendezvous? To find out, we need to begin by going back to November of that year, when I walked into PC World and bought a brand new HP Intel Pentium 4 Personal Computer.

"What do we need a new computer for?" Georgina had screamed when I struggled through the door with a big box, knowing my fondness for buying merchandise because of the bright, attractive packaging.
"For... um... multi-media stuff," I mumbled.
"We only use it for emails," Georgina retorted.
"*You* may only use it for emails," I snapped, "But *I* need to stay at the cutting edge of technology."

Georgina picked at a freshly peeled tin of sardines and continued to sneer at me as I wrestled with monitor cables, printer software and a webcam which flatly refused to come out of its vacuum-sealed packaging. Nine hours, and three quarters of a bottle of whisky later, I was finally online. Georgina was in bed by then.
"Have you heard of this thing called You Tube?" I yelled out from the living room. "It's fantastic. People can upload video to the internet. It's like having your own TV station!"
"Step away from the computer," Georgina shouted. "For God's sake, Brian, it's two thirty in the morning!"

But I was hooked. My tired, doddery old laptop and 56 kbs dial-up connection were now forever consigned to the bin and I had arrived, hyperventilating with excitement, on the brink of what was soon to become known as the "explosion of User Generated Content". Now anyone, anywhere, could record any old crap, and upload it to the internet, to be gobbled up by a huge worldwide audience.

I sat and consumed this brave new world deep into the early hours of the following morning - breathing in every pixel of its addictive vista. Audio downloads, video downloads, the world was entering the early stages of "Web 2.0", and I couldn't get enough of it.

What I didn't know was that what had previously been but a brief daily visit to the computer in the corner - to check my emails, or to quickly read the morning news online - would now be replaced by marathon coffee-drinking sessions, in which, for hour upon hour, I would slowly be reduced to the level of a hunched, bleary-eyed nocturnal beast.

I finally crawled into bed at about four am, waking up Georgina with one of my usual "Brian has entered the bedroom" farts, before sliding under the duvet like an over-excited walrus. I tossed and turned, and sweated, which was unusual for me, because I normally sleep quietly like a baby, gently curled into the foetal position.

"What is it?" Georgina mumbled into her pillow, resigned to the fact that a conversation was inevitable.
I turned over, propped myself up on one elbow and faced her in the darkness.
"This is going to sound strange," I said. "But I've had a premonition."
"What?"
"I think I may have been put on this Earth to upload total bollocks to the internet!"
Georgina was momentarily intrigued.
"What kind of bollocks?" she asked.
"Oh, I don't know… step aerobics for zebras, sex tips for pandas…"
"What?"
"First things that came into my head," I said.
"Good night," said Georgina and she turned over and went back to sleep. About two years later, we recorded a podcast in which I casually mentioned "sex tips for pandas" again. What happened after that turned out to be the very first step in our bizarre

globetrotting adventure, and the reason that we finally ended up in that taxi in Hong Kong.

INTRODUCED BY A CLOWN

But before we hear more about that, we must first go back even further. Because our own personal story actually begins three years earlier, at a small comedy club in Crouch End called Downstairs at The King's Head.

"Downstairs" has been around even longer than The Comedy Store. It was founded by drama lecturer Huw Thomas and musician Peter Grahame, and the ethos of this great little club is the same today as it was when it first opened its doors in 1981. Then, the "alternative comedy" circuit was young and most of the emerging comedy clubs were intimidating bear pits for the performers, with audiences actually encouraged to bait acts. Huw and Peter wanted to create an atmosphere that supported and celebrated all performance styles, and to ensure that audiences were made to feel welcome and part of the event. The emphasis was on a variety of entertainment and value for money, and if you'd visited "Downstairs" in the early eighties you'd have seen early performances by Eddie Izzard, Julian Clary, Paul Merton, Alexei Sayle and even old beardy Hagrid himself, Robbie Coltrane. In fact there are very few famous comics who haven't played Downstairs at The King's Head. Even U.S. comedy superstar Robin Williams turned up to do a gig once. But on that evening it was me that was on stage trying to get laughs. Frankly, I wasn't having much luck.

I was appearing with an actor called Andrew Barclay, with whom I'd scored minor success a year earlier when together we'd written and produced a late night comedy series for Channel 4 called Pets. But our own double act still needed rather a lot of work.

ANDREW: The messenger has brought a message, on his horse.
BRIAN: What does it say?
ANDREW: Nothing, it is a horse, it cannot speak.

One of the things that kept me smiling during that gig was the site of Georgina sitting at one of the tables in the front row. She was laughing politely and grinning a cheeky grin. And after the show I was introduced to her by a mutual friend called Joey. It wasn't long before I realized that Georgina was actually the only person in the room who shared my sense of humour. And that included my performing partner Andrew. Georgina and I got on really well and, since she was looking for work at the time, she rather impertinently offered to help Andrew and me in our production office at Elstree Studios. Georgina has never been backward at coming forward.

She said she could give us a hand with "PR stuff". We weren't entirely sure what kind of "PR stuff" she was talking about, but we said we'd give it a try for a couple of weeks. Before I knew it, I was involved in a good old-fashioned office romance.

Georgina believes that because she and I met at a comedy club our relationship was straight-away built on a foundation of sharing humour.

She'd split up with her actor boyfriend about two and a half years before, and had not been terribly gregarious since. She only went to The Kings Head on that night because her old friend Joey was tenaciously adamant that getting "out of the house" was a good idea.

It was undoubtedly Joey's enthusiasm and friendship that brought Georgina and me together. We really should thank her with a drink some time, but Joey spends most of her time overseas touring with Cirque de Soleil. How many couples can say that they were introduced by a clown? In our case I guess it was strangely appropriate.

When Georgina saw me walk on stage that night - in the guise of my miserable, lethargic comedy character, "Lucky Lizard" (which incidentally I hated playing) – she says it somehow made her feel secure – she felt immediately that we might share something.

UNIMPORTANT GOALS

Georgina had worked as an actor herself, but she'd avoided getting up on stage since a serious road accident about ten years before had left her bereft of the courage she felt she needed to open herself up once again to the scrutiny of an audience. Outwardly, she seemed confident and outgoing, but in her mind she says she felt very insecure. She'd no idea how much that night was going to change her life - that she'd again be plunged into the nerve-jangling world of performance - and that she'd love it.

Chatting to me after the gig Georgina seemed relaxed and happy. The miserable, insecure character I'd been playing on stage seemed to her to have the same mental attitude she herself had had for so long - that performing was a bit of chore, something that had to be done, but not necessarily enjoyed. She seemed to immediately relate to this. In Georgina's own words, "My soul had taken a battering, and that evening Brian began to caress it back to life."

Before Georgina and I met she'd displayed all the outward signs of a career-minded PR person, working for a blue-chip promotions agency and achieving a series of unimportant goals. She worked 10 hours a day, drinking profusely, going for long lunches, pitching to companies and generally following a life so repetitively mundane it made her feel like weeping.

Like most people, Georgina had worked in that job for no other reason than to pay the rent - painting by numbers in a superficial world where no-one asked you how you were and, if they did, they really couldn't be bothered to listen to the answer.

In 2000 Georgina found herself sitting in an office deciding how to get column inches for Ovine and Bovine News, and each day the urge to add comedic value to her inane existence was getting stronger. One morning, when charged with organizing press clippings for "a flea collar for disreputable cats", she suddenly realised that there must be more to life. So she quit.

On Monday morning she'd been organizing a party for a book about ergonomics. By Tuesday lunchtime she'd handed in her resignation. She probably should have stayed in that relatively safe job, but Georgina's sanity was way too important to her – she'd started to find comedy in everything that presented itself, and knew that leaving that mind-numbing office environment was the only way to move her life forward.

The day Georgina met me at The Kings Head she was working as a temp in central London, and her parents had just bought her a brand new PC. Yes, believe it or not, until 2002 Ms Sowerby was completely computer free.

Georgina's leap into the internet age had actually begun just one evening before she met me, when she'd set up her first ever email account away from the office. Fate must have been taking a hand here. When she scribbled down her brand new email address for me - hoping to the heavens she had remembered it correctly - she tried to play it cool, secretly saying to herself, "How fabulous am I to have one of these squiggly things in the middle of my name, so that people can correspond with me in a technological manner in keeping with the twenty-first century".

When Georgina got home from the gig that night, she opened Outlook Express for the first time ever, and immediately found an email from me. She was flattered that she'd been the first thing I'd thought of when I got home from the gig, and was delighted that her ability to flirt had not become entirely extinct during the preceding couple of years. She shoots, she scores.

Meanwhile, I was completely smitten. I suggested that Georgina take the day off work and that we go somewhere for a drink. Her reply was an oddly traditional one, like a line from a high school musical.
"Do you have any wheels?" she asked.

FIRST DATE NERVES

Our first date was as entertaining as I had expected it to be. I took Georgina to a famous pub in St.Albans called The Fighting Cocks – which is one of the oldest inns in the country. I thought she might be impressed, but I'm not sure she was. Georgina drank way too many

Red Bulls, and I just sat and stared at her like a love struck puppy. This simply had the effect of making Georgina feel awkward and she immediately thought her mascara had smudged into panda eyes, or that she had a piece of cabbage stuck between her front teeth. But I didn't notice her embarrassment. I just stared some more.

Half way through the evening I suggested we go for something to eat. Maybe a pizza. Georgina said she'd rather sit and watch TV, and asked how far it was to my house. An hour later we were sat on my sofa, with a bottle of Merlot on the table between us.
"Why aren't you drinking any wine?" Georgina asked me.
"Because I have to drive."
"Where are you going?" she asked.
"I've got to drive you home, haven't I?" I said.
"Don't worry," she said. "You can have as much wine as you want."

YOU'RE NOT JOSEPH

In that typical "first date" kind of a way we chatted about our childhoods. I told Georgina I'd grown up in the sixties, in the London borough of Tottenham, but that despite this tough urban setting, most of my childhood memories were of trees and grass and sunshine.

I told Georgina I'd always fancied myself as a bit of performer. My best friend Richard Comerford and I used to bomb around the streets of Downhills Park dressed as Batman and Robin, and in the evenings we'd set up a stage in my parents' garden and would perform a comedy double act - copied word for word from that of Leslie Crowther and Peter Glaze, in the kids' variety show Crackerjack.

Here's the only gag I can remember from those little shows in the garden. It was probably the first joke I ever told in front of an audience:

BRIAN: What's the name of The Lone Ranger's horse?

RICHARD: Silver.

BRIAN: Well, he used to be called Silver, but he's been out in the rain all night.

RICHARD: So, what's he called now?

BRIAN: Rusty.

I was always at the front of the queue when they were casting the school plays, and my mum and dad were endlessly dragged to the school to watch me performing in various dreadful shows, most of which seemed to require me to wear a towel on my head. When Andrew Lloyd Webber and Tim Rice wrote Joseph and the Amazing Technicolor Dreamcoat, they had no idea how much the show was going to boost the sales of colourful bathroom towels.

THE GREAT FABRICATOR

I'd started the ball rolling, so now it was Georgina's turn to tell me all about herself. She said she'd been living in London for around 15 years now, but she still missed the small village in North Yorkshire where she grew up. She said it was – and still is – very tiny. Blink while driving through it at 29 mph and you'd miss it completely. But luckily, it wasn't too far removed from the city of Middlesbrough, so when Georgina was in her teens there was no shortage of places to go and party in white stilettos and fake tan.

Georgina's little home town was not crammed with public amenities. It had a post office – which was located in someone's front porch - and a small pub. So, there were only two jobs in the village, and Georgina did both of them. She began by working in the pub, serving scampi and chips in a basket to "townies", then worked as post mistress, handing out stamps and pensions to little old ladies and farmers. Georgina had exhausted the entire village job market before she had reached her 17th birthday.

With all its quaintness and charm, such a small village was never going to challenge the creative powerhouse that was Georgina Sowerby. As much as she loved the place, she always knew that she'd have to move on sooner or later – though she says that an elastic band attached to her heart pulls her back there, almost every day of her life.

Georgina's future would probably have been fairly predictable and mundane had she stayed in North Yorkshire. Not much call for comedy at a village fete in which the only prizes given out are for bonny babies and best fancy dress. Not that Georgina didn't have a crack at the fancy dress herself. In fact her very first performance - in the village fancy dress competition at the age of three - was as a bird. The costume was completely made out of newspaper. Her mother being a costume designer and her dad being an architect meant that Georgina's fancy dress costumes were ingenious beyond belief, but in that first competition her appearance was swiftly halted when her parents spotted little wet patches under the bird's eyes - she had been secretly crying inside her uncomfortable little origami masterpiece.

Georgina had fond memories of her life in North Yorkshire - summer fetes, agricultural shows, even a farmer who named all his calves after the girls in the village. As in many rural villages, time seemed to run more slowly, and in during the winter they were regularly snowed in. The narrow roads were sometimes blocked by furious blizzards and the school bus was often unable to collect Georgina and her school friends, leaving them to spend their day excitedly digging tunnels and having adventures in huge banks of drifted snow – a perfect escape from lessons, without the need to make up fibs.

It had been a reassuringly safe and comfortable place to begin your life, but not one of great contrast or excitement. So, just like me and my friend Richard, she'd fabricated fantastic games and adventures in the woods and fields surrounding her home. She said she was certain that that was where her creativity and desire to perform had come from.

One day the garden would be made out of sweets, then it was a fairground, or a department store into which Georgina stole quietly like a thief. Every day, she participated in elaborate imaginary events and made up a myriad of different roles for herself to play.

Like me, Georgina also "found fame" at school. When asked to take in "something red" for Show and Tell, she took a huge Danish wooden horse - one of the many fabulous items on display in her parent's house. That night the school cleaners moved it while tidying up the classroom and the next day Georgina declared that this was "magic". Of course, this placed Georgina firmly at the centre of attention, a position she quickly learned to maintain and enjoy. Meanwhile, the cleaners aided and abetted her special powers by changing the wooden horse's position at least three times a week. Her role as The Great Fabricator was established.

Georgina loved entertaining others as a child. From an early age she interviewed people with the intensity of a news journalist. She found she was able to hold people's attention with jokes, and quickly discovered that being funny could be a valuable commodity.

Exactly as I did when I was at school, Georgina told the other kids in the playground that she had a secret joke book, and she absorbed funny stories like a sponge, to later relate as currency. "Funny" made you friends a lot quicker than handing out fruit gums. And it was cheaper.

Just as I remember that gag from Crackerjack, Georgina remembers the day, aged four that she rushed home to tell her parents her first ever joke.
"What time did the Chinaman go to the dentist?" she asked her dad.
"I don't know, what time did the Chinaman go the dentist?" he politely responded. Little Georgina took a deep breath and proudly delivered the punchline: "Half past two."

She remembers falling on the ground with laughter, while her poor dad was left to figure out that she'd actually meant "tooth hurty". Not the most PC of punchlines today, rendering young Georgina's original version both funnier and less racist.

Georgina told me that it was as early as those days that she decided she wanted to be an actor. Many grow out of it. Not Georgina. She was determined to turn make-believe into a career. So, at the age of 18, she chose to study drama at university in London.

Three years of acting was going to be bliss for a born drama queen like Georgina. She loved, and still does, the camouflage of pretending to be someone else. What could be better than having your thoughts given to you on a page? She said it still made her bubble inside when she pretended to be someone else, but wondered, like so many actors, if it was because she wasn't happy being herself.

Georgina stayed at my house that night, and we talked bollocks about our childhoods deep into the early hours. It was a relaxed and familiar time, during which a happy and inexplicable bond was quickly formed. We giggled and swapped stories. Georgina twice fell off the sofa, whilst hooting at my inanities. Friendship was unavoidable. Laughter was an aphrodisiac.

MESSY DIVORCES

The following week Andrew and I went up to Edinburgh for a four week run at the Gilded Balloon Theatre and, after our first show, Georgina turned up at my Edinburgh digs with a suitcase packed for 3 weeks.

By this time, Barclay and I had more or less agreed that if fame as a double act was going to strike, it would surely have stricken us at least ten years before. He also seemed unreasonably angry that Georgina had quickly taken over his role as the main "partner" in my life.

Soon afterwards I had a huge row with Andrew and we stopped working together; later disbanding our production company at Elstree. I've been through two divorces with former partners, but the split with my comedy partner Andrew was by far the worst "divorce" I've ever had to endure. I'm on reasonably friendly terms with both of my ex-wives now, but Andrew and I haven't spoken for years. Never go into business with your best friend. It's a recipe for disaster.

Immediately after Edinburgh 2002, Georgina moved the contents of her wardrobe, and all three of her toothbrushes, into the small semi-detached house I was renting near the studios in Elstree. Mainly because I had a garden and she didn't. Or so she said. Our relationship had developed an unusually quickly. One minute Georgina wasn't a part of my life, the next she was all encompassing. It felt natural and comforting to have her around. At the same time, she provided a jovial audience, and a willing comedy conspirator. Within a few short weeks we were working, eating, sleeping and playing together. We understood each other and didn't ask too many questions. We didn't want to tempt fate by discovering anything dreadful. Making someone laugh can be highly addictive, but also allows you to be superficial. We felt safe in allowing the complex part of "us" to develop over time. We had connected, and for that we were both grateful. It seemed we had both really needed a friend. We lived together in Elstree for about six months. Then, in the spring of 2003, we moved into the flat in North London.

Georgina and I loved Crouch End. The town had grown up as a tiny hamlet on the old medieval route from London to the north of England, but most of it was built in the late 19th century, so it had a deliciously Victorian flavour. It was only a few miles from the City of London, but Crouch End felt more like a country village, with a large red brick clock tower dominating the centre of the Broadway. There were loads of bars, restaurants and pubs, and it was surrounded by woods and parks, so the place had a very rural atmosphere. There was a drama school, an art school, and a recording studio in a converted church, which was once owned by Dave Stewart of the Eurythmics.

Crouch End was full of famous faces and media types, and it had featured in many, many books and films before this one. The movie Shaun of the Dead was shot in Crouch End, and Nick Hornby's High Fidelity was originally set there, and in one of Stephen King's short stories, Crouch End was the location for an interdimensional time portal. Bob Dylan once considered buying a house in Crouch End. If it was good enough for Bob, it was good enough for us.

Chapter 2
Streaming Radio

Fast forward back to November 2005, where Georgina snored, pig-like, next to me, as I stared up at the high, ornate ceiling of the bedroom and tried in vain to comprehend the mind-boggling possibilities of uploading endless crap to the internet. Should I make a short comedy film and put it on YouTube? Should I record one of our live comedy shows at The Kings Head, and stick it on a server somewhere?

I drifted off into a fitful sleep, dreaming of Oscar ceremonies at which all of the awards were given out to people who had made micro-budget B-movies on camcorders, and embedded them on their websites.

Over the next couple of months, internet broadcasting was never far from my thoughts. As a TV writer I had a half-decent list of credits to my name, but I was getting increasingly sick of pitching script ideas to commissioning editors with acne on their faces or development producers who were so young they weren't allowed in the newsagents more than one at a time. The prospect of being able to reach a large audience without having to go through this humiliating and dehumanising process was extremely alluring.

"But how do you make money out of it?" asked Georgina next morning, "What's the point of making a programme for the internet, when no-one's going to pay to see or hear it?"

"I don't know," I said.

I knew there must be some way in which we could exploit this revolution in web broadcasting. Maybe we could tie it in with our creative training business? At this time, Georgina and I were earning much of our income from the online marketing of writing workshops with well-known comedy scriptwriters. Our most popular workshop was with BBC script associate Keith Lindsay, who was then co-writing the first series of Green Green Grass with Only Fools and Horses creator John Sullivan. Might there be some way of broadcasting these workshops on the internet?

THINK TANK

Time is meaningless in cyberspace, but in the real world Spring was turning to Summer and, at the end of May, while Georgina was visiting her mum and dad, I decided to go off on one of my little solo seaside jaunts for a few days. I needed to do some thinking. You can't do serious thinking in London. There's too much going on. Too many car alarms going off. You need a soundbed of seagulls squawking to be creative.

I booked a cottage on the Suffolk coast and headed off with my laptop. Last time I'd done this, the result had been a short stage play, which I'd later had produced in Edinburgh, so I had a good feeling about this excursion. Whilst meditating in monk-like solitude, I was going to come up with a business plan to end all business plans. A hard-hitting New Media, web broadcasting strategy for Brian and Georgina.

I was in Southwold for six days. It was a pleasant week, the sun shined constantly, and I spent most of the time in a pub called the Sole Bay Arms, drinking Adnams Best Bitter. Lots of Adnams Best Bitter. They make it there, you know. Just over the road from the pub, in the Adnams Brewery. If I'm honest, I came up with bugger-all that week. Except wind. I rang Georgina.

"How's the New Media think tank going?" she asked.
"Extreeeeeemely well," I hiccupped back at her.

"I've been thinking," I said. "Now, this is just an idea, shoot me down in flames if you like. But, what about starting an online radio station? For new comedy writers and performers? Like our fringe show, but on the internet."
"Great idea!" said Georgina.

Interestingly, Georgina's memory of this same conversation is that it was *her* who suggested the idea to me. Not the other way around. But that's not important right now. Because at the exact moment we were having that telephone conversation, something momentous was happening on the internet. A website called

Engadget was announcing to the world that Apple had added a new feature to their software for the iPod.

The article said this:

> iTunes 4.9 adding support for podcasts
> Posted May 23rd 2005 7:05AM by Peter Rojas
> Filed under: Portable Audio
>
> Steve Jobs just revealed at the All Things Digital conference that iTunes 4.9 will add support for podcasts. With one click you'll be able to subscribe to different feeds and have them automatically delivered to your iPod. You'll be able to search through a directory of available podcasts (producers will be able to register their podcasts with the iTunes Music Store), but users will have the option of adding whatever feeds they want to iTunes.

An awful lot of people saw that post. But I didn't. The very first book on podcasting had also just been released - the award-winning Podcasting: The Do it Yourself Guide, by Todd Cochrane. But I didn't see that either. I was too busy wasting my time in a pub in Southwold. Even more alarmingly, when I got back to London, I was going to start an online radio station.

DIGITAL NIRVANA

The next date I wrote in my diary was 9th June 2005, when I could be found slumped in front of my computer, totally exhausted. I'd been sitting there for almost 48 hours, and I hadn't had a wink of sleep during that time. Every twenty minutes or so I would run around the room celebrating like Johnny Wilkinson after converting a try. Moments later I was disconsolate, defeated, weeping into my mouse mat. I was trying to work out how to stream audio onto the internet.

Had I known, when I started out, how complicated it is to stream audio, I suspect we would never have started our online radio station *Comedy 365*. But I was hopelessly naïve. I had no idea that the road to digital Nirvana would be so rocky, or that it would pass along a learning curve that was as steep as the north face of the Eiger.

Georgina says I am pig-headedly determined. Whereas she tends to put things off for a year or two, I grab ideas by the scruff of the neck and wrestle them into fruition. My problem, however, is that I tend to get projects off the ground *too* quickly, without always thinking them through with the amount of attention to detail they deserve. I suspect this is why I am not a millionaire.

After what seemed an eternity of sleepless nights and failed attempts, I discovered a piece of software which could effectively stream MP3s for me. It was called SAM Broadcaster and after a few online tutorials I was on the air. SAM is a virtual audio studio, with all the functions of a real radio station. You can schedule and play programmes, promos, jingles, and even fade up a microphone and talk to the world live on air. Within a couple of days, I was ready to broadcast. One small problem. No content.

Despite this minor detail, I was like a child on Christmas Day with my new radio station. I sat in the living room, my headphones clamped to my head, recording voiceovers, reading scripts and mixing music.

HOSPITAL RADIO

At the age of 17, I'd worked on a small radio station called LHBC, at the Whittington Hospital in Highgate, and like most kids of that age I was quick to adapt my voice to an irritating mid-Atlantic drawl, in order to sound as much like a Radio One disc jockey as possible.

"You are listening to London Hospital Broadcasting, your very own hospital radio station, I do believe."

The "I do believe" was critical. It was the part of the voiceover that made you sound like Tony Blackburn or David "The Kid" Jensen.

My co-host Mike Haynes and I used to present the Saturday Morning Chart Show and, as far as I can remember we did it with the same eleven records for two years. Mostly we played a track called "I Know What I Like (In Your Wardrobe)" by Genesis. We just loved those records with bits of the title in brackets.

Mike and I also co-presented a show for a while at a hospital for mental health in Friern Barnet. You haven't lived until you've hosted a live radio phone-in for the patients in a psychiatric ward.
"Who's that on the line?" Mike would say.
"It's John."
"And what's your request, John?"
"I don't have a request. I was just wondering if you had any cigarettes."
In one programme I put a call through to the studio, and a quiet, shy voice simply said: "The voices told me to do it."

Hospital radio has brought a lot of pleasure to a lot of people over the years. All of them DJs and none of them patients. But, looking back, I think working in hospital radio was one of the most formative experiences of my life, and it probably goes a long way towards explaining why I so readily took to the idea of starting an online radio station, and later a podcast.

INTERNET RADIO

Georgina and I kicked off our radio station by recording some live fringe shows at The Kings Head in Crouch End, and editing them into 15 minute programmes. But the only way we were going to get what broadcasting marketeers would soon be calling "compelling content", was to go public and announce the launch of Comedy 365 to the world. On the 29th June 2005, Georgina sent a press release to *The Stage*. The following day they published this:

Web radio station to showcase original British comedy:

An internet radio station has been launched with the aim of showcasing new British comedy writers and performers. Comedy 365 has been created by Brian Luff, who runs a regular sketch night in London, with his co-producer Georgina Sowerby.

Luff said: "There are very few ways for new writers and performers to expose their material to a broadcast audience. We hope this move will help change that, and give some talented newbies a taste of writing for a real radio audience.

This is a natural extension of what we have been doing with fringe comedy and this is the perfect way to show people the kind of talent that is around at the moment in an accessible way.""

The station will broadcast programmes from 7pm to midnight every night, featuring material from the club nights, as well as musical spoofs and performances from specialty acts.

Sowerby added: "We have been producing live fringe shows for new writers and performers for three years. Comedy 365 is a way of taking some of that new talent and exposing it to a much bigger audience."

It was a fantastic plug, and we soon started to get material sent to us from writers and performers all over the world. A week later, Comedy 365 was broadcasting nightly, with a looping schedule of material from John Dredge, Richard Cray, and an hilarious comedy team from Canada, Data Radio. There was also a promising new double act called Fetto and Palmer. It all sounded great. But we didn't have any listeners.

Actually that's not 100% true. We had three listeners. We never found out exactly who they were, or where they came from, but we did suspect that one of them might be MI5 in Lambeth, checking that we weren't broadcasting secrets to enemies of the State. One night our audience peaked at eight. Then immediately went back down to three again. But I was unperturbed. Every night, I still went and sat in front of that computer, and streamed comedy out to a staggeringly disinterested world.

HARNESSING THE CRAZE

Despite our lack of listeners, we continued to get media coverage, thanks to Georgina's ingenious press releases and enthusiastic phone calls. And it was while I was scouring the web looking for mentions of Comedy 365, that I stumbled upon the article that was to change my, and Georgina's, life.

It was on the UK comedy website, Chortle on the 6th July 2005.

In Pod we Trust
Comics hit 10,000 downloads

A group of London comics has harnessed the craze for podcasting to reach a five-figure audience. For the past month, Stefano Paolini, James Dowdeswell and Diane Morgan have been releasing a thrice-weekly topical show called Whack My Bush on the internet. The five-minute comedies were incorporated into Apple's key iTunes site on Saturday – and notched up more than 10,000 downloads in just two days. The show's success launched it straight into the global podcast charts at number 21.

I got very excited when I read this article. I dashed around the flat, hopping up and down like a Telly Tubby with a sugar-rush and shouting "That's it! That's it!" Georgina thought I had re-discovered penicillin.

I realised at that moment that we had the right product, but we were simply delivering it in the wrong way. We had to start podcasting Comedy 365. How hard could it be? Even President George W. Bush had just started podcasting, or at least the White House had begun syndicating his weekly radio speeches. If it was possible for that moron, then it was time that Brian and Georgina had their own podcast.

Needless to say, I then didn't sleep for another 48 hours while I tried to work out how to create something called an "RSS feed". I shouted, I punched the desk, I tugged furiously at what was left of my hair, and I shovelled peanut butter sandwiches into my mouth. It was during this meticulous research process that Georgina and I first came across the name Adam Curry – an ex-disc jockey from Guildford - who claimed to have come up with the concept of podcasting in the first place, and a man with whom we would one day publicly cross swords.

THE FINER POINTS OF PODCASTING

We also came across the name Chris Skinner, who appeared to be regularly producing a podcast called Simulacrum. We emailed Chris and a few days later we were sitting in a smoky pub with him, in London's West End.

Chris was a young radio producer who had stumbled upon podcasting a few months earlier and he'd been syndicating Simulacrum ever since. The premise was simple. Chris sat in front of a microphone and pretended to interview famous people. These so-called celebrities were played by friends and colleagues of his, who neither looked like, nor sounded like, the people they were meant to be. In other words it was bollocks. Total bollocks.

Chris's humour was pretty hit and miss, but some of the episodes were very, very funny, and he had already been nominated for one of the very first podcasting awards. Over several pints of Fullers London Pride, Chris filled us in on some of the finer points of podcasting. In return, we agreed to syndicate Simulacrum via our own podcast feed, which was to be called Comedy 365, in memory of our still-born internet radio station.

Comedy 365 was destined to become the platform for hundreds of episodes of Sowerby and Luff podcasts, but we didn't know that then. Nor did we know that following one of those podcasts we'd receive an intriguing email about pandas from a man on the other side of the world.

Chapter 3
Waxing Georgina

"What do you want to do with your life?" Georgina asked me, out of the blue, while we were waiting for our Tandoori takeaway in the Crouch End Curry Club one evening.

"That's a strange thing to ask a man waiting for a chicken jalfrezi," I replied.

"Tell me," she said.

I deeply inhaled the aroma of sizzling garlic, and thought about it for a moment.

"I suppose I'd like to see more of the world," I said. "I'd like to travel. Meet people. Learn more stuff… about stuff."

"Me too," said Georgina, "Let's get on a plane and fly around the world!"

"We can't afford to," I said.

"Why?" asked Georgina.

"Because," I said, "We're spending all our money on audio recording equipment."

"Let's go to America, or Japan or Australia!" Georgina insisted again.

"Have you ever seen the movie Field of Dreams?" I said.

"Yes," replied Georgina.

"If you build it they will come!" I said. "It's the famous quote from the film."

"Isn't that something to do with baseball?" asked Georgina.

"Yes," I said. "The guy in the movie builds a baseball field, but he doesn't really know why he's doing it. He just has a gut feeling that it's a good idea."

"So, what's that got to do with us going travelling?" asked Georgina.

"We just need to have a little faith," I said. "I don't know why I'm investing so much energy in this podcasting thing. I just have a gut feeling that's it's leading somewhere."

We picked up our Indian takeaway and headed back towards the flat. Georgina gave me a very strange look indeed.

On 9th July 2005, we set up a podcast hosting service with a small American company called Liberated Syndication. 24 hours later we uploaded the very first Comedy 365 podcast. In those days the four young guys running Libsyn still had day jobs. At the time of writing, they're serving around 70 million audio downloads a month.

The first Comedy 365 podcast was just over 13 minutes long and began with Georgina's dulcet tones: "Fresh new comedy talent, broadcasting live from London. This is Comedy 365."

Extraordinarily, the very first performer to be showcased in that inaugural podcast was future Perrier Award winner Laura Solon. Recorded Downstairs at The Kings Head in June 2005, Laura's hilarious routine "Stories" was to become part of the act that would win her the coveted fizzy water prize at the Edinburgh Festival just 6 weeks later. So, not a bad start for our first podcast.

SKETCH CLUB

By the time Laura had become a regular performer in our fringe showcase, Georgina was single-handedly producing the show. She looks back fondly at her days running Sketch Club, but organising those weekly performances also took a massive amount of time, and a hell of a lot of patience. The endless phone calls to line up acts took at least a full day every week, and then there was the logistical nightmare of comedians who decided not to turn up at the very last minute. Of course, Georgina couldn't moan at people for not showing up, because Sketch Club was a fringe show. The fringe is financed by what is known as "profit share", and in a half-filled 80 seat pub theatre, with 6 acts on the bill, everyone's got a pretty good idea how much profit there's going to be.

I've been involved with a lot of profit share shows over the years. I first performed at The Kings Head in 1992 in a weekly sketch night called Bloody Mondays. That gig proved to be the breeding ground for a whole franchise of sketch teams, collectively called Comedy Factory, with whom I appeared on the London and Edinburgh Fringe throughout the early nineties. The best known profit share sketch night in those days was probably TBA at the Gate, which launched its founders Andy Parsons and Henry Naylor into a long-running BBC radio career as one of the UK's best loved double acts.

As a member of Comedy Factory, I performed at TBA several times, and the pace and style of that gig laid the foundations for many successful sketch nights which were to follow in the capital, including Sketch Etc and of course our very own Sketch Club.

Some weeks Sketch Club had more acts than The Royal Variety Performance and the show over-ran by about an hour. Other weeks, there were only three of us, running around on stage like headless chickens and battling to fill an hour. My favourite fallback item for when the show was way too short to charge the audience a fiver, was to shuffle on stage in the guise of a character called The Sixties Poet.

This long-haired troubadour was a bespectacled cross between John Cooper Clark and Roger McGough, and he used to hammer his way through a bunch of ironic poems which explained why the Swinging Sixties were shit.

We looked like twats with flowers in our hair.
The Sixties were crap. I know cause I was there.

Twiggy was too skinny
You had to be a midget to drive a Mini
Monty Python's sketches were too zany
David Bailey's photos were too grainy

Jumping Jack Flash a bit over-excited
My love for Marianne Faithful... unrequited
Soft drugs were over-rated, hippie culture odd
Buddy Holly never made it to the sixties, lucky sod.

Sketch Club was all about creating a group vibe. Up and coming acts joined the show one by one, over a period of months and years, and some eventually joined forces to become established comedy teams. The Runaway Lovers are a fine example of this. They all joined Sketch Club as individual acts - John Roy, Lawry Lewin,

Clare Warde and double act Colin and Fergus - but started improvising and writing together to become a hugely experienced sketch group, with great ideas and huge talent.

Many of these performers have since gone on to feature in some of TV's more cutting edge comedy shows of the last couple of years, and it all started over a pint of lager at *Sketch Club*. Georgina and I held regular auditions and only the best acts were showcased at our gig. As a result of this initial sifting process, the night quickly gained a reputation as one of the most consistently quality comedy gigs in London.

Sketch Club was a tightly rehearsed show, with a huge variety of performers and styles, and I like to think we were pretty good judges of talent. Some performers, like Laura Solon, Richard Thomson, and Eirlys Bellin shone with a bright light. It was a joy to watch them perform every week and it made all the hard work worthwhile.

You know instinctively if someone's going to be funny within the first two seconds of them starting their act. Like venturing into a new house and instantly knowing if you'd like to live there or not. Even the way some performers walk onto the stage can tell you all you need to know about them. Comedy is so much about confidence. You need to be brimming over with the stuff. Audiences can smell fear. If you give them even the smallest whiff of it, you're dead. Fear makes the audience feel uneasy, and if they're uneasy they sure as hell won't laugh at you.

As well as new acts, many established comedians came and tried out new material in our live shows. Even Russell Brand came and did a 5 minute slot, while he was in the final stages of overcoming his drink and drug problem. Russell was modest and humble. He quietly introduced himself, then went and hid in a dark corner of the club. When I introduced him, he launched himself onto the stage like a whirlwind, comedy guns blazing. Russell summed up, for us, the typically huge contrast between comedians on and off the stage - switching the performance button on with a click, cooking on gas for 10 minutes, then retreating back into the shadows. Quiet and, dare we say it, sweet, for us Russell perfectly encapsulated the dichotomy of the shy clown.

Sketch Club was a joy. It was a genuinely funny and inspiring evening, for audiences and acts alike, and we were very proud of it.

PAINTING ON THE RADIO

As well as Laura Solon, the first ever podcast on Comedy 365 also featured Stupid Stupid Eighties, an hilarious Human League parody by Richard Cray's band Dogs Must Be Carried. We met Richard at Sketch Club, and were amazed at the back catalogue of funny songs he had in his attic. Richard's a perfect example of the kind of unsigned act who benefitted quickly from the global rise of podcasting. He's since started to distribute material via his own small record label and he now helps us to produce The Sowerby and Luff Show on an almost daily basis.

Finally, in that initial show, was a sketch called "Painting with the Van Vons" by Canadian outfit, Data Radio. It featured an oil painting lesson on the radio – an idea that Georgina and I found completely hilarious from the very first time we heard it. It's difficult to explain how weird it was for us to listen to comedy material, penned and recorded three thousand miles away, going out in our little podcast. Sowerby and Luff's world of comedy was starting to widen with every email we received.

Immediately after uploading that first show, Georgina and I added the Comedy 365 feed to a website that Chris Skinner had told us about called Podcast Alley, and over the next couple of weeks Libsyn's stat tracking revealed that our first ever podcast had achieved around 350 downloads. So in 3 weeks, our audience had gone from 3 to 350. Now we could see what all the fuss was about. Podcasting did actually work.

My only appearance in that first show was to read a short promo for Sketch Club at the end. Alas, it wouldn't be long before Georgina would have trouble wrestling the microphone away from me. Indeed, turning the recording equipment off at the wall was often the only way she could get me out of the flat to go and do the weekly shopping.

A HOLIDAY HIT

Ever since my hospital broadcasting days I've clearly had something of an obsession with radio. Even when Georgina and I had been on holiday in Lanzarote earlier that year, I'd somehow become embroiled with that island's curious little radio station.

One evening, we were sitting in the bar of our hotel, listening to the strangled stylings of a local karaoke singer, who we shall call Reg. He was an ex-pat Brit who had escaped the hurly-burly of being an out of work musician in London, to become an out of work musician in the Canary Islands. After the gig, we got chatting with Reg at the bar, and he invited us to visit his "studio" the next day. I've never been one to spend my holidays slumped next to a swimming pool. Georgina can remain inert for long periods of time, like a sloth on Night Nurse, but I can never keep still for longer than 5 minutes. The idea of relaxing next to a pool for 14 days is a form of torture for me. It was Georgina's job to soak up the sun, mine to wear a knotted handkerchief on my head and abhor the heat. Close as we are, in many ways Georgina and I are the proverbial chalk and cheese.

The following morning I left Georgina snoozing on a sun lounger, jumped into our hire car, and bumbled off into town. Reg had converted most of his holiday bungalow into a recording studio and was scraping a living writing advertising jingles and emailing them to London. I'm always keen to find shared areas of interest with my drinking buddies, so I scoured my brain to try and find some connection between myself and the music industry.

The only thing I could think of was my own slim involvement in the writing of the theme song for my Channel 4 series, Pets. The subtitle of the series had been "Every dog has its day, but this isn't it", so I had suggested to the composers that they write a song called "This Is My Day". Andrew scribbled some lyrics, and the boys quickly came up with a brilliant pop track - not dissimilar to the theme music to Friends.

"I wrote a pop song once," I said proudly to Reg, in the hope of impressing my new musician pal.

"Wow," he said, "What was it called?"

5 minutes later we had downloaded "This Is My Day" from the Pets website and were listening to it over a beer in Reg's back garden. The track's sunny, happy atmosphere sounded great in the hot Canaries sun, and Reg suddenly got very excited.

"You could get a big summer hit with this in Lanzarote," he said. "Come on, I'll drive you up to the radio station!"

"Can we pick up Georgina on the way?" I asked

"Sure," said Reg.

UK Away FM was the local English language radio station for Lanzarote and Fuerteventura. "Where exactly is the studio?" Georgina and I asked, as Reg's ancient car turned off road, and began to drive over increasingly large rocks and boulders.

"It's up there" he said, and he pointed ahead towards a huge towering volcano.

"The views are fantastic," he said, "You can see the entire island from up there!"

Georgina went very pale. "I'm sorry, I really don't do heights," she said.

I'd once tried to take Georgina to a press event in a restaurant at the top of a very tall building in London, and she had actually passed up the opportunity of free food and drink, rather than be in such a high place. She was genuinely terrified at the thought of it. It was like a scene from Alfred Hitchcock's Vertigo.

"Just drop me here", she said and leapt out of the car.

"A radio studio on a volcano?" I said to Reg. "Isn't that dangerous?"

"It's a dormant volcano," he said and somehow that made everything normal again.

Half an hour later we pulled up outside a small white building on a sharply inclined red soil slope.

"Why does it have to be up so high?" I asked, almost gasping for oxygen. In reply, Reg pointed to a tiny radio transmitter on the roof of the building. As soon as we were inside, he introduced me to the Station Manager and Head of Programming, Phil.

Phil was a craggy-faced go-getter who got up at the crack of dawn every morning to present the breakfast show. He then spent most of the day bombing around Lanzarote and Fuerteventura selling radio advertising to small local businesses. Then he raced back to the studio and did the drivetime show. The man was practically a one man radio station and he seemed to be making a pretty good living from it. I think Phil may have inspired me more than I know during the formative months of Comedy 365, a few short months later.

Reg waved the CD he'd burned of This Is My Day.
"I have in my hand," he said to Phil, "the biggest holiday hit this island has ever heard!"
Phil slid the disc into a CD player. "This is great," he said. "Can we play it?"
"I guess so," I said, "As long as you pay all the usual royalties to the guys that wrote it. Including me."
"Oh we don't pay royalties," smiled Phil. "That's how we stay in business."
"You're pirates?"
"Of course we're pirates," he said. "Would *you* pay royalties if you ran a radio station in the middle of nowhere?"

I rang London and spoke to the guys who had written the song and to Stacey Smith, who had recorded it. The track had never had any radio play since appearing in the Channel 4 show, and they all seemed think they had nothing to lose.
"Where's the radio station again?" asked Stacey.
"On top of a volcano in Lanzarote" I said.

An hour later, while Reg and I were driving back to my hotel, he switched on the car radio. Phil was on the air, and he was already playing This Is My Day. Georgina and I were in Lanzarote for another 10 days or so, and every single time we switched on the local radio during that time, they seemed to be playing This is My Day. I was the only record plugger on the planet to get a thousand radio plays and not earn a single buggering penny from it. But that track became the soundtrack to a great holiday. Not that Georgina saw very much of me. I was way too busy playing with my radio chums.

UP AND RUNNING

Comedy 365 made UK Away FM look like Radio One, but at least it was up and running and it had 350 listeners. We started to get material sent to us from all kinds of bizarre new comedy acts. There was a low-tech sketch show called Executive Slippers. There was the strangely-named Totally Depressed Show. But our favourite, by far, was a writer/performer called John Dredge, who sent us an hilarious series of programmes called simply Things, which John had originally recorded for a small community radio station in London called Resonance FM. The show was about nothing in particular, and seemed to perfectly fit the slowly-emerging brand of Comedy 365. Dredge has since contributed regularly to LBC, and is slowly finding fame via his own video shows on YouTube.

In a similarly surreal vein, we also received The Adventures of Tea Man, from a theatre group in Philadelphia, and a very slick radio sketch series called Blue Pepper, which had recently been turned down by the BBC.

More compilation shows like these followed, and we managed to put out a completely different mix of material every day. We could see the audience slowly building, as we added our feed URL to as many podcast search engines as we could find, but when we submitted our show to the Apple iTunes podcast library, we heard nothing. We knew from reading about Whack My Bush on Chortle, that we'd only get our audience to really grow if we were listed on iTunes, so we patiently sat back, and waited for our listing to appear.

Every day, Georgina would check the iTunes library to see if Comedy 365 was there, and every day it wasn't. iTunes seemed to be a law unto itself. If they decided they were going to list your show they would. If not, there seemed to be bugger-all you could do about it. Comedy 365 simply didn't show up on iTunes. Weeks passed, and eventually we forgot all about it.

Chapter 4
Borrowing from Bennsy

I was becoming increasingly obsessed with improving the technical quality of Comedy 365, which wasn't easy with a budget of zero. I was freelancing at the BBC at the time and I rang up an old telly friend of mine called Alan Benns. I knew that Bennsy had a load of old broadcast equipment lying around in his loft, and I had a feeling he'd lend it to me.

"Why should I let you borrow it for nothing?" he said.
"I'll give you a credit," I said. "You can be Comedy 365's Technical Supervisor."
"A credit eh?" said Bennsy.
"Yep."
"Do I have to do anything else for this proposed credit?"
"Nope."
"In that case," he said "You've got yourself a Technical Supervisor!"
"Welcome aboard!" I said. Telly people will do anything for a credit.

Next thing I knew, the flat was crawling with wires, microphone stands and mixing desks. It didn't look like a home any more. The living room looked more like a cross between a radio studio and Dr Who's Tardis. If Georgina opened a cupboard door, it knocked over a mike stand. Simply walking to the window meant crossing a river of cables wider than the Amazon, and every time Georgina went anywhere near the computer, I barked something at her.

"Don't touch anything!" I would say and then I'd add, with a slightly mysterious air, "It's encoding."

Other PC's soon began to appear. Then a laptop. Suddenly, everything in the flat, including the kettle, seemed to be either encoding, uploading, downloading, front-loading or rear-ending. Georgina stayed quietly out of the way. She had forged a small space for herself, next to the television, from where she didn't move for several days at a time, except to occasionally venture out and forage for food around the microwave.

The upshot of all this activity was that the voiceovers between the comedy clips were now starting to sound a lot more professional and I was recording some of my own material. The only problem was that I was getting rather obsessed with the whole thing. I even turned down freelance work, and before long my bank manager began to get rather twitchy.

THE BIG SQUEEZE

One evening, Georgina suggested that we should do a programme of our own. Why was Comedy 365 spending so much time and effort promoting the talents of other performers? If Brian and Georgina's flat was going to look like a BBC outside broadcast unit, then wasn't it time we used it for the Brian and Georgina Show? I was sceptical at first, but agreed to think about it. Still not entirely understanding the nature of podcasting, or why her life was suddenly, exclusively, dedicated to it, Georgina went surfing around on Google, trying to source good examples of the genre. It wasn't long before she stumbled upon Dawn and Drew.

Dawn and Drew were a young married couple from Wisconsin who did a regular podcast, and everyone on the internet seemed to be raving about their show. Georgina downloaded a couple of episodes and played them to me. When I first heard The Dawn and Drew Show I couldn't believe my ears. I'd been brought up in broadcast television, so I was used to everything being slick and well-produced. Dawn and Drew were so laid back. There were no production values, there was no script, there was barely any content at all. They just chatted to each other, and listened to messages that people had sent them.
"Oh, for fuck's sake, *we* can do this!" I screamed at Georgina. "What are we waiting for?"

On the 20th July 2005, we set up two of Bennsy's microphones on the dining table in the living room, and we recorded the first ever episode of our inaugural podcast, which we decided to call Sowerby and Luff's Big Squeeze. It was fairly tightly scripted, but not very well rehearsed and featured the dull, rumbling accompaniment of a fleet of W7 buses pulling up at the bus stop outside our flat. We did an opening link, a couple of sketches and then, for added tension, we played Trivial Pursuit at the end. That was it.

Here's an excerpt:

> BRIAN: I can't find the running order. What did you do with the running order?
>
> GEORGINA: I haven't done anything with the running order. I gave you the running order.
>
> BRIAN: You didn't give me the running order.
>
> GEORGINA: I gave you the running order.
>
> BRIAN: She hides things.
>
> GEORGINA: I do not *hide* things.
>
> BRIAN: You hide things. You hid my glasses.
>
> GEORGINA: I moved your glasses. I tidied your glasses. I did not hide your glasses.
>
> BRIAN: You hid my glasses.
>
> GEORGINA: OK, where did I hide your glasses?
>
> BRIAN: In that… "thing".
>
> GEORGINA: Thing?
>
> BRIAN: That "thing" that came with my glasses.

GEORGINA: Your glasses case.

BRIAN: How am I supposed to find my glasses in my glasses case??? That's the last place I'd think of looking for my glasses. You hid my jacket.

GEORGINA: I did not hide your jacket.

BRIAN: You hid my jacket.

GEORGINA: On the coat rack.

BRIAN: We have a coat rack? Where's the coat rack?.

GEORGINA: In the cupboard in the studio.

BRIAN: Aha! So you admit you hid my jacket. You hid my jacket inside the cupboard in the studio.

GEORGINA: No.

BRIAN: Behind a closed door.

GEORGINA: What?

BRIAN: There was no possible eye-line between myself and the jacket.

GEORGINA: You're insane.

BRIAN: You hid my lager.

GEORGINA: I put your lager in the fridge.

BRIAN: I never put my lager in the fridge.

GEORGINA: Why?

BRIAN: There isn't time.

We recorded ten 15 minute episodes of Sowerby and Luff's Big Squeeze over the next few days, and we uploaded the first one to the Libsyn server on 25th July 2005. Georgina and I talked about anything and everything we could think of, and in one episode I can even remember Georgina waxing her legs. Those ten shows were the only podcasts we ever really planned to record.

So it would look like we worked for a real production company, we signed off every show by saying that The Big Squeeze was "produced by the British Podcasting Corporation for Comedy 365". I even registered the name and I set up a web page which looked a little like our podcast was produced by the BBC.

About a week after the first Big Squeeze went onto the podcast feed at Libsyn I noticed that someone had left a comment on our Libsyn blog page. Excitedly, I clicked on the link.
"You're shit," it said. I quickly hit delete. I'm sure I blushed.
"What was that?" asked Georgina.
"Oh, nothing," I said.

Despite this rather worrying and brutal feedback, Comedy 365's daily audience had now climbed to around 2,000. Meanwhile, 6,000 miles away in Hong Kong, a chap called David went into an electrical store and bought himself a shiny new iPod.

Chapter 5
Giving CPR to Chickens

Three days after Laura Solon won the Perrier Award in Edinburgh, her agent rang me.

"We'd like you to remove Laura's act from your podcast," she said.

"We have Laura's permission to broadcast it," I replied confidently.

"That was before Laura was a Perrier winner," said the agent. "Now you need *our* permission."

"Why isn't Laura ringing me herself?" I said.

"She doesn't *have* to ring you," said the agent. "She doesn't have to ring anyone ever again. She's won the Perrier Award."

I argued with the agent for about ten minutes then I shouted at her and put the phone down. Which probably wasn't a very good idea, as that particular agent represents most of the well-known comedy talent in the UK.

"What was all that shouting?" asked Georgina.

"I just told Avalon to fuck off," I replied.

"What?" moaned Georgina. "They're the biggest comedy agent on the planet!"

"Yes, I know," I said.

"And you told them to fuck off?"

"Words to that effect, yes," I said.

Georgina laughed. But she also looked a little perturbed. I think she thought I'd gone insane.

OUR FIRST FAN MAIL

Against my better judgment, and still spitting blood, I took Laura Solon's act off the Comedy 365 podcast feed, and we made our first enemy in showbiz, if there is such a thing. Enemies quickly become friends again if there is some money to be made.

Georgina and I got pretty depressed that day. We felt that Sketch Club had been one of the gigs that had made it possible for Laura to test and develop her award-winning material, and we wanted to feel that we'd played some small part in her huge success. Instead, we'd simultaneously had a smack on the wrist and a slap in the face, and we felt quite sorry for ourselves.

But something cheered us up that day. Because that was also the day on which our very first fan letter arrived by email. A very special moment, particularly considering that rather nasty comment that had been posted on our blog page a few weeks before. Of course, we had no idea that this email would be the first of a veritable downpour.

From: "Andre"
Sent: Thursday, 1 September, 2005 1:28 PM
Subject: Congratulations for the show

Hello there. I would like to congratulate you on your excellent shows, and I hope that you keep on doing them. Could you tell me where you do your shows exactly?
Yours sincerely, a Valued Listener.

For some reason I replied by informing Andre that we recorded our programmes in a broom cupboard. Next day, he emailed back again to ask where we studied to be disc-jockeys. Then he requested an autographed picture, and signed off by saying, "You have a listener that is in Spain now."

A genuine fan letter, and a request for an autograph to boot. Georgina had often been asked for autographs before, but previously all the hunters had been under the impression that she was Helena Bonham Carter. The buzz of getting real fan mail was amazing. We couldn't get over the fact that someone, somewhere, had actually enjoyed listening to our inane ramblings at the dining room table. That week, exactly a year after first tracking results for the word "podcasts", Google was now finding more than a hundred million hits on the word. So this was getting serious...

THE GAY LEGS

By now, we had recorded 24 episodes of The Big Squeeze and the penny had finally dropped. This show was not going to be about reading scripts, telling jokes and doing hastily-penned comedy sketches. It was going to be about the way in which Georgina and I viewed the world, the fact that we didn't take life too seriously, and about the things that happened to us every day in our relationship. But most importantly, it was going to be about connecting with the audience and making friends. Thousands of friends, all over the world.

By mid October 2005, Comedy 365 was "Podcast of The Week" in Time Out Magazine. Meanwhile, I had cured most of the initial sound problems we'd encountered by taping the show in a converted flat with paper-thin walls. Instead of recording in the front living room - the one right next to the bus stop - I set up a WAV recorder, a four channel mixer, and two good quality studio microphones in the smallest room at the rear of the flat. By hanging heavy rugs on the walls, I was able to achieve the kind of "dead" sound that even a professional recording engineer might have been be proud of.

Meanwhile, The Big Squeeze was taking on a life of its own. We wanted to give it a more intimate feel - one that involved the audience more - so we started telling them that we were recording the show in a small Irish pub in N8 called The Gay Legs.

Locals will know that there isn't actually a pub in the area called The Gay Legs. The name is just Bennsy's nickname for a real Crouch End boozer called The Harringay Arms. Get it? Harrin*gay* Arms, Gay Legs.

Since we began, The Gay Legs has been interpreted, and spelt, many ways by our poor, confused, overseas listeners. Gaylicks, Gaelics and Gaylex are just a few examples from emails. Maybe Georgina and I should learn to speak English more clearly.

To help create the illusion of broadcasting from a pub, we spent an entire evening in the Harringay Arms, with our little portable tape machine sitting on the table between us, recording endless stereo sound effect beds that we'd be able to play under our voices during the programmes. Eventually, I think Georgina and I actually began to believe that we *were* in The Gay Legs while we were recording the show, and the warm, cosy atmosphere of that little London local became very much a part of the Big Squeeze brand.

Many a mysterious package has since been sent to Sowerby and Luff, care of that pub. Some of our listeners assume that we virtually live in the place, and the more astute of them have tracked down the address on the internet. The look on the landlady's face was priceless when we first went in there for a pint and were handed a parcel from New York. She's been polite enough never to ask why we appear to be using her hostelry as some kind of PO Box.

The couple who run The Gay Legs are very protective of the "stars" that drink in there. Eagle eyed punters have been known to spot cast members from the TV soap EastEnders, BBC newsreaders, and occasionally even the voice of Bob the Builder himself Neil Morrissey. Georgina was once sitting drinking with the famous Irish comedian Sean Hughes, when a paparazzi photographer came into The Gay Legs to take a picture of Sean. The landlord snatched the camera right out of his hand, and threw him into the street.

WHAT COLOUR IS YOUR TOOTHBRUSH?

A couple of the things that really started to build the audience for The Big Squeeze, and generate huge feedback, were the stupid competitions and surveys we began to run. We never offered any prizes or rewards for taking part, but no-one seemed to care. All they wanted was to hear their name being read out on their MP3 player.

Once, I pretended that Georgina had bought a baby gerbil as a pet, and we asked the listeners to come up with a name for it. The "Name That Gerbil" emails continued to come in for weeks and weeks afterwards. (Richard Gere being the most popular suggestion.) A few weeks later we asked the listeners to tell us the colour of their toothbrushes. It seemed the more trivial the question, the more feedback it would generate. Unable to cope with the volume of emails on that subject, we eventually had to add a dedicated Toothbrush Colour Survey to our website.

From: "Mark"
Subject: Toothbrush Colors

Here are some cold hard facts. Oral B, which is a big dental brand in Australia and America, produces 730,000 blue toothbrushes per year, with red coming in at second with 650,000. The rest of the colours, in order, are lime, orange, lilac, aqua, purple, pine, white, black, sky blue, pink, then all of the preceding colours combined with white, then various combinations of two colours.

Georgina's International Database of Toothbrush Colours is now the largest in the world, and is often used by dental professionals and students alike in presentations and essays. Or so she says.

Sometimes we caused controversy over the most pointless of subjects. We were inundated with emails, for example, when I casually mentioned that if you divide zero by zero, the answer would be zero. It became immediately obvious that a small percentage of the audience for The Big Squeeze were mathematicians, and the debate raged for many weeks.

From: "Christopher"
Subject: Zero divided by zero

Brian, Brian, Brian........ Brian! I just listened to The Big Squeeze, and heard you say "Zero divided by Zero = Zero". Oh dear. You cannot divide a sum of money, or anything else come to that, by zero. Try it and your calculator will blow up. Gospel.

Georgina made a promise in one programme that she would answer every single email that was sent to us. This probably wasn't the most sensible thing she ever said, but so far she's managed to keep her promise, with the exception of three particularly filthy emails about a donkey, which she wisely chose not to answer. Over the months we gradually built up pen pal-like relationships with our most regular listeners. We knew when they were going on holiday. We knew when they had arguments with their partners. We even knew when their sons were having their Bar-Mitzvahs. Georgina tried her best to come up with entertaining replies to their emails, spending at least a couple of hours each morning answering messages from all four corners of the globe.

Luckily, Georgina is a morning person. By the time I've crawled out of bed she's usually answered dozens of emails. While I'm wallowing in my pit at the far end of the flat I can often hear her chuckling over the latest rubbish sent in by one of our regulars.

I tend to do my work at the other end of the day. I'll often sit up editing programmes or writing ideas until the early hours of the morning. The fact that Georgina's a morning person and I'm an evening person means that there's always something going on in our flat. It's like having two shifts on the factory floor. Except that we don't have to clock in. It does mean, however, that we always have to record in the afternoon, when we are both equally awake.

A lot of people used *The Big Squeeze* to pass the time while they were at work or in high school. Once, we asked the listeners to tell us exactly what they were doing while they were tuned in, and we got some surprisingly specific replies:

From: "Silvan"
Subject: What I'm doing...

Sanding blocks of Styrofoam into various strange shapes, for school credit. Oh, also eating some chocolate-coated coffee beans.

SLEEPLESS IN SVENDBORG

While becoming ever more deeply immersed in the world of what clever people were now calling "on-demand audio", we continued to support ourselves by running comedy writing workshops every couple of weeks in London. It was through the website for one of these workshops that we received an unexpected email from a man in Denmark called Micael.

"Would you like to come to Demark," he wrote, "and present one of your workshops at the Svendborg Comedy Festival?"

Georgina looked up Svendborg on the map. It was a tiny seaside town in the south of Denmark.

"It doesn't look big enough to have a comedy festival," she said.

I peered over her shoulder at the map. "It doesn't look big enough to have a post office."

One of the rules of working freelance is if you're offered a job which you don't really fancy doing, you quote an unrealistically large fee and demand first class accommodation. Unfortunately this ploy didn't work with Svendborg. For reasons best known to them, they were determined to have Sowerby and Luff at their comedy festival.

A few weeks later, our plane touched down in Copenhagen, and a train whisked us across a fjord to a place called Nyborg, where we were to be met by Svendborg's "King of Comedy" Micael.

Micael was a painfully polite man of about 40, with a shiny bald head. As we climbed into his tiny car at Nyborg station, Georgina and I looked at each other as if to say "What the fuck are we doing here?"

During a long and uncomfortable car journey to Svendborg, Micael explained, in perfect English, that he was a huge fan of Monty Python, and that it had always been his dream to run a comedy festival in Denmark.

"Why didn't you hold the festival in Copenhagen?" asked Georgina.

"Because this is the *Svendborg* Comedy Festival" Micael replied, with quite staggering logic.

It slowly became clear that with only a tiny amount of support from Svendborg Town Council, Micael was financing this extravaganza himself. He dropped us at our hotel and said he looked forward to working with us the next day.

Svendborg was clean. Disgustingly clean. If it had been any cleaner you would have had to wear white rubber boots and a surgical mask to walk down the street. We ventured out that evening, and the entire town was deserted. We walked for what seemed like miles and neither saw nor heard anyone. Eventually we walked into a restaurant and ordered two pizzas.

"What's this on the pizza?" asked Georgina when dinner arrived.

"Peas," said the waiter.

Georgina giggled and whispered in my ear. "Who puts peas on a pizza?"

"People in Svendborg," I whispered back.

We didn't sleep very well that night. It was too quiet. And clean. The next day we rose early and after a healthy breakfast of bacon, eggs and peas, we walked though spotless, silent streets to the medieval town hall in which the comedy festival was to take place. The doors were locked and bolted, and there was a chain across the outside.

"I can't see any publicity for the festival," said Georgina. Like a vampire, Micael suddenly popped into view out of nowhere, making us both jump.

"There is a poster!" he said, and he pointed at a small A4 photocopy, stuck hastily to a brick wall with Bluetack.

"Svendborg Comedy Festival," it said. It looked as if Micael had made it himself the night before.

"Where is everybody?" we asked.

"They will be here soon," he said. "They are sharing a car from Sweden."

It soon became clear that there were so few attendees for our workshop in Denmark, they were able to share the same car. Even more bizarrely, they were coming from another country.

"Comedy is very popular in Sweden," said Micael.

Our hearts sank. We'd apparently flown half way across Europe for nothing, and it was quite possible that our host was a fucking lunatic. We were led into a large meeting room, with a high, echoey ceiling, and supplied with warm bottled water and biscuits.

"When will the people from Sweden be here?" asked Georgina.

"Any minute now," said Micael, and sure enough, ten minutes later we were joined by a small group of Swedish people, who wanted to talk about comedy with Sowerby and Luff.

We usually began our workshops by going around the table and asking each person in turn to tell us a little about themselves. I kicked off with our host, who was sitting at the far end of the table, looking a little nervous.

"My name is Micael," he said, "I am the organiser of the Svendborg Comedy Festival."
He obviously couldn't think of anything else to say about himself, so we moved on swiftly.

Next was a middle-aged lady sitting at the other end of the table. She was blond and strikingly good-looking, and explained that she was a highly successful comedian in Sweden, who had for many years fronted her own television series. It has to be said, this was not the kind of background information we usually get from the budding comedy writers who attend our workshops in London.

"Why are you here?" I inquired politely.

"I am a big fan of Monty Python," she said.

The group from Sweden were friendly, funny and forthcoming, and the day passed surprisingly quickly, as the seven of us chatted about various theories of comedy writing. But at the back of my mind was a nagging question – where was the rest of the Svendborg Comedy festival?

When the workshop finished at around five o'clock, Micael led us all downstairs, and into a cavernous wood-panelled hall, with a stage at one end. In the centre of the stage was a microphone on a stand, and sitting around a single table in the middle of the room were seven or eight elderly locals.

"Who are these people?" I asked.

"This is the audience," said Micael.

"The audience for what?" I asked.

"You," he said.

It transpired that two of the people in the audience were Micael's mother and father. They sat and patiently waited for the show to begin.

"Do they speak English?" asked Georgina.

"A little," said Micael.

I looked at the blond TV lady from Sweden. "Will you get up and do five minutes for them?" I pleaded.

"No fucking way," she smiled.

At that point, Miceal put on a face mask and a top hat.

"I'm afraid," I whispered to Georgina.

"It's OK" she said, "I promise I will get us out of here alive!"

Not surprisingly, neither Georgina nor I speak Danish, but we managed to follow Miceal's act. First he told a couple of jokes, then he sang a little song. Then, to my utter horror, he introduced me. "Ladies and gentlemen, all the way from London, Mr Brian Luff."

I walked slowly onto the stage, accompanied only by the sound of my own footsteps and Georgina giggling in the back row. I began with an old warm-up routine I had once seen MacKenzie Crook do at a club in Hammersmith.

"You're probably wondering why there are so few people here," I said. "Well, we *were* expecting a coach party of people from Hull."

Georgina was now literally sobbing with laughter, but the rest of the room was as silent as the grave. I continued.

"I was wondering if one of the tables here wouldn't mind *pretending* to be the coach party of people from Hull."

There was only one table in the room, so I edged towards them.

"Would you guys like to be the coach party of people from Hull?" I asked.

"Pardon?" came a quiet voice. I heard a thud, as Georgina fell off her chair.

That was the climax of the Svendborg Comedy Festival. Even as we write this, we still can't quite believe that it actually happened. But the good news was that Miceal asked for our invoice at the end of the day, and paid us immediately. He even invited us back the following year.

"Will it be in Copenhagen next time? Georgina asked.

"Of course not" said Micael, "It is the *Svendborg* Comedy Festival."

It is one of our greatest regrets that we didn't take any recording equipment to Denmark that week, as the comedy night in the old town hall would probably have made one of our funniest podcasts ever.

Chapter 6
Stalking Colin Blunstone

"When are you at your happiest?" Georgina asked suddenly, while we were out shopping in Crouch End Broadway.

"That's an odd question to ask a man pushing a trolley around Budgens," I said.

"Tell me," Georgina insisted.

"When I'm in the aisle with the crisps and the Tortilla chips," I replied.

"Not in Budgens," snapped Georgina. "When are you at your happiest in life?"

I chucked an industrial-sized bag of cashew nuts into the trolley and thought about it for a while.

"When I'm travelling," I said. "I love staying in hotel rooms."

"So do I," said Georgina. "But why?"

"It's like living in a bubble," I said. "That's why rock groups become completely addicted to touring. They forget how to live in the real world."

"And what are we escaping from when we travel?" asked Georgina. This shopping trip was turning into a session on the psychiatrist's couch.

"Everything," I said. "Ex-wives, mortgages, money worries. In a hotel you don't even have to worry about cooking food or doing the laundry. Everything's done for you."

"Like being in prison?" asked Georgina.

"Isn't it the real world that's the prison?" I said cryptically.

"Maybe that's what our podcast is really all about," said Georgina. "Escapism."

"For us or for our listeners?" I asked.

"Both," smiled Georgina.

Inspired by our Svendborg adventure, and ever more addicted to suitcases and hotel rooms, we decided it was time we took The Big Squeeze on the road. Clearly, what we needed to do was to start talking bollocks about stuff that was going on in the outside world. So, we scoured the listings magazines and newspapers for the most cringe-making and kitsch event we could find, and eventually plumped for a 1960's weekend at Butlin's in Bognor Regis. Believe me, until you've seen a seventy-five year old woman in an electric wheelchair, dressed as Cilla Black, you haven't lived.

We drank weak lager out of plastic glasses and watched a succession of overweight, grey haired men in matching gold lamé suits, strum their way through songs that had propelled them into the pop charts forty years earlier. Then we recorded a podcast about it. It was a mixture of genuine review and surreal exaggeration, and it got a great response. At one point I suggested that Georgina had disappeared around the back of the Bob the Builder house at Butlin's with all five members of Dave Dee, Dozy, Beaky, Mick and Tich - and had "pleased them all in special ways."

One night, Georgina and I wandered into one of the Butlin's music venues and caught the end of a performance by a legendary band called The Zombies. I pompously explained to Georgina that this was, of course, not the 1960's line up of the group, and that the band could only achieve the genuine sound of The Zombies if graced by the unique voice of the original lead singer Colin Blunstone. At which point a woman sitting at the table in front of us turned around and announced, "This is Colin Blunstone."

"I think you'll find it isn't," I smiled confidently.

Being too shy to walk up to the lead singer after the gig and ask him who he was, I asked Georgina to go into Butlin's Customer Service the following morning and inquire "if there was a Mr Blunstone staying on site."

"I'm afraid I can't pass on that information for security reasons," said the assistant.

"I don't want to know his room number," said Georgina. "I just want to know if it's the real Colin Blunstone or a tribute artist."

"You might be a stalker," said the assistant.

"I am not a stalker," said Georgina. "Why would I want to stalk a man with dyed hair who is old enough to be my grandfather?"

"I don't know," said the assistant, who was now becoming a little annoyed.

"Look," said Georgina, "If I was going to stalk Colin Blunstone, don't you think I'd know if he was the real Colin Blunstone, or someone who sounded a bit like Colin Blunstone? A stalker would know that kind of thing."

"I'm sorry," said the assistant, "I can't help you. Anyway, he checked out this morning."

In that week's podcast we offered a Butlin's teabag as a prize for anyone who could tell us if Colin Blunstone was currently appearing as Colin Blunstone in the UK tour of The Zombies, and one of the listeners sent us a link to the official Colin Blunstone website, featuring a photograph of him singing at Butlin's that very Saturday night. We asked the listener for his address, so that we could send him the teabag, but he never replied. We still have the teabag.

BOLLOCKY BANTER

Our audience was now effectively writing The Big Squeeze for us, and our little 15 minute podcast soon became a 30 minute show, in which the highlights were invariably curious subjects raised by our listeners.
User Generated Content was on the rise, and it had found its way into Brian and Georgina's spare bedroom in Crouch End.

Every week, Georgina would read out her latest list of subjects for the "Talking Bollocks" section of the programme. She kept a big A4 notebook, full of bits and bobs that had intrigued her, or made her laugh during the week, and we'd invite the listeners to add to it.

From: "Virginie"
Subject: An addition to your world famous list…

Please talk about very small dogs, the kind you can sit on, or step on, without even realizing it.

There was never any shortage of subject matter, but it was also around this time that listeners first began to invite us to go and stay with them.

From: "Joel"
Subject: Sowerby and Luff

The other day I downloaded several episodes of your show... quite by accident, mind you. Much to my surprise, I found myself laughing my arse off at your brassy bits of meaningless mad, and bollocky banter. If you ever find yourselves in Vancouver, Canada, you have a place to stay and all the crème de menthe you can drink.

    It wasn't long before we'd had enough emails like this to begin to seriously contemplate the idea of taking The Big Squeeze on tour, and going and meeting one or two of our devoted listeners in the United States. Meanwhile, in order to create the illusion that we were already spreading our wings, we started to experiment with simple audio soundscapes, to apparently lift ourselves out of The Gay Legs and into the real world.

    By far the most popular of these was the episode in which we pretended that the entire show had been recorded while we were having a day out in the car. We supposedly got hopelessly lost in the countryside, and the programme slowly descended into a massive argument between Georgina and I, while I drove the car and she navigated with a map. (A programme based on a not entirely fictional episode the week before.)

    The listeners were so convinced that we had actually recorded the show in a motor car, and had a genuine row, that we then decided to try a load of other unlikely scenarios. In one show, Georgina "tied me to the bed", and spent the entire show spanking me. In another, we did a spoof of the TV series Most Haunted, and pretended that we were on a ghostbusting vigil in a dark and lonely location called Yarm Barn.

    One week, with the help of a few seagull sound effects, we even pretended that we were recording the show stark bollock naked on a nudist beach in North Wales. Feeling guilty that we'd defrauded the listeners, we then taped the next show *actually* naked. But we never referred to it during the programme. When Georgina "gave me a tattoo", live on air, not a single listener questioned whether it was for real. We didn't have the heart to tell them that the sound of the painful tattooing device had been achieved with an electric toothbrush.

>From: "Logan"
Subject: Brian's Tattoo

Could you put a picture of the tattoo up on your website? I'm sure that your myriad of listeners are interested to see how it turned out.

The more experimental we became, the more feedback we got.

From: "Mark"
Subject: Bed-tying podcast

Your recent bed-tying podcast had me wetting myself on the train into Waterloo this morning (much to the disgust of my fellow commuters). Great imagery. Keep them coming.

We now lived in a world where a man on a train could listen to me being "spanked" by Georgina, whilst pulling into Waterloo Station on a Monday morning. It was weird. But it was going to get a whole lot weirder.

CORPORATE CAPERS

Georgina and I were still financing our podcasting activities mainly by running writing workshops at a church hall in Crouch End. We also organised the occasional corporate workshops, in which we ran team-building exercises using comedy writing and performance. Getting people to write, then perform stand-up or sketches in front of a large audience of their work colleagues is an excellent test of bottle for client-facing staff. At least, that's what it used to say on our website.

We'd spend the morning teaching clients a series of tried and tested comedy writing formulae, then get them to apply those formulae to short sketches set in their own places of work. These events usually went pretty smoothly, but one weekend we ran a workshop for a well-known financial services company from the City of London. We had no way of knowing that one of the scenes our students penned featured a rather delicate situation involving a member of middle-management who was about to get fired. Worse still, everyone in the company knew he was going to get the sack, except him. That was the joke. And it would have been an extremely funny joke, except for the fact that when the group performed their sketch in front of the entire company that evening, the guy who was about to get fired was sitting right in the front row.

I'm sure there are many ways to tell a man that he's going to lose his job, but this had to be one of the worst. Needless to say, the gentleman in question was not amused and, of course, Georgina and I were mortified. When we run similar workshops now, we always tell that little story as a cautionary tale about the dangers that comedy can pose in a corporate environment.

We've also been asked to get involved with comedy-driven activities for the purposes of promoting products, and over the years we've employed a surprisingly large number of comedians for such gigs. In many cases, the good money a comic can earn from this kind of work can far outweigh their earnings as a comedian on the circuit. It's known in the business as "milking the corporate cow."

One client engaged us to employ a team of comedians for the purpose of promoting the white rum Malibu in around 120 different pubs and bars around the UK. The promotion involved a huge logistical operation, in which we had to recruit, train and write scripts for over 20 comics, as well as organising all their travel and accommodation for a period of 12 weeks.

Inspired by shows like Trigger Happy TV, and working alongside a creative agency called The House, we created "Anti-Seriousness Squads", whose job it was to burst into bars with megaphones and announce to the startled people of that town that they were "far too serious".
Only by sampling the miraculous alcoholic beverage Malibu would these folks become suddenly and converted to "A Life Less Serious". As you can imagine, this was a fairly thankless task for the

comedians involved, but the activity scored a high level of increased sales for the stuff, and eventually the campaign won a prestigious marketing award.

Dozens of up-and-coming comedians came in and tried out for those Malibu gigs. I particularly remember two auditions. Robin Ince (later Ricky Gervais's famous sidekick) was considered "a little too quiet and shy" by the client, and Justin Lee Collins actually removed his trousers and hopped around the room on one leg. Despite this extraordinary display Malibu loved Justin, but when he was offered the work he turned it down, "because there was too much travel involved." Poor Justin has since had to make do with his own primetime comedy series on Channel 4.

Other notable members of our "Anti-Seriousness Squads" included Tom Price – more recently the star of Channel 5 sketch series Swinging, Lawry Lewin from BBC sitcom The Life and Times of Vivian Vyle and inspired New Zealand stand-up Jarred Christmas. I bumped into Jarred quite recently and he confided in me that it had been "that bloody awful Malibu gig" that had enabled him to give up his day job and turn professional as a comedian in the UK. It's great to know one's doing one's bit for the funny men and women of tomorrow.

Chapter 7
Gloopy Love

"Manchester United has paid a mammoth twenty million pounds for their new defender. We can't imagine why the club would hand over such a huge amount of money to a long extinct hairy mammal who looks like an elephant."

So began one episode of The Big Squeeze in the late winter of 2005. It wasn't the best joke we'd ever come up with, but Georgina and I were slowly getting the hang of this podcasting lark. By then, we were dedicating almost all of our time to running Comedy 365 and recording our own podcast. But Christmas was coming, and our bank managers could not be kept at bay for ever. As in many long term relationships, arguments are most likely to kick off over money matters. "The Money Monster" we call it. Such disputes are generally pretty fruitless and destructive.

Being creative can be a fucking burden sometimes, and Georgina and I would no doubt have had a much easier life if we'd been a couple of lawyers, or maybe a dentist and a chartered accountant. But then we wouldn't have met each other. Unless, of course, Georgina had been a dentist and I'd been brought in to prepare her annual tax return. Or maybe she'd been called upon to perform some painful root canal work on one of my back molars.

When The Money Monster reared its ugly head in Crouch End, there were days when we both felt bad-tempered and irritable, and didn't want to record The Big Squeeze at all. Other times, we had to tape the show even if we were both feeling unwell. Georgina says I'm at my most humorous when I feel like shit. I suspect she might be right. Sometimes when we went into that little room to record a show, it felt like a prison cell. We stood there glaring at each other like mindless idiots, without having as much as the first line of the programme loaded into our brains. Motivating yourself to be entertaining when you're feeling like crap isn't easy, and forcing out a laugh, when your head feels like it's full of Polyfilla, is not the kind of therapy either of us would recommend.

SHOWBIZ FAMILIES

My dad has always been quietly horrified that I haven't settled into a more steady and well-paid profession, but it is at least partly the fault of my family that I've ended up in this industry in the first place.

Yes, I admit it. I come from a "showbiz family" of sorts. My mum and dad actually met while singing together in a swing choir, which had been put together to entertain British troops at the back end of World War II. When the war was over, The George Mitchell Singers stayed together and became extremely famous - appearing in hundreds of BBC radio and TV shows, and even the occasional movie. My mum and dad did dozens of radio broadcasts, and in 1948 my dad was a backing singer in Here Come The Huggetts with Jack Warner and a teenage Petula Clark. Dad's autograph book is filled with the signatures of stars like Noel Coward and Irving Berlin. It must be worth a fortune.

After the war my Uncle Alan also joined the singers, and he stayed as a member of the group until the early 1970s, which was when he first took me to the BBC to watch camera rehearsals for The Dick Emery Show - a comedy series he was appearing in at the time. After five minutes sitting in a real BBC studio I was hooked. This had to be better than working for a living.

Georgina, too, was "backstage" from as early as she could remember. The smell of scenery paint and the wonder of costume storage rooms enthralled her. Just as my parents met in the entertainment business, Georgina's mum and dad also met in the theatre. Her dad, Malcolm loved his amateur acting, and mum, Barabara designed all the costumes. Georgina quickly learned her way around Middlesbrough Little Theatre, and her parents always seemed to be involved in one way or another in the productions there.

When she was six, Malcolm designed and built the set for a production of King Lear, and she spent her time following him around on the stage and watching rehearsals. Little Georgina sat in the auditorium for the technical run through of Lear, and her dad suddenly became worried that she might be frightened by the famous eye gouging scene. He hurried to remove her from her seat before the bloody torture took place on stage, and he remembers her saying quite calmly "But Daddy, my favourite colour is red."

So, both Georgina's and my family backgrounds were a little unorthodox. Her family were theatrical and creative, and she grew up in a house that had paintings of hogweed on the wall and Egyptian hieroglyphics decorating the bathroom. Staying at friends houses when she was young, Georgina was always amazed how conventional her friends' parents were. Her own family weren't exactly a "hippy commune", but her upbringing, like mine, was far from conformist or dull.

Barbara met Malcolm, during her first ever acting role, and they immediately fell in love. He'd just returned from Switzerland, where he'd been working as an architect, and he was about to start designing buildings in Sheffield. Georgina says the pairing was "wonderful fate".

Like me, Georgina grew up in rich and fertile soil for creativity. She also had a vivid imagination and when the truth didn't excite her, "little white lies" played an important part in her world. They still do, I can assure you. And that can often come in very handy in the creation of an improvised comedy show.

In 1973, after half a lifetime working in the entertainment business, my uncle Alan finally decided that the freelance life of a singer was too precarious for him, and he went and got himself what my dad would call "a proper job". Barely a month later, I left school and started work in the television industry. One out. One in.

BUY US A DRINK

As a mostly freelance writer and producer, I've never been in employment for more than about 6 months at a time, and I've become accustomed to having a fairly erratic income. So, if Georgina and I were really serious about this podcasting lark, we'd have to come up with a convincing way of generating revenue through Comedy 365. There was still no sign of our feed in the iTunes charts,

so we weren't getting enough listeners to go after sponsorship. We had to be inventive. I asked my dad for some ideas.
"Get a proper job," he said.

After an evening sitting in the real Gay Legs drinking Guinness, Georgina and I came up with a plan. Since people thought we were recording in a pub, maybe they'd buy us drinks. Then we could read out the names of the people who were getting the beers in during each show. The following day, I set up a shopping cart on our website which enabled listeners to click on two beer glasses and buy each of us a pint. Before the day was out, one of our regulars had bought both of us a drink.

So, now we were technically professional broadcasters, with a revenue generating radio show. But freelance work, as ever, was looking thin on the ground, and The Big Squeeze wouldn't be enough to see us through Christmas. What we needed was a bigger audience and a real sponsor. Fueled with enthusiasm after our drink-buying idea, I came up with another scheme for generating revenue. We would sell sponsorship for The Big Squeeze on EBay.
"It'll never work," said Georgina.
"It'll work," I said.
"It'll never work," she repeated.
Ten days later I checked EBay and howled with joy.
"We've got a bid! We've got a bid!"
"How much?" Georgina asked.
"A pound," I said, and slumped back into my chair.

BIG FISH

While I was online that morning, I also checked iTunes, like I did every day, to see which podcasts were currently in the Top 100. I'd generally start searching from the bottom of the chart upwards, hoping that one day I'd discover that Comedy 365 had slipped in at number 98. But I rarely scrolled up higher than 50. What was the point? We weren't going to be there. Which is why, for the past few days, I had failed to notice that Comedy 365 was sitting proudly at number 14.

"Fuck!" I yelled. Georgina came running out of the bathroom wrapped in a towel, imagining that I had accidentally cut my finger off with a power tool.

"What's the matter?" she panted.

"We're in the top twenty on iTunes!"

We performed a victory dance around the flat, but we didn't really know what our new-found chart status meant. I dashed back to the computer and, for the first time in a week, checked our download stats. Big Squeeze 43, in which we discussed giving CPR to chickens, had racked up over 10,000 downloads.

From: "Mark"
Subject: Woman Resuscitates Chicken

A retired nurse saved her brother's chicken by administering mouth-to-beak resuscitation last week after the fowl was found floating face down in the family's pond. "I breathed into its beak, and its eyes popped open," she said, but admitted that she did not know how to find a pulse on a chicken.

10,000 listeners. Now that was an audience. And certainly a clear improvement on those three people tuning in to Comedy 365 back in the summer.

Next day we got an email from a listener in Canada. We were 23 in the Canadian iTunes chart. A week later we entered the USA chart at 12, and by the end of November 2005 we had overtaken The Simpsons podcast to sit at number 3 in both the USA and UK charts. As far as I remember, that day only BBC DJs Chris Moyles and Chris Evans were keeping Comedy 365 from being the top podcast in the United Kingdom.

Georgina and I went into overdrive, and quickly launched a brand new weekday programme in addition to The Big Squeeze. We named it The Rush, and it was supposedly recorded at the W7 bus stop outside our flat. It took the format of a daily "drivetime" show, for people to listen to during the rush hour on their way to work. Before long, The Rush was pushing nearly 100,000 downloads a week.

So there we were, talking to a daily audience as large as a small local radio station, and we didn't even have a proper studio. Podcasting was still in its infancy, and it was looking like we were about to become a couple of its very first celebrities. But Sowerby and Luff were still only big fish in a relatively small pond. All of that was about to change. Because the next day, Ricky Gervais announced to the world that he was going to start podcasting. Our little cottage industry was never going to be the same again.

OUR FIRST SPONSOR

It was December 2005, and Georgina and I were excited to note that downloads of our podcast had now passed the two million mark. Meanwhile, I was once again keeping the bank manager at bay with a couple of weeks freelance work making TV trailers for My Name is Earl in German and Swedish.

At the end of the month, one of our listeners emailed to suggest that we should regularly give out a text number in our shows, as most of our audience listened to us while on the move.

When we approached a texting company called Essendex, we were amazed to discover that they had actually heard of our podcast, and they offered us a completely free text number and account in exchange for giving them the occasional plug in our programme. In its small way that was Sowerby and Luff's first ever commercial sponsorship and, looking back, it was the first time we ever started to think of our podcast as something that might one day pay the mortgage.

Ironically, the Big Squeeze text service never really took off. We got the occasional daft little message, but our listeners tended to want to send us long, rambling emails full of trivia, jokes and extended incidents from their private lives - material they really couldn't be bothered to write on a keyboard the size of a postage stamp.

GLOWERING GEORGINA

Of course, all of this activity was running in parallel with our normal everyday lives and despite our unexpected online fame, we still had all the usual stresses and strains of living together and being in a long-term relationship. Georgina says that sometimes, for effect, I would deliberately try and put her in a bad mood before we started to record. She says I'd be rude, sarcastic or simply try and irritate her into a reaction. We'd often start the show not even looking at each other across the microphones – Georgina red-faced and fuming.

I'm sure it must have been evident in some of our podcasts that we were genuinely loathing each other. I'll admit, my so-called "wit" can often misfire and be quite hurtful, and many of our throw-away comments, which listeners might have perceived as funny, were actually continuing an argument we started before the programme. Or even from the previous week.

I'm extremely short tempered, and Georgina has a great line in glowering. But sometimes this combination can lead to some great moments in our podcasts. We've had lots of emails in which listeners have asked if we sometimes record the show after a big row. Our replies have always been honest. We have so often glared at each other while happily reading out funny emails. But this is probably to be expected if you live, work and record together in one relatively small place.

TEN PAIRS OF PANTS

In the run up to Christmas 2005, we decided to step outside the Big Squeeze format and make a series of podcasts which would give Georgina a chance to make use of the various funny accents and voices she can do. So, we created another new series.

In Ten Pairs of Pants I pretended I was traveling around the country, trying to persuade women to give me a pair of their knickers – a fairly thin and sexist premise, admittedly. However, in every town I visited, the girl I met was actually played by Georgina. She would show me around her town then, of course, refuse to give me a single item of her underwear and send me away with my tail between my legs.

I supposedly travelled to Manchester, Newcastle, Bristol, over to Ireland and to numerous other UK cities, all without leaving the comfort of the little studio in our spare room, and all the while stretching Georgina's use of character voices and accents to the limit.

Astonishingly, Ten Pairs of Pants got around 50,000 downloads per week, and remains one of our most popular podcasts ever. The only accent Georgina had real trouble with was Middlesbrough, which is ironic, because that's where she comes from. Half way through that programme we just gave up and went to the pub.

STATS AND SITCOMS

Around this time we launched our first comprehensive audience survey, using a company called Podtrac. Listeners were encouraged to visit our website and fill in a 10 page questionnaire. We were surprised how many of our regulars took the trouble to do it. Once the number of respondents had passed 500, the results began to be taken seriously by potential sponsors and advertisers, and for the first time a picture began to emerge about who our listeners were and where they came from.

We were interested to learn that over half of our audience was in the United States, and that it was predominantly male. It also became apparent that the majority of our listeners used our podcasts like a breakfast show, while on their way to work, or as a drivetime broadcast when they were on their way home. The results of this survey really helped us to pitch our programmes with the right tone, as for the first time we were able to visualize our listeners while we were recording.

Ever keen to road test new ways of recording the Big Squeeze, one week we actually wrote a U.S. sitcom episode in the style of Seinfeld. Of course, this extended the prep time for the show from 2 hours to around 4 days, but we wanted to be seen to be pushing the envelope of what a weekly podcast could achieve. Big

Squeeze – The Sitcom was also a scenario which played on our regular listeners' increasing curiosity about the real-life relationship between Georgina and me.

"Are you two married, shacking up or just acting?" asked one email. But we never seriously discussed our ex-partners, ex-wives or skeletons in the cupboard. That wouldn't be cricket, now would it? Anyway, it was a lot more fun to continue to keep everyone guessing.

Here's a snatch from that completely fictional sitcom episode:

BRIAN: My ex-wife wants more money for the kids.

GEORGINA: Ouch!

BRIAN: I can't afford to send her any more money. My outgoings are already going out further than my incomings are coming in.

GEORGINA: Mm.

BRIAN: My outgoings need to start going out less than they are going out. Not going out more than they are going out.

GEORGINA: Then you can go out more.

BRIAN: What?

GEORGINA: Reduce your outgoings, and then you'll be able to go out more.

BRIAN: Yes.

GEORGINA: Then you'll become more outgoing.

We did occasionally let slip the nature of our real-life partnership, but we thought it was far more important that our listeners created their own fantasy picture of our lives. Mind you, sometimes the fantasies could go a little far.

> From: "Wes"
> Subject: Get out of my head!
>
> Last night I had a very odd dream. I dreamed that I flew on a dragon's back to London, and had tea with you two. There was also marmalade. It was very strange, especially since everyone had their clothes on - something very unusual in my dreams. Bugger off and let me sleep!

How about this one:

> From: "Kerri"
> Subject: My Dream
>
> I don't know if I should tell you this, but I'm going to anyway. You might be freaked out, you might be flattered, or you might just laugh. Here it is: I had a sex dream about you two! Georgina and I fooled around for a while, which was very sexy. Then, after a while, Brian joined us. Unfortunately, that's when things went downhill. At least for me. Brian started to have sex with Georgina, and I basically got left out. Once you both finished, you said you were tired and went to bed and just left me there, all hot and bothered and extremely frustrated. For some reason, you slept in separate beds, which I found weird. When I asked you why, you said there was no reason to sleep together because you both hated to cuddle. Georgina, I was thinking, maybe we could both explore our bi-curiosity together. If it's anything like my dream, it'll be sexy as hell. You'll just have to leave Brian at home.

Charming. Thanks Kerri. Occasionally, Georgina's sexy messages to her adoring male listeners incurred the jealous wrath of her fans' own partners:

> From: "Susan"
> Subject: Podcast smooches

I have to protest at Georgina sending my husband podcast kisses. I was already peeved with you when he insisted that we spend our last night out sans kids listening to your programme. It's not that I didn't enjoy it, but it didn't exactly set the right tone for the romantic dinner I had in mind. Anyway, podcast smooching is more than my ageing ego can bear, so lay off.

COSTUME DRAMA

Inspired by Merchant Ivory, we even turned our hand to costume drama for one of our podcasts - penning an historical radio play about the fictional seventh wife of Henry VIII. Needless to say, Georgina played wannabe wife number seven and I played Henry, using my very best Ray Winstone voice. Here's a short clip, in which Henry talks about his innate fear of getting old, a speech which I think exactly reflects my own views on the subject.

> HENRY VIII: I intend to become very old indeed. The physicians in this place wouldn't dare let me die, anyway. I'd have 'em executed. But old age is a terrible thing. You wake up in the morning and every part of you either aches, itches or throbs. The arse is the worst. Sometimes it burns, sometimes it bleeds, sometimes it just gently hisses. But it's always there, the arse. Saying "listen to me, focus on me, don't forget about me" - the epicentre of your aching, itching, throbbing universe. Then there's the sores. Bed sores, cold sores, sore bollocks, sore feet. When you're young, you don't even notice your body. With age comes a terrible acquaintance with the flesh.
>
> My prick turned bright canary yellow once. I never found out why. It eventually returned to its regular hue, after passing, one by one, through all the colours of the rainbow. At Yuletide in 1543 it went bright purple and began to flash. Drawing on years of medical experience, the Royal Physician put a leech on it. And I can assure you, the last thing in the world you want sucking on your knob on Christmas Day is a leech. Excruciatingly painful. It cleared up the problem though. Eventually. Shortly afterwards I had the physician burned as a witch at Greenwich. The leech and I still communicate regularly by letter…

My sexual performance has become terribly disappointing. These days, if I have intercourse twice a year I refer to it as "multiple orgasm". Even the king of England cannot pass a law to extricate himself from the sheer Gothic horror of getting old.

THE CHRISTMAS SINGLE

After a long pre-Christmas session in the pub, our musical guru Richard Cray and I came up with the ridiculous idea of putting out a free-to-download Sowerby and Luff Christmas Single. I rang a very hungover Richard the next day and asked him if he had any unused original songs lying around in his attic. Ten minutes later he emailed me the lyrics and an MP3 backing track for one of his old compositions, Gloopy Love – a daft sound-alike of Yummy Yummy Yummy by The Archies.

 I immediately rang in sick to my freelance job, and loaded the track up in my N-Track studio software. It took me a while to build a vocal booth in the hallway in the flat, but I finally got a decent sound by hanging a fluffy rug over the front door and propping a double mattress against the entrance to the kitchen. While Georgina was at Sainsbury's that afternoon, I gargled with gin and recorded a guide vocal. I played it to her when she got back.

Oh my gloopy love, oh my gloopy love,
Oh my love for you is ever so gloopy.

Oh my gloopy love, gloopy gloopy love,
Oh my love for you will never go soupy.

Gloopy love is true love especially when I make it with you.
I feel nice and gloopy and I hope you're feeling gloopy too.

 "What the fuck is this?" snapped Georgina.
 "It's our Christmas single," I grinned.
 "It's shit," she said.
 "Don't worry," I said, "It'll be fine when the multi-tracked harmonies are put on it."

"And who's going to do the multi-tracked harmonies?" she asked.

"You are," I said.

Georgina howled her way through 20 or 30 takes of the song, and after a few more overdubs we recorded an intro which pretended that we were going to Abbey Road Studios to tape the song. We even faked a photo call on the zebra crossing outside the studio, which ended with Georgina supposedly being run over by a car.

Two days later we uploaded Gloopy Love to the Comedy 365 feed and in the run up to Christmas 2005, without one single radio play, the Sowerby and Luff Yuletide Single racked up over 30,000 downloads.

Chapter 8
Fluffy and not so fluffy

"If the universe is expanding all the time, does that mean that if you get up in the night to go to the bathroom it's a slightly longer walk than it was the night before."

Another cringe-making one liner from The Big Squeeze, circa Christmas 2005.

Around that time we also talked about sumo wrestling on ice and airbags for parrot fish. But that Yuletide there was a far more significant event in the fast-emerging podcasting industry. Apple launched their very first portable MP4 player the iPod Video. Like many other emerging podcasters worldwide, we spotted right away that hundreds of thousands of punters would be hungry for video content for their new toys on Christmas Day, so we pulled out all the stops to come up with an idea for a video podcast or "vodcast".

It simply wouldn't be practical to video the Big Squeeze. The nature of the show would need a proper TV studio with at least 3 cameras. So we needed a small-scale, simple TV idea. Above all, it needed to be cheap. It was now four years since I'd co-produced the puppet show Pets for Channel 4, but the idea of doing another daft puppet series had never been far from my mind. But it was Georgina who suggested the idea of buying a couple of crappy old glove puppets on EBay and shooting a Punch and Judy style video show, in a studio the size of a shoebox.

A couple of days later a jiffy bag arrived in the post containing three glove puppets: a rabbit, a lamb and a mouse. It wasn't long before we had christened them Dr Rabbit, Nursey Lamb and Bleak Mouse, and begun to fashion odd little props for them. Meanwhile, a quick call to Bennsy secured a PD-150 video camera and a suitcase full of lights.

The following day we arrived at Bennsy's house in Teddington to discover that he had stayed up most of the night converting his attic into a miniature TV studio. Georgina and I then spent the next three days under hot lights, with our arms propped painfully inside an impromptu puppet theatre, improvising inane dialogue for a flea-bitten rabbit and sheep. It was both the most hilarious and painful experience so far in the great podcasting adventure.

DR RABBIT: What are you holding in your hands, Nursey Lamb?

NURSEY LAMB: It's a test tube, Doctor.

DR RABBIT: What's the test tube for Nursey Lamb?

NURSEY LAMB: I'm using it as a magnet, to try and attract a Bunsen Burner.

Bennsy and I worked through the following night editing it all together and speeding up the voices, until Dr Rabbit and Nursey Lamb were completely unrecognizable as having anything to do with

Sowerby and Luff. Sometimes Bennsy and I laughed until we cried as those cuddly little creatures seemed to take on a life of their own. There's something quite addictive about hearing a cute little rabbit say a four letter word. But would anyone else get it?

     We eventually edited ten 5 minute episodes of "Fluffy TV", and launched the first one on Christmas Day 2005. The response was amazing. This small-scale, silly show was obviously custom-made for viewing on a TV screen the size of a matchbox. By the time all ten episodes had been uploaded, we started to get emails like this:

    From: "Lucan"
    Subject: Fluffy TV

    I work at WebTrends in Staines. We all love Nursey Lamb and Dr Rabbit so much we had a bit of a Fluffy TV party last night, and watched each episode back to back on my TV (plugged in to the iPod). For health and safety reasons we paused between each one, so we wouldn't die from lack of oxygen.

It took Georgina and I quite a while to get our heads around the idea of a Fluffy TV party, then we got this email from Germany:

    From: "Amanda Wilson"
    Subject: Fluffy TV

    Just thought you'd love to know that Fluffy TV is being successfully used to teach German students English. So don't be too shocked if you bump into a German talking about her "minge" or singing "Cumbubble Corner". Cheers, Amanda

It should be explained that Cumbubble Corner was nothing more than Dr Rabbit repeating a rude word as many times as he could in 15 seconds. It may not have been rocket science, but let it never be said that the work of Sowerby and Luff is not educational. There have now been 22 episodes of Fluffy TV and, at time of writing, the series has racked up almost a million downloads. The show has even attracted some fan mail from a genuine Hollywood producer.

From: "Ali LeRoi"
Subject: Fluffy TV

Hi, I'm the executive producer of America's TV Show Everybody Hates Chris. I LOOOOOOOVE Fluffy TV and have been searching the web looking for early episodes. This is the funniest thing I've seen in years. You've got me hooked.

BAGGAGE AND BOOZE

It was an exciting time. But it was also Christmas, which is generally the most stressful time of year and, as a result of our baggage from former lives, the festive season invariably brought all manner of unpleasant pressures to bear. Georgina and I would often squabble over the most trivial of things.

But our most frightening arguments always came when Georgina wasn't able to record Big Squeeze because of drinking too much. She went through a particularly tough time in 2005, when the pressure of impending court cases and unreasonable legal threats by her ex-partner were, in her own words, "holding her hostage in her mind". This led to many extended drinking bouts to block the pain - the results of which usually left her completely incapable of getting out of bed, let alone being able to be the life and soul of a party on the internet.

All this was made worse by Georgina's complete denial that she had a problem. Her day to day life became regularly punctuated by long periods of painful sadness, exacerbated by alcohol. Needless to say, this often severely hampered our recording schedules and deadlines. I would fly into rages, frustrated by how her drinking was taking the fun out of a really exciting time in our lives. I would often yell uncontrollably at her, when all she really need was a hug.

All of this, in turn, was followed by Georgina's astonishing ability to stop drinking at the drop of a hat, without an ounce of regret. She'd often bounce into the studio ready to take the comedy world by storm - a completely separate person from the dour, sullen character the day before. I know that Georgina has recorded Big Squeeze shaking and sweating with the torment of alcohol withdrawal, none of which was missed by our most regular and eagle-eared listeners. I'm sure that if you listened to all the episodes of Big Squeeze in order, they would be a fairly accurate map of the extreme bio-rhythms of Georgina's life.

At times, the podcast became Georgina's way of communicating pain to the world, even though she tried to hide it behind a façade of humour. But "funny" is not always a big enough screen to mask all of our anxieties or remorse. I found it increasingly hard to cope with the strain of Georgina's drinking and ironically, in order to cope with it, I started to drink way too much myself. I remember one weekend I discovered a half empty vodka bottle that Georgina had hidden in the laundry basket in our bedroom, before slipping into one of her deep sleeps.

I poured the remaining vodka away, and threw the bottle into the dustbin. I then immediately walked round to the off licence, and bought myself a bottle of whisky. I poured myself a large one and placed the bottle on a shelf in the kitchen. Worried that Georgina might be tempted by this when she woke up, I then hid the whisky behind a cupboard in the living room.

So, now Georgina was hiding booze from me and, at the same time, I was hiding it from her. Brilliant. The flat was becoming like a surreal Easter treasure hunt, in which the bunnies were hiding Scotch and vodka instead of chocolate eggs.

CLEAN UNDERWEAR

Georgina believes that one reason for her problem with alcohol was a serious road accident she had while working as an actress in her early twenties. She was appearing in a play called Casanova, and a colleague was giving her a lift to rehearsals on the back of his motorbike.

On the way to the theatre, a car drove through a red light and hit the bike Georgina was riding on. She still doesn't know exactly what happened, only that she was thrown off the back of the bike, and flew about 30 feet through the air before landing on another car coming in the opposite direction. It's a miracle she wasn't killed.

Georgina's first memory after the crash was of laying on the ground staring up at the sky, and telling the surrounding group of faces that they must on no account try to move her. She heard someone say that she should be taken to the pavement, as she was blocking the road, but Georgina's Girl Guide experience kicked in and she made it quite clear to the surrounding Good Samaritans that they shouldn't move anyone who may have broken something. There was actually a thigh bone sticking out of Georgina's leg, but she says it didn't hurt at all.

Her body somehow took away the pain with endorphins or with some kind of natural, shock-induced happy pill. She remembers feeling completely in control and simply thinking to herself, "What the fuck?"

Two paramedics scraped her off the road, and chatted as they gave her pain killers and oxygen. Georgina remembers making jokes. The body must produce some very clever hormones in times of stress, and she particularly remembers noting to herself that wearing clean underwear, no matter what your mother tells you, has no relevance whatsoever when you have a serious accident - the ambulance people simply cut your knickers off with scissors, and never look to see what brand they are, or whether they're clean or not. They're far too focussed and professional for that.

Georgina was on a hospital trolley when she called her friends Lynne and Joey, and calmly asked them to bring in her nightwear and a toothbrush. She was very practical, asking them to let her family know where she was. Georgina's mum always thought she'd instinctively know if anything happened to Georgina or her sister. But she didn't. It came as a huge shock to her. It's a message no parent ever wants to hear.

Georgina says her time in hospital was quite different from anything she'd ever known before. Having been fit, busy and active she was suddenly plunged into a world of doing absolutely nothing, and doing it very slowly indeed. For a long time, Georgina couldn't move at all. Her leg was completely snapped into two pieces, and she had to be kept artificially active by what she named a Womble – a machine covered in a sheepskin coat that constantly kept her leg moving and prevented the blood from clotting.

One minute Georgina had been learning lines and trying on costumes, the next she was being wheeled around by friends and nurses in a hospital ward. That's how fast your life can change, and that's why both Georgina and I believe you should always embrace life and live right in the moment.

Georgina became great friends with the nurses, knowing them all by their first names. She even chatted to the little old ladies who surrounded her. Georgina spent much of her stay in the orthopaedic ward, so many of the other beds around her were taken by elderly geriatrics who had fallen over and broken their hips.

When you're completely immobile at the age of 23 it's extremely incapacitating mentally, as well as being a physical nightmare. With no form of escape for weeks, Georgina was forced to rely on others to wash her hair and hold her leg while she went to the loo. She remembers this as being a humiliating, but at the same time quite liberating experience.

She learnt to trust and appreciate the hard work of others, but most importantly realised how much her friends and family meant to her. Hospital visitors became a lifeline. The first time Georgina's sister washed her hair after the accident, she remembers it as an almost religious experience. She says it was the small gestures and the kind thoughts that kept her from going insane during those days.

The accident left Georgina in a wheelchair for over four months, and at one point her doctor told her she might not walk again. As you can imagine, this news was like a red rag to a bull for Georgina, and only served to make her more determined to make a full recovery.

Georgina was appalled by peoples' attitudes to someone in a wheelchair, and this was exacerbated by the fact that she was only in one for a relatively short period. Four months is nothing compared with a lifetime, but she was still barred from pubs and restaurants because she was considered a fire-hazard.

"People don't communicate with you when you're the height of a child," Georgina remembers. In shops her mother was often asked to "move *her* out of the way". Or, she'd get withering looks, as if she couldn't possibly be human and intelligent if she was in a wheelchair.

Angry though she was, Georgina was able to laugh off incidents like these. It's difficult to take yourself too seriously while you're being prodded in embarrassing places by doctors or treated like a child. She even remembers giggling to herself while having to hold her own leg underwater in a swimming pool, because it kept floating uncontrollably to the surface like a balloon.

When Georgina finally moved onto crutches and went to a nightclub with her friends, the bouncers wouldn't let her in because the metal frames supporting her body were considered by security to be a weapon. She had to argue her case by announcing that if she were to use them as such, she'd fall over, defeating the purpose of the exercise. Georgina believes this experience, and others like them, enabled her to never again "take shit from anyone".

After her accident Georgina was a tenacious little bugger. She didn't let a day go by without practising her walking or doing the endless exercises that would bring her leg back to full strength. She remembers that when she first walked again it was an odd experience – she wobbled like a penguin, and was about as graceful as a hippo. But she learned to laugh at herself and that gave her a lot of strength.

Of course those long weeks and months of inactivity left Georgina extremely bored and frustrated, and it was during that period of her life that she first remembers turning to alcohol to block the pain. The only physical memento of that car accident was a six inch scar on Georgina's thigh, but the long term effects were a lot more to do with her dependence on alcohol during the most stressful times in her life. From bitter experience, Georgina knew only too well that her body was completely unable to tolerate alcohol, even in relatively small amounts, and she was painfully aware of the consequences if she submitted once again to temptation.

The trouble was, Georgina connected alcohol with confidence. She felt that with it she could talk freely and audaciously, and she didn't think she was interesting or funny when she was sober. Her overriding sense of infallibility when pissed, or on the way to being pissed, gave her a strength that she didn't feel she had when sober. Georgina described the hit of the first drink as the most pleasurable feeling in the world. It wasn't that she didn't know when to stop. It was that she was physically incapable of stopping, once she had started.

Listening back to old recordings of our programmes made Georgina realise that drinking just made her reactions slow, and caused her to mistime her cues and gags. But sometimes she couldn't hear the drink speaking. That was when it became the most dangerous.

Regularly recording the podcast was slowly giving Georgina the strength to stop drinking for good. Emails describing how our show had helped others through difficult times re-enforced this feeling, and motivated her to realise that she had to help herself. Georgina's desire to use her imagination and sense of humour to good purpose was being fulfilled and with it her destructive bouts of drinking began to become less frequent. Ultimately, it was the generosity of our listeners that helped her stop.

Now she had a reason to be lucid, and every week the podcast became more and more her salvation. Family and friends listened instead of judged, and her new found honesty unearthed support from all quarters. Breaking the cycle of addiction was difficult, but Georgina's optimism and strength that she has shown throughout her life, surely brought her through. Now she was in control.

Chapter 9
Squeezy Marmite

For Sowerby and Luff, it was now a New Year, and 2006 kicked off with both good news and bad. The good news was that we received more emails for a single podcast than ever before. Mainly because Georgina said the words "soapy tit wank". The bad news was that the BBC threatened to sue us.

Yep, some bright spark in the legal department at Television Centre noticed that we'd registered the web domain "British Podcasting Corporation", and that the website we'd set up bore a striking resemblance to the BBC News site. So, quite literally, the writs begin to fly. Not having access to a heavyweight media lawyer, Georgina and I made a grovelling, unreserved apology to Auntie Beeb and promised we'd never do it again.

To: BBC Litigation Department
Re: Use of BBC copyright material

Thanks for your email. It was not our intention to pass ourselves off as the British Broadcasting Corporation, or to cause any genuine confusion with members of the public, between ourselves and the BBC. In accordance with your letter, we have today placed the following disclaimer, in a prominent position, on our website:

"The British Podcasting Corporation is in no way associated with, or endorsed by, the British Broadcasting Corporation, or any of its wholly-owned or partly-owned subsidiaries."

Yours faithfully
Georgina Sowerby and Brian Luff

Our actual view was that it was a total, unforgivable waste of license-payers' money to spend time threatening legal action against a fictitious organisation that was so clearly a spoof of the BBC. The corporation is famous for its own comedy shows, many of which are satirical and relentlessly take the piss out of anything that moves. But sadly, the Beeb often seems unwilling to be satirised itself. It's also possible that they were genuinely pissed off that they hadn't thought of this rather clever domain name themselves and registered it, as we did.

PODCAST FODDER

Georgina and I find the oddest things amusing. Even a litigation letter from the BBC. We know that life is invariably stupid and pointless, and we're not threatened by it. We revel in it. We were only saying the other day - when ITV announced they were looking for men and women to take part in *Wife Swap* - what a strange couple we are. We're simply not concerned with day-to-day stuff like "Who does the washing up?" or "Should the toilet seat be left up or down?"

Day to day bickerings are little more than fodder for our podcast, not genuine reasons to argue. We're the sort of people who laugh at the end of a friendly debate, then simply go off to write it down in the notebook for future reference. I've often wondered if we could market this technique as counseling for couples with marital problems. Even our most trivial day-to-day business is also that of our listeners. I'm certain that hearing Georgina and me squabble about underwear left on the bathroom floor brings our audience closer to us. They can relate.

We saw a quote once in some dreadful American book on working relationships. It said, "For couples who work together, the unresolved argument from the night before can overflow into the workplace, making the office a messy mash of domestic discontent." But Georgina and I harness that energy of dispute and simply rework it for our podcasts.

This is an excellent way of airing your grievances and, weirdly, of getting genuine advice from people. We air our dirty laundry in public much like they do on those mid-morning talk shows for brain-dead housewives. But, we like to think we do it with a little more humour and intelligence. We are our very own *Vivian*

Vyle Show, or maybe Jerry Springer, but without the trailer park trash and transsexual, illegitimate children.

Georgina and I were once described by a listener as the Richard and Judy of the podcast world - a comparison that appalled us at the time - but on a very simple level it might just be true. Their ability to skip around the edges of a tempestuous relationship, as they continue to broadcast together, is based on the feeling that deep down they must really love each other. It can't all be for the cameras and the money. Can it?

STATESIDE BANTER

Our American listenership was building by the minute. In fact we were constantly being emailed and told that our Stateside regulars were starting to get serious problems with their speech patterns.

> From: "Charlie"
> Subject: My Accent
> I've been listening to your talk show for so long that my accent wavers in and out of a British accent and my friends hate it. But I love it, so keep up your glorious talk show and please reply on the air.

We're convinced that one of the reasons our banter seemed to go down so well in the United States was that the Americans didn't have a clue what we were on about. And of course there was the swearing.

> From: "Darin"
> Subject: British Swearing
>
> Why on earth is it so darn funny to hear British people swear? Ya'll can say "shit" or "fuck" and that cracks me up! Why isn't it as funny when I say it?

A combination of local references and strong British accents meant that at least half of what we said probably flew way over the heads of most of our American listeners. But they didn't care. For them, that was half the fun. And *The Big Squeeze* was free, so the price was right.

Chapter 10
Paparazzi on the M1

"What's your greatest fear?" Georgina asked me one afternoon, as we rummaged around the tape and DVD section of one of the cluttered charity shops in Crouch End.

"Is this another of your impromptu therapy sessions?" I replied.

"Yes," said Georgina. "Now tell me, what is your greatest fear?"

I picked up a faded old VHS copy of Vic Reeves Big Night Out, and carefully considered my reply.

"My greatest fear is of being ordinary," I said.

"Ordinary?"

"Yes. I think I'd rather be dead, than be ordinary," I mused.

I pointed at the cover of the tape. "Look at this guy," I said. "Vic Reeves built a career out of being extraordinary. He completely re-invented comedy. He took old-style variety and modern alternative humour and he did them both at the same time. No-one else had thought of doing that. He changed the world."

"So, you want to change the world?" asked Georgina.

"No," I said. "I just don't want to be ordinary. What's your greatest fear?"

Georgina answered without hesitation. "Of losing my imagination," she said. "Of not being able to dream."

"That's a bit deep," I said.

"I'm a very deep person," said Georgina.

I suddenly noticed that the old lady serving in the shop was listening intently to our conversation. Embarrassed, I handed her the Vic Reeves tape.

"I'll take this," I said.

"That'll be fifty pence," she smiled.

When I got it home, I opened the box and it contained a VHS of Jane Fonda doing step aerobics in a leotard.

PAY PER DOWNLOAD

Around this time Ricky Gervais decided to start charging his listeners for his podcast. Of course, we assured our loyal audience that Big Squeeze would remain free for ever, but shortly afterwards we got an email from Audible.com, the very same company who were producing Gervais's series. They said they were looking for more comedy content, and that they liked our show. This propelled Georgina and me into something of a quandary. Having announced that we'd continue to podcast free, we were now being offered an opportunity to charge for what we produced. Who knows, maybe we'd make a fortune by marketing our content via Audible?

We went for a meeting with Chris McKee, the MD at Audible UK, and explained our dilemma.
"No problem," he said. "Carry on producing the free shows, and at the same time make a series for us, which you can charge for." This seemed a fair solution, so we immediately brainstormed some ideas with Chris, and very quickly came up with Sowerby and Luff's Sex Guide, which was to be a series of six 30 minute audio shows in which we talked dirty. The series launched about a month later, and featured Georgina's and my A-Z of Sex. Not the most original idea we've ever come up with but, hey, we needed the money. Last time I looked, Sowerby and Luff's Sex Guide was still flying high in the iTunes Audiobooks "Self Development" Top 100. Which is funny in itself.

Chris rang me and asked if we had any other content that Audible could market. The only thing I could think of was a novel I'd written a few years before. But I'd have to record it as an audiobook.
"I've got this audiobook," I said.
"Great! What's it called?"
"It's called Sex on Legs," I said.

It took me around two weeks to re-write Sex On Legs to work as an audiobook, and a further eight days to record it. It takes rather longer than you'd imagine to record an entire novel. Every single chapter tends to be riddled with fluffs, breaths, re-takes and the sound of pages turning, so the editing process seems never-ending. When I finally delivered the MP3 files to Audible, Chris came up with an excellent PR idea.

"I've looked into it," he said, "and as far as I can see, this is the first novel to go to premium download audiobook without first being printed in book form."

I was a little dubious. "Are you sure?" I said.

"Absolutely. I'll get our PR chaps to send out a press release straight away!"

The following week, Chris sat in his office with a journalist from *The Financial Times*, and told the story. To our amazement, during the next couple of days, every single national newspaper picked up the story from the FT, and before long, this appeared in *The Times*.

Novel release on podcast site

The first audio-only novel has gone on sale, after a British author decided to release his book as a podcast without a paper edition. Sex on Legs, a 75,000-word comic novel is being sold online by Audible UK, the company best known for selling podcasts by Ricky Gervais.

Brian Luff, a London-based comedian, by-passed traditional publishing houses by pitching his novel directly to Audible. He believes that listeners will pay £9 for the book, a sci-fi thriller about a sports commentator and the possibility of a zero-minute mile.

I love the way it says, "He *believes* people will pay £9." Who would have thought that the most famous newspaper in the world could be so bloody insulting to a budding author.

When *The Independent* ran the story a couple of days later, they wanted a photograph to accompany the article. They couldn't find one they liked on the Sowerby and Luff website, so their picture desk rang Audible, who in turn gave them my mobile number. That morning Georgina and I were somewhere on the M1 between North Yorkshire and London, and I was driving, so Georgina answered the phone. She quickly explained to them where we were, then turned to me.

"It's The Independent, " she said. "They want to send a photographer, on a motorcycle, to photograph you on the motorway." I genuinely thought she was winding me up.

"No, honestly," she said. "They want to know if we can pull into the Service Station just outside Leicester, and they'll take the picture there."

Feeling like we were at the centre of a small media circus, we pulled into Leicester Services, and a man in a leather jacket sat me in a flowerbed, holding my laptop, and took 400 photographs of me, using a motordrive camera with a satellite dish attached to the top. Moments later he was back on his Yamaha and hurtling towards London.

Now and again experiences like this give Georgina and me a tantalizing taste of what it might be like to be just a tiny bit famous.

"Did I spot you two in Camden Town yesterday?" asked one email.

"Did I see you on the telly last night?" asked another. One morning I was on the Central Line - one of London's most overcrowded, unreliable and unpleasant underground routes - when I noticed that the young man sitting opposite me was mouthing something. I took off my iPod, and looked at him with a puzzled and slightly concerned expression.

"Are you Brian Luff?" he asked shyly.

"Er... yes?" I replied.

He took off his iPod as well. "I'm just listening to you and Georgina right now!" he smiled.
It was the first time I'd been recognised as a result of the podcast. I was so surprised I think I was probably a little rude to the poor chap.

"How weird is that?" I said.

"I've got to get off here," he said, and he quickly shook my hand and jumped off the train at Queensway. I don't really know why I was so surprised. We know that many of our audience listen to the podcast on the London underground in the rush hour while they're on the way to work I just wasn't expecting to sit opposite one of them.

Over the years I've worked with a lot of famous faces, and have sometimes been in their company when they've been approached by members of the public.

"That bloke over there is staring at me!" a famous ITV sports presenter once said to me in a pub in Tottenham Court Road.

"Of course he's staring at you," I said. "You're on network fucking television every night of the week."

"Well, I don't like it," he said.

I could understand exactly how he felt, but deep down I was a little jealous.

Of course, many celebs love to be stared at. I worked with that great British eccentric John McCririck many moons ago, and he would talk so loudly in pubs that you'd swear he was using a megaphone. John wasn't happy until everyone in a public place was staring at him, and I wasn't at all surprised when he volunteered for Celebrity Big Brother several years later. For him, being on television 24 hours a day was his idea of heaven. As an old friend of John's it does sadden me, however, that he's now known to a whole generation as "that fat, sexist nutter off Big Brother", and not as an award-winning sports journalist – the thing that made him famous in the first place.

As more and more press coverage began to appear for my audiobook Sex On Legs, controversy was beginning to brew. In particular, a science fiction author from Detroit called Scott Siegler emailed me to say that it was *he* who had first podcast an audio novel without initially going into print. Audible argued that he'd been giving his book away for free, whereas we "believed people would pay £9", but Mr Siegler could not be appeased. Eventually, Audible changed the wording on the online blurb for Sex On Legs, and everyone was happy:

> "You heard it here first! This Audible exclusive is only available in digital download format. The book can be heard but not seen..."

Downloads for Comedy 365 now topped 2.5 million and, as an experiment, we finally decided to shoot a video version of The Big Squeeze. I thought Georgina looked very good on camera, but the exercise only served to prove to me that I have an excellent face for radio. I think many of our female listeners were rather disappointed to see me on camera in living colour. I have a tall, dark and handsome voice, but unfortunately it's produced by a short, fat, ginger body.

PISTON-PUMPIN' THRILLS

Ever since we'd started recording podcasts, Georgina and I had dreamed of finding a sponsor, but as it turned out our first real sponsor found us.

From: "Jonathan"
Subject: Sponsor for Comedy 365

Time Warner Cable wants to run a campaign across a number of podcasts including yours. This campaign would be targeted to specific geographic regions within the US. About 23% of your listeners would fall within the target area, amounting to about 51,000 downloads per month that would carry the ads. Does this sponsorship sound like something that would interest you?

This email was a turning point for Georgina and me. Up until that point we had, in our heart of hearts, still viewed The Big Squeeze as a sideline – just a bit of fun - but now there seemed to be a genuine opportunity to earn a full-time living from that cramped little studio in our flat. The Time Warner money was not exactly life-changing, but it was a start.

A second sponsor followed soon afterwards, and in Big Squeeze 79 we found ourselves reading some appallingly badly-written endorsements for a new motorcar called the Honda Fit.

"Get your high-octane, piston-pumpin' thrills from a gas-sippin', low-emissions vehicle! A lean, mean, clean machine that delivers 38 miles per gallon on the freeway! Burn, baby, burn!"

Dear God! Would we read out *anything* to stay in business? Luckily, many regular listeners actually thought this ad was a spoof, so we kind of got away with it.

TAKING THE BLAME

Ever since our first date, Georgina and I had loved exchanging daft little tales about our childhoods, and when we did this in our podcasts, we were often sharing the stories with each other for the very first time. By far my own favourite is the story of when Georgina's parents were involved in building the set for a local production of The Sound of Music. Georgina's dad had spread out two large canvasses in the garden, on which he was painting a couple of giant Nazi swastikas for the final scene. It appealed to his odd sense of humour when he noticed Georgina and her little sister - both blond haired and blue eyed - running happily in and out of these stark fascist symbols, as the paint dried slowly in the English summer sun. So, he took a couple of photographs to chronicle the scene.

Strange to say, those photographs were *never returned* from the chemist, and the Sowerby family still imagine to this day that they are suspected of being Neo-Nazi sympathizers. The Sound of Music story illustrates how our material was becoming ever more personal and family orientated, and as a result more listeners felt that they wanted to share their own personal family moments with us.

From: "Daniel"
Subject: Ello

I have just finished serving in the Singapore army for two years, and I'm about to return to Perth, because my mom and dad have migrated there and that's where my family is now based. I'm in a state of absolute turmoil - leaving the close knit relationships that I have made in Singapore. Being down and gloomy, your wacky, crazy pub babble put a smile on my face and left me feeling great. Thank You. Lots of love to both of youzzzzzzzzz. Daniel from Singapore, Going to Perth Western Australia, tomorrow.

We loved getting emails like this. But on the down side, we also received a number of emails which directly blamed us for damage to property or personal injury. The first of these was alarming, but fairly straight forward.

From: "Jonathan"

When Georgina, said "soapy tit wank" I sprayed my coffee all over my computer screen. The cost was £250 to replace the monitor. IT WAS WORTH IT!

The next suggested that our show may have placed one of our London listeners in direct physical danger.

From: "Andrew"
Subject: Old man

Coz of you two, I nearly got into a scuffle with an old man with one arm. I was gazing into space, listening to your show on the underground, and smilin' and a smirkin' away.... when I realised I was looking towards an old man. I realised, as I focused on him, that he had half an arm missing, and that the stump was on display. He had been looking back at me all this time - which I was completely oblivious to - but as he got up to leave the train, he lurched towards me and waved his arm at me, shouting. I was pretty much unaware of the whole thing up until that moment, as my headphones were blocking out what he said - so all I saw was him sticking his stump in my face and mouthing "Wanna take a better look?" So, a pretty surreal end to my commute to London.

Just as we were getting over that bizarre tale, we received this one from the North East of England:

From: "Matthew"
Subject: Note to Brian and Georgina

You guys are doing a great job and I really enjoy the show, however I am blaming Georgina for breaking my foot. Whilst listening to her swear like a sailor, I fell over, and went two days in agony. I finally went to the A&E, where they told me I had been going around on a broken foot. You guys are the best.

In our defence, The Big Squeeze did also seem to have healing properties, some of which appeared to reach as far as Iowa.

From: "Maria"
Subject: Kneecap Therapy

When I injured my kneecap at work and had to have surgery, you guys are what I listened to while I was in the hospital to help detach from the pain. I listen all the time when I am at physical therapy. My therapist even plugs my iPod into his computer and everyone in the clinic listens.

One listener, Sarah from Oregon, even suggested she should get her doctor to write a prescription for Sowerby and Luff as an anti-depressant. It was a very odd feeling, while we were standing in front of a couple of microphones in North London, to think that we were so intimately interacting with the lives of strangers on the other side of the world. But we slowly began to get used to it. But nothing could have prepared us for our next set of emails from an intense young man in Vermont, USA.

Chapter 11
Saving Bobby's Life

From: "Robert"
Subject: Fluffy TV got me fired

My name is Robert DeAngelis, and I have to say thank you, because you got me fired from my job. I was listening to your podcast and my boss caught me for the third time, and fired my ass. I hated that fucking job anyway, and it was all worth it! Best Regards, Bobby

Wow! Did we really get this guy fired? This wasn't funny anymore. Then this one arrived a few days later:

From: "Robert:
Subject: My dog

I have some bad news. I live in woods about a mile or so from town, and about twice a week I go out running, and listen to your show while I jog with my dog Bandit. We were running down my street when I had to stop to adjust the volume on my MP3 player, and a couple of deer ran across the street, which happens all the time. But my dog freaked out and ripped the leash from my hand and went on the chase.

Too bad a truck beat him to it, and killed him. I guess the good news is that Bandit was about 8 years old, and had bad arthritis. About the only thing he liked to do was walk with me, and even that was a challenge for him. Oh well, shit happens. He led a great life. Your show keeps me laughing, and I guess I should thank you, because if I wasn't listening to your show I would have run after my dog and got hit too! Lets hope that the next few weeks bring better luck!!! Just thought you'd like to hear that. Bobby.

This email genuinely freaked us out. Depending which way we looked at it, we were either responsible for killing Bobby's dog, or for saving Bobby's life. Either way, it didn't make us feel too comfortable. Georgina replied, saying that we were very, very sorry, but at the same time gently suggesting that it might all be the product of a rather over-active imagination? Bobby replied right away.

> From: "Robert:
> Subject: My dead dog
>
> This is a picture of me and Bandit a few years back. I would have gotten a picture that was updated but it was the only one I could find. I don't want you to think you killed my dog... but I was listening to your show when it happened. But you didn't kill him, the truck did. I wish I was making these things up, but sadly I'm not. Love, Bobby

Then Bobby wrote to say that he was thinking about getting a new puppy, and that if it was a girl, he was going to name it Georgina. He signed off by saying "I'm sure Bandit is listening to your show, because what other show would be playing in Heaven. None, because yours is the BEST ON EARTH!!"

About eighteen months later, we came up with the idea of visiting Bobby in the States. We were keen to meet the dog that was named after Georgina. But he never replied to our email. So, Georgina did a little research, and before long discovered a web page on MySpace for a lad she thought might be Bobby's brother. After making several connections via the web, it became apparent that at the time Bobby had sent us those strange emails, he was working from home for his *father's* company. So, had his own dad fired him for watching Fluffy TV at work? We doubted it. And of course, as soon as we doubted that, we began to wonder if all the other emails from Bobby were for one purpose only. To wind us up.

Maybe we did save Bobby's life. We'll never know. But the whole episode taught us to be a little more cautious about messages from our listeners, and to take some of the stuff they sent us with a very large pinch of salt. It would appear that our listeners, influenced by our own wayward imaginations, were now throwing themselves into the fantasy world of Sowerby and Luff as much as we were. It was as much an escape for them as it was for us.

Meanwhile, we weren't going to let Bobby piss on our parade, because the biggest thrill of doing our podcast was always going to be the feedback we got. There were people who emailed from work, there were young mothers who listened while breast feeding. There were invites to weddings, announcements of births, even proposals of marriage. I guess we enjoyed the sheer randomness of who we communicated with. Like pen pals from another continent, but with no introductions necessary.

Then there were the bizarre coincidences. Like Edgar from France, who went on a visit to South America, and discovered that someone he met in Mexico listened to us every day. Or Stephanie, who invited us to her wedding even though she lived in America. Georgina wore a hat for the programme that week, in celebration of the event, and Stephanie asked to see a photograph of it.

Then there was Emily, who actually sent Georgina a birthday cake from New York City "care of The Gay Legs pub in Crouch End." Somehow it found us, and luckily the real owners of the pub are always happy to hold onto parcels for us.

Everyone takes their small part in the huge suspension of disbelief that is Sowerby and Luff. Emily in New York was to become one of Sowerby and Luff's closest friends and most avid contributors, and we'll be hearing a lot more about her later in this book.

We were thrilled by the fact that so many strangers willingly joined in with our daft little podcasting game. They wanted to be on our team. They wanted to be part of the fun and, in turn, we welcomed them into our world and became a part of theirs. Georgina and I now knew people from all four corners of the globe.

There was a bunch of new recruits from the Israeli army who listened while they travelled back and forth to basic training. There was a bomb disposal expert in some army base somewhere that we weren't even allowed to mention. We even heard from soldiers in Iraq, who literally listened to us talking bollocks while they were being shot at.

FUNNY WOMEN

In spring 2006, Georgina and I were pleased to be asked to act as judges in the semi-finals of the Sheila's Wheels, Funny Women competition in London. Having performed on the fringe ourselves, it was a rather uncomfortable experience to have to sit in a room with a group of comedy professionals and decide which comedian was funnier than which. I think some people enjoy this Roman Emperor, thumbs up, thumbs down experience.

Clearly Simon Cowell revels in it. But I think we found it an unenviable responsibility. Who is to say what's funny and what isn't? Surely, it's the individual sense of humour of every single audience member that makes this decision. Comedy is, after all, the most subjective art form in the world.

Georgina and I have certainly never based our own material on what we think other people will find amusing. We simply set out to entertain each other. If the audience happens to like it as well, then that's an added bonus. Most comedy writers and performers would say the same thing. Trying to please everyone is a recipe for disaster.

BAD KARMA

In the usual vain attempt to keep our bank accounts in the black, we were persuaded to run some commercials for Titan Poker in our podcast, and we quickly ran up over 100,000 downloads for them. To our amazement, we started to receive letters of complaint from a handful of our listeners, accusing us of promoting gambling. It had genuinely never occurred to us that anything we promoted might show us, personally, in a bad light, but this feedback made us realise that our brand was now firmly established in the minds of many of our audience. These listeners felt that we, ourselves, would not approve of gambling, so our programme should not be running commercials for Titan Poker. "You know it in your hearts," said one email.

True, Georgina and I rarely gamble above and beyond a lottery ticket on a Saturday night and a flutter on the Grand National once a year. And even when we do play cards on a Sunday evening, after Antiques Roadshow, we only tend to play for matches or pennies. But we have no serious moral issues with gambling itself. We thought long and hard about whether we should remove the Titan Poker commercials from our show, and then the decision was made for us, because the promotion failed miserably and Titan refused to pay any of the podcasters involved a cent for the campaign. I suddenly remembered one of those TV trailers I'd made for My Name is Earl. It was as if *karma* itself had stepped in, and our selfishness and lack of morals had been punished.

Ironically, the very next week, I was hired as a freelance producer to work on television coverage of the British Poker Open at Riverside Studios in London, and in the space of 7 days I met 20 of the top poker players in the world. I even interviewed a few of them. These are people who can sit around a table laden with a million dollars in chips, without showing a hint of emotion, and who can calmly watch their lives change on the turn of a single card. I met a young man from Holland who had earned so much money playing poker that he now lived in a castle. What amazed me was how ordinary he was. Just a shy young chap who considered that he was quite good at playing cards.

Thinking back to Sowerby and Luff's Titan Poker dilemma, I asked him about the morals of online poker. He explained to me that online professionals often logged on via multiple computers, thinking nothing of playing against nine or ten opponents at the same time. These cynical pros would wait until the bars chucked out at around eleven thirty at night, then go online and start playing poker. They sensed which of their opponents were rank amateurs and had maybe been drinking, and would prey only on these individuals, at the same time swiftly pulling out of games with any opponent who looked like they might know what they were doing.

In this way - playing only against a handful of mugs - they could routinely empty the bank accounts of casual punters, and earn hundreds of thousands for themselves every year. So, maybe our listeners were right to be concerned for the morals of Sowerby and

Luff. Meanwhile, our beloved local soccer team Spurs signed Mansion - one of the biggest gaming and casino websites in the world – as their shirt sponsors. The club won alarmingly few games after that, and eventually sacked their manager half way through a match. Maybe our old mate *karma* was on the prowl again.

THE PISSING VIRAL

In the year or so since we'd started podcasting, many large companies had begun to take on-demand media seriously - as a place to spend their sponsorship and advertising budgets - and the future was slowly beginning to look a little rosier for start-up online producers like ourselves.

One area which was expanding rapidly was the viral – industry jargon for a short, punchy film that would be rapidly passed around on the internet because of its humorous, often quite explicit, content. The most successful virals were now getting 10 or 20 million downloads, and advertisers now thought nothing of spending fifty to a hundred thousand pounds on creating a short piece of video that would never appear on broadcast television.

Georgina and I got caught up in the viral revolution in the late summer of 2006. We were hired as writers by a company called Maverick to come up with ideas for a viral for a PSP game called Gangs of London. In this game, young violent gangs battled for supremacy on the streets of the capital. It was gruesome, it was bloodthirsty, and it was about as far from the Sowerby and Luff brand as you could get. But hey, we'd always liked a challenge. The brief was to create a 60 second, humorous movie that would appeal to the shoot 'em up generation.

We sat in a baking hot, airless meeting room in the West End, and brainstormed ideas for two days, and it was Georgina who finally came up with a rather unexpected approach.
"Look, this game is all about protecting your territory, right?" she said.
"Yes…"
"So, what if these gangsters literally *marked* their territory?"
"Marked?"

"Like dogs, yes. In the street."

"Let me get this straight," I puzzled, "you want to film a bunch of violent gang members pissing in the road?"

"To mark their territory, yes."

"A pissing viral?"

"Yes. The strapline could be 'You've marked your territory, now fight to keep it!'"

I wasn't sure if Georgina was joking. But we called the client into the room, and they absolutely loved the idea. A few weeks later a talented young commercial director called Elliot Goldner shot *Mark Your Territory* in a bleak, rain-soaked alleyway in East London. The minute-long movie - featuring a sinister drum and bass underscore - showed a couple of teenage cockney gangsters skidding to a halt next to a BMW belonging to a bunch of the meanest looking yardies you've ever seen.

The cockneys jump out of the car, quickly urinate over the wheels of their rivals' motor, then speed away. When the yardies discover what's happened, instead of using their sawn-off shotguns for revenge, they quickly re-mark their territory by pissing over their own car again.

Somehow, we'd managed to come up with a non-violent promo for one of the most violent video games ever devised – an achievement we were quite proud of. When Mark Your Territory was released, it topped the viral movie charts for 4 weeks. Our first number one. We'd come a long way since I went into PC World and bought that new computer.

PROPPING UP THE FOOD CHAIN

Our first number one didn't make *us* rich, but vast amounts of money are spent on New Media nowadays. There are cameramen to be paid, camera assistants, producers, assistant producers, directors, first assistant directors, second assistant directors, make-up people, caterers, runners, but bottom of the food chain is always the writer. Everyone in a TV studio gets paid more than the poor fucking writer.

The reason that jobbing writers, and to some extent jobbing actors, get paid so little is because everyone thinks that *they* could do it themselves. The skill sets are not so easily identifiable as, say, the man who builds the scenery or the sound recordist. Both of these people have clearly attended some kind of specialist training course in order to use their power tools or press that record button at just the right moment.

But if you're an actor, or a scriptwriter, people frequently say to you, "Oh, I've done a bit of acting myself." Or, "perhaps you'd like to take a look at my novel some time." Legendary comedian Peter Cook had a great response to such a commonly uttered comment. If someone said to him "I'm writing a novel," he would simply reply "Neither am I."

We used the fee from writing that viral to buy some new recording equipment for the studio. Normal people would probably have used it to go on holiday, or to get some new curtains for the living room.

We bought all our audio kit at a famous little music shop in Crouch End called Rock Around the Clock. One afternoon we were in there buying an expensive new cardioid microphone and a flashy pair of headphones, when Georgina suddenly whispered in my ear.
"Do you think we're delusional?" she asked.
"What do you mean?" I replied.
"Well, who are we *really* doing all this for? The listeners, or ourselves?"
"You mean, is this just an elaborate form of self abuse?" I said.

"Yes," said Georgina. Are we just jerking off?"
"Does it matter?" I asked.
"What if we are?" she replied
I considered the proposition: "Podcasting as a form of masturbation. Discuss."
"Well?" probed Georgina.
"I think the trick is not to think about it," I said. "We've done 99 shows, so we might as well do 100."

I gave my credit card to the guy behind the counter, and waited with my fingers crossed to see whether it would be declined.

That week we did indeed record Big Squeeze 100. It was incredible how quickly our first year of podcasting had gone, and how fast we'd arrived at that initial milestone. We'd now sat and talked bollocks for over 50 hours, and the strange activity was being funded, to some extent, by a variety of obscure advertisers. Our centenary programme featured a half-hearted Sowerby and Luff endorsement for the recently-released Superman DVD Smallville. As usual the script was abysmal, but we did what we could with it.

GEORGINA: This show is brought to you by Smallville.

BRIAN: I *love* Superman...

GEORGINA: The Complete Fifth Season on DVD.

BRIAN: It's the series where Clark Kent faces the rogue Kryptonians...

GEORGINA: Brian loves Superman...

BRIAN: Lex Luther launches a vicious political campaign...

GEORGINA: He's very excited about this.

BRIAN: And "The Fortress of Solitude" rises.

GEORGINA: He's been waiting for this DVD to come out for weeks.

BRIAN: It includes all 22 episodes, deleted scenes, and commentaries, plus an exclusive "behind-the-scenes" look at the making of the 100th episode.

GEORGINA: OK, I'll get it for you.

BRIAN: I can't wait!

GEORGINA: Smallville: The Complete Fifth Season, out on DVD from September 12th.

BRIAN: Yes!!!

At least it wasn't promoting gambling or prostitution. Around the same time, Big Squeeze became one of the first podcasts to experimentally be distributed onto mobile phones, but unfortunately the damn things could only cope with 10 minute clips from our programmes – encoded at such a low quality it sounded like Georgina was suffering from a severe speech impediment. But the important thing was that we were at the very cutting edge of technology. Or so we were told by the pimply young enthusiasts at Mobipod.

THE END OF THE LINE

We were having an absolute ball with our podcasting, but in September 2006 the Comedy 365 bank account finally ran dry. My credit card was declined in Oxford Street while trying to buy a piece of audio editing software. Reality check. We'd landed a string of advertisers and revenue generating deals, but there still wasn't enough money in the podcasting industry to sustain two people living in the most expensive city in the world.

After recording Big Squeeze 107, we slumped down on the sofa, cried a little, and reluctantly took the decision that it was time to stop podcasting. It had been an adventure, but we had to be realistic. We couldn't live on fresh air any longer. Even a couple of half hour programmes a week were taking a massive amount of time to prepare and produce. The time commitment could be as much as two or three days a week if you included Georgina's time responding to emails and my time editing programmes and creating idents and sound effects. And even the small amount of income we received generated administration time and bookkeeping.

The crunch came when on the last day of September I was offered a long term contract with Big Brother producers Endemol. If I took the job, there simply would not be enough time to continue to produce new programmes for Comedy 365.

That night we went to bed feeling overwhelmingly depressed. We'd come so far. Stopping The Big Squeeze was going to leave a huge gap in both of our lives. But there was no alternative. We had to give up podcasting for good.

Chapter 12
Health and Safety

With help from Richard Cray, I built a daily schedule of old episodes for the *Comedy 365* podcast feed, and like UKTV Gold we became a repeats channel. Before long, emails started to come in asking if we were OK Where had we gone? Were we sick? Georgina answered as many as she could. Then something very odd happened. We began to notice that downloads of the original old shows were increasing by the day, and our chart position in the iTunes Top 100 was actually improving. We still had much to learn about the concept of "time-shifted" content.

Georgina was constantly amazed at my ability to look on the bright side of life. But I could also get deeply despondent and morbid about the most irrelevant of things. Like many depressives, I frequently felt that the world was out to get me. Just me. I got annoyed when the flat was untidy and then even more angry if Georgina tried to it tidy up. I believed that the London Underground system was hot, overcrowded and airless specifically to annoy *me*. I knew that everyone else in London had to put up with the same thing, but I didn't notice the other people.

Life constantly got on top of me, and when I got depressed, I tended to eat way too much. Come to think of it, I tended to eat way too much even if I wasn't depressed. During the podcast Georgina often made bitchy little sideways references to my weight - which annoyed me intensely, probably making it quite funny to listen to. I suppose deep down she only said it because she was worried.
"I don't want to lose you," she said. Although how she could ever have mislaid a 230 lbs man, I couldn't imagine.

Georgina used to say she'd love me whether I was 230 lbs or 330 lbs, but I was unclear as to where these very precise parameters come from. Did that mean she'd stop loving me if I tipped the scales at 331 lbs? Or that she'd have walked out on me if I suddenly dropped to a super trim 150 lbs?

"I want your body to have as much energy as your mind," Georgina said to me once, while we were wandering around the boating lake at Alexandra Palace. "You can endure a mental workout, but you get out of breath running for a bus."

She was right. I was getting horribly out of shape. But I didn't think of myself as a fat person. Other people were fat. I was simply a bit overweight.
"You're stubborn beyond belief," Georgina said. "You want everything in the world to be categorised, but you totally refuse to fit into any category yourself."

Georgina was convinced that it was mainly the fact that I was overweight – my poor self image, if you like – that was one of the main things that made me depressed. I wasn't sure whether I agreed with that, but Georgina knew me better than anyone, so I took what she said seriously.

What worried me, was if I stopped being depressed I wouldn't be able to write funny stuff anymore. I'm told this is a common worry among writers with depression, and an awful lot of books have been written on the subject.

The British comedian Stephen Fry made an excellent television documentary about it. I know that several years ago, when I briefly took a course of anti-depressant drugs, I was unable to write a word for months. I was at the back end of a particularly unhappy relationship, and I'd gone to see my local GP, who had diagnosed me as suffering from "non-reactive" depression. In other words, the doctor believed I was the kind of person who was liable to get depressed whether I was content with my life or not. It was just a chemical thing in my brain, he thought. I now believe this to be a completely incorrect diagnosis, because when I finally separated from that particular partner my depression lifted almost overnight. It wasn't the chemicals in my head that had been making me depressed, it was the woman I was living with.

Believing I had a chemical inbalance, the doctor prescribed me with an anti-depressant called Seroxat. I'd never heard of it at the time, but the drug has since become notorious. Seroxat was one of the world's biggest selling and most successful anti-depressants, and the doctor in question assured me that the drug was "completely non-addictive".

He was wrong. I, along with thousands of other poor bastards around the globe, soon discovered that Seroxat had a very dark side – thousands of users getting hopelessly hooked on the stuff, and suffering horrific withdrawal symptoms when they tried to come off it. For many it lead to self harm and even suicide. But very little warning of these terrible side effects accompanied the drug. Even doctors, like my own local GP, were initially unaware of the drug's potentially lethal effects.

Within a few days of taking the stuff, I was unable to work, unable to concentrate on anything more complicated than tying my own shoe laces, and I was as impotent as a eunuch. The last person in the world I wanted to consult was the idiot who had given this stuff to me in the first place, so after a few short weeks I took myself off the drug.

The following day I had to travel abroad for a meeting, and I spent my first night Seroxat free, on my own, in a Sheraton Hotel. It was like that scene in the movie The Wall, when the rock star character, played by Bob Geldof, finally goes completely insane. I chewed my pillow.

I banged my head against the wall. I clawed at my own skin. I wept. I laughed. I screamed. I dribbled. For one brief instant, I toyed with jumping out of the window. Luckily the room was double glazed, and the window didn't open.

I experienced those sensations for about four days afterwards. Even weeks, months later, I continued to suffer dizzy spells and felt sick. I've felt seriously depressed many times since that occasion, and there is no better incentive to snap out of it than to remember what can happen if you make the mistake of consulting a doctor. I'm convinced that the doctor I visited
nearly cost me my life. I've had a serious mistrust of all things medical ever since.

THE EVIL EMPIRE

Anyway, I started the job at Endemol, and within days I was once again climbing up the fucking walls. But this time I didn't need an unpleasant drug experience to make t happen. I'd heard Big Brother's production company jokingly described as "The Evil Empire", but nothing had prepared me for actually working there.

I personally experienced a distasteful arrogance among many of their staff. A lot of the people I encountered were rude, obstructive and self serving, and this created one of the most unpleasant working environments I have ever come across. Others may have had a very different experience working at Endemol. I'm only speaking for myself.

I was heavily involved in the live streaming of Endemol programmes onto the internet. At this end of the media, television is produced incredibly cheaply, and the resulting low levels of staffing put people under intolerable pressure.

In particular, I was responsible for the web transmission of one show in which 2 young members of staff were performing the functions of about 10 production staff. They were crammed into a studio the size of a cupboard, with a small computer which doubled as a gallery for 3 cameras and an editing suite.

During the production, the two of them acted as floor manager, cameramen, producer, director, vision mixer, sound recordist, graphics operator and video tape editor. They also wrote and edited the scripts and even put make-up on the presenters. And they did this five nights a week with no cover from any other staff. I asked them what would happen if one of them went off sick.
"We can't go off sick," they said.

The electrical equipment on that particular production was, in my opinion, also a health and safety nightmare. There were cables and wires everywhere, and more trip hazards than an Iraqi minefield. While I was there during one internet transmission, a senior member of staff was being shown around. He managed to trip over a cable leading to a computer modem, and nearly took that evening's transmission off the air.

I quickly became deeply miserable working full time for Endemol. It was regular money, but I missed working with Georgina and I had serious misgivings about the way the company treated its staff. But there was the occasional highlight. I worked on Endemol's reality hairdressing show Celebrity Scissorhands, in which a bunch of B-list celebrities cut the hair and clipped the toenails of a bunch of C-list celebrities.

This all made for fairly obnoxious viewing, but it was in aid of Children in Need, so it wasn't a total waste of time. I managed to get Georgina signed up to be one of the victims and before she knew it she was having her fingernails painted, on live television, by infamous "love rat" Darren Day.

Unfortunately, Darren swore so much during this section of the programme that almost every piece of dialogue was removed from the transmission, which meant that Georgina's delicious "talking dirty" moments with the star never made it onto the air.

Such untransmittable moments are removed from live reality programmes by a small team of editorial staff called "compliance". Ironically, it was a similar team of compliance people who, only a couple of months later, dropped Endemol firmly in the shit when they failed to remove allegedly racist comments by Jade Goody from Celebrity Big Brother.

So, it was all right for Ms Goody to be a racist bully, live on air, but Darren Day couldn't say a rude word to Georgina before the watershed. What a strange little world we inhabit.

A ROUGH PATCH

I walked out of Endemol a week before Christmas 2006. I didn't have another assignment to go to, but I'd rather eat my own head than ever work for that organisation again. That very day Georgina and I received an email from someone called Laura. She said that she'd "had a real rough patch" lately. Her husband had cancer, work was going badly, and various other things. Laura said that listening to Sowerby and Luff's daft little podcast helped her forget about all of that for a while and just laugh.

"You don't know how much I need it, and appreciate it," she said.
After reading an email like that, there was no way we were ever going to stop podcasting again.

Chapter 13
A Bigger Squeeze

One way we were able to exploit the growing interest in podcasting commercially was to offer modest consultancy services to small companies and individuals who wanted to follow in our footsteps and promote themselves via podcasts or vodcasts on iTunes. The first private client we landed was an extremely unlikely one - a successful businessman in his mid fifties called Phil, who had always dreamed of performing comedy.

Phil had never been near a stage or a television camera in his life, but his over-the-top personality and ugly-but-strangely-appealing looks seemed to have some potential. Phil had a head like a hard-boiled egg, and a face like Woody Allen.

Phil's company hired us to teach him stagecraft and camera technique, and to generally groom him in the ways of the podcaster. So a few days later Bennsy, Georgina and I took Phil out filming for the first time on the streets of North London. The idea was that Georgina would bowl up to people in the street and ask them to come over and be interviewed by Phil. He would then fire embarrassing questions at them about their sex lives.

The first time Georgina and I directed Phil on the streets of Camden Lock he was truly awful. He found it impossible to focus on what he was doing for more than a few seconds, and even the relatively simple task of holding a microphone seemed completely beyond him. Bennsy and I had to spend hours and hours cutting together the footage, and even then the resulting 6 minute programmes were virtually unwatchable. Despite this fact, Phil continued to hire Georgina and me to help him to shape and brand his podcast. We even came up with a name for his show and art-directed the logo for his designers. Then we showed Phil's IT people how to set up an RSS feed and launch his podcast onto the iTunes platform.

Now, you wouldn't think the story of this wannabe would be worth mentioning in such a brief history of podcasting, would you? Except for the fact that Dr Cockney's Sex Survey is now one of the most successful podcasts in the world. Remarkably, Phil has still not learned how to hold a microphone properly.

THESAURUS WALRUS

Feedback from our audience research at Podtrac had taught us that most people listened to our podcasts on the way to work, and actually wanted them to be longer. We always relied on audience feedback to improve The Big Squeeze and considered that even one solitary email might reflect what hundreds of listeners were thinking. If something was pleasing or annoying one listener, it was probably having that same effect on fifty others. Or a thousand. So, if the listeners wanted longer programmes, that's what we'd give them.

In early 2007 we extended our podcasts to around 45 minutes, and re-branded Big Squeeze as The Big Big Squeeze. We were confident that the addition of that extra word would make all the difference. But we also came up with a load of new content and some new characters.

From: "Kari"
Subject: TW
Thesaurus Walrus is fabulous, I cannot get enough of him!

Thesaurus Walrus was an extremely sneaky creation, because he enabled us to create a sketch without having to sit down and write a script. I would simply put on a stupid squeaky voice, Georgina would give me a word, and I would list as many words as I could think of that meant the same thing. All I needed was a Thesaurus opened at the right page. TW was also quite a sad character, constantly asking to be doused with water to stop him from "drying out" in the pub, and he quickly started to get floods of fan mail of his own. Kim from Delaware emailed to say that "she laughed so hard she cried."

Another of our most popular items was regular appearances by Derek Fake-Séance – a fairly obvious piss-take of TV medium

Derek Acorah. In The Big Big Squeeze, Derek's first appearance was in an item called Sandwich from Beyond the Grave.

I like to think that my wildly caricatured impression of Derek Acorah was reasonably accurate, but Georgina and I also prided ourselves on doing impressions of celebrities that sounded absolutely nothing like themselves. Like Georgina's wild stab at sweet Scottish actress Hannah Gordon, or my dreadful Ray Winstone, who sounds much more like Bob Hoskins.

THE WHITE LODGE

I've never claimed to be able to act. It's just "Brian trying to do a funny voice". I did go to Mountview Drama School in my late teens, but sadly not to study acting. I spent most of my time climbing ladders and burning my fingers while attempting to adjust stage lights. But while I was at Mountview I met an actor who turned out to be something of a mentor in my life - and to whom I know I owe a huge debt in terms of what I've been able to achieve since.

Forbes Collins is probably best known for his role as King John in Tony Robinson's brilliant and innovative BBC childrens' series Maid Marion and Her Merry Men. But back in those days Forbes was one of the most prolific fringe theatre directors in London, and a well- known face in many of the best-known television series of the day. Blackadder, Doctor Who, Lovejoy, Minder, Forbes used to pop up in them all.

Meanwhile, he had an extraordinary talent for persuading his fellow actors to take part in numerous hair-brained profit share shows. I think Forbes viewed me as a young prodigy, and he would invariably give me the job of stage manager on these theatrical events. Sometimes, if he was feeling generous, he might even dub me "producer" - but either of these jobs generally meant little more than being in charge of making the tea or going out and buying cigarettes for the cast. If I performed these duties well, I would occasionally be entrusted with the sound desk or even the lighting panel.

Forbes's big house in Finsbury Park, The White Lodge was regularly filled with an unlikely repertory company of talented people. I can remember sitting wide-eyed in Forbes's overgrown back garden listening to a seemingly never-ending stream of showbiz tales from his famous friends.

Burt Kwouk chatted about filming Return of the Pink Panther with Peter Sellers. Don Henderson told of playing General Taggi in Star Wars, and Forbes himself shared his experiences of working with the legendary Franco Zefferelli, in Lew Grade's Jesus of Nazareth. Forbes actually had a Call Sheet from that movie framed and hanging in his kitchen. It showed his name, in a single scene, alongside Laurence Olivier, Ian Holm and Anthony Quinn.

I remember those days with enormous affection, and I'm sure I was inspired by them. One afternoon, during a break in rehearsals for a Forbes play at Hoxton Hall Theatre, I recall a young actor from the cast sitting at a piano and banging out a couple of songs he'd just written.
"What do you reckon?" he asked.
Everyone seemed to agree that they were quite catchy.
The actor was Richard O'Brien, and the songs were destined to become part of the score for The Rocky Horror Show.

After much nagging, Forbes eventually allowed me to play the occasional small part in his shows. I remember appearing as Nately in his extravagant fringe production of Catch 22, and one Christmas I even got a part in the panto.

That holiday season it was Aladdin, and the reason I remember that year so clearly is because the panto was produced by Martin Campbell - a fresh faced lad who would one day direct the James Bond movies Golden Eye and Casino Royale.

So, it's not difficult to see why I might have been inspired by those early days on the London fringe. For over a decade, Forbes produced spectacular, critically-acclaimed fringe shows with no budget whatsoever. No one ever got paid, and virtually everything on the stage was either begged, borrowed or stolen. But people loved those shows. They adored them because they were inventive and crammed with great ideas and great performances - and that's what tends to happen with Art when there are no commercial pressures.

Forbes taught me that if you have a little imagination, and unstoppable drive, anything is possible. But the most important commodity on the fringe is the ability to bullshit. Years later, while I was co-producing a touring version of Sketch Club in Edinburgh, I devised a splendid piece of fringe bullshit that I hope Forbes would have been proud of.

THE GHOST IN THE CAVE

We were appearing in a venue that was then called the Gilded Balloon Caves, which was in the supposedly haunted vaults of the Old Town in Cowgate.

Edinburgh is famous for its ghost tours around these very vaults, so I wondered if we could get away with telling the press that our comedy show was haunted. Before I wrote a press release, I went on one of the official ghost tours, and jotted down a few notes as I went.

As luck would have it, one of our cast was only in Edinburgh for the first week of a three week run, so I informed the media that she had "walked out" of the show because she'd been freaked out by a ghost on the stage.

"Singer Quits Fringe Show" was the first headline to appear in the press, and over the next few days the story was picked up by almost every national newspaper and one daytime TV talk show, making us one of the most written-about shows in Edinburgh. To this day, when Georgina and I read something about ourselves in print we call it a Caves Ghost.

CONFESSIONS OF A PODCASTER

Georgina sometimes worried how much she and I lived vicariously through our podcast. It seemed to be the one hour of the week that we were actually *obliged* to talk to each other. Sometimes it was an awkward, uncomfortable hour, other times an absolute joy. Whoever said sharing your life with thousands of strangers would be easy?

Was there anything we wouldn't talk about? I'm not sure there was. Like a lot of humour The Big Squeeze was innately confessional. By being completely frank and open we let the audience in.

They got to know us, and we got to know them. I think one of the major selling points of Big Squeeze was that we were *not* professional broadcasters. In producing a show that was a little "raw" Georgina and I were offering a genuine alternative to the slickly-produced, re-packaged commercial radio shows that were our competition.

Chapter 14
Name That Bird

Perhaps the most stupid of all the regular features in our podcasts was Name That Bird. But as we were finding out more and more, the more inane the item, the more popular it became. Every week, we'd simply play the same irritating, high-pitched sound effect of a bird, and Georgina would try and guess what it was.

> From: "Jake"
> Subject: Name That Bird
>
> This has been annoying me for quite some time, cause I think I know the bird! So every time it plays I've been yelling at my computer "It's a seagull! A seagull damn it!" For to me that's what it sounds like. It sounds like a baby seagull. But I could be wrong.

This utterly pointless competition, with no prizes, ran for weeks and weeks. Gary from Colorado suggested it might be a cardinal. Daniel from Idaho reckoned a spotted thick-knee. Julian suggested the common drongo. In every podcast Georgina would dutifully read her way through seemingly never-ending lists of obscure bird names, sent in by our loyal regulars.

Dean suggested emu, dodo, ostrich, pelican and flamingo. Laura suggested avocet, fish eagle, reed cormorant, green pigeon, stilt, and white headed vulture. When Georgina finally guessed it was a plover, after months of trying, the aforementioned Julian was listening to us on his iPod while sitting his mock GCSEs. At the exact moment she "named that bird", a plover was mentioned in his exam paper.

This extraordinary coincidence posed two important questions for Sowerby and Luff. One: What the hell were we doing with our lives? And two: What the fuck was Julian doing listening to an iPod while he was sitting his mock GCSEs? Even after the bird was finally guessed, the emails continued to flood in:

From: "Paul"
Subject: Name That Bird

I haven't caught up to the most recent episode yet, so don't know if you've guessed that bird yet. But it could be a red-billed hornbill or a superb starling. Otherwise, there is another bird which nests on the ground and fakes injury to lead predators away from its nest. But I don't know what it is called.

Name that Bird was what many comedy writers like to call a repetition gag, and repetition is at the heart of a lot of the material we create for our podcasts. Audiences love repetition.

SAY IT AGAIN

Just like the clothes we wear, comedy goes through certain fashions at certain times, and at the moment it's undoubtedly repetition that's strutting its stuff on the catwalk. Like Ali G asking a scientist if the biggest number in the universe is "A million, million, million, million, million, million, million, million, million…"
Like Alan Partridge calling across that car park to his friend, "Dan! Dan! Dan! Dan! Dan! Dan! Dan! Dan!" Like Stewie in Family Guy trying to attract the attention of his mother, "Mum! Mum! Mum! Mum! Mum! Mum! Mum! Mum! Mum! Mum!"

Shows like Little Britain turned repetition into an art form. The episodes were almost identical week by week, with just a few variables carefully adjusted in order to keep the audience onside. Human beings love repetition because it makes us feel safe. In a chaotic and uncertain world it's sometimes good to come home to a comedy show in which you know exactly what's going to happen next, and when.

Georgina and I are very aware of this when we play a game like Name That Bird week after week. Our regulars feel reassured by the level of predictability. We know this because every time we change a single thing, we get an email from someone, somewhere, begging us to put it back. Most of our lives are governed by routine, and sometimes it's nice to have a reliable soundtrack on your iPod which fits into your very own groove.

The world is an insane and dangerous place, and the swirling log we cling onto in the whirlpool is invariably some kind of repetition. For Neanderthal Man, it might have been something as simple as the steady, rhythmic drip of water outside the cave. For our listeners, it may be the stupid, squawking sound of a plover, at the same time every week, on their MP3 player.

ON THE TELLY

Georgina and I had been running comedy writing courses for almost 5 years, so we were well used to talking about humour in terms of theories and formulae. We took part in several television documentaries which focused on our comedy students and followed their progress from workshop to first gig. We made the first of these documentaries, The Test with Granada Television, whose programme followed our first-time student Paul Wooding from stand-up workshop to on-stage debut at the Comedy Store in only a few short days.

London Weekend Television then shot another reality-style show with our student Keith MacDonald as he prepared for his first gig at the Comedy Café in London. When Keith appeared on stage that night we were both supposed to be filmed in the audience "mentoring" him. But instead, I spent the entire bloody evening sitting in an aeroplane on the tarmac at Milan Airport.

Bennsy and I had been filming in Italy the day before and we got so delayed on the way back I never got to see Keith's momentous comedy debut. Embarrassingly, the incident was actually featured in the documentary, making yours truly sound like something of a globetrotter. In reality, it was the only foreign filming trip I went on that entire year.

As a result of these two TV shows Georgina and I were for a while in great demand on the cheap documentary circuit, and we actually turned down quite a few similar offers to appear in virtually identical shows. But there was one programme we were extremely keen to take part in for two reasons. One; because it was just the sort of telly Georgina and I loved watching ourselves, and two; because we thought that with a bit of luck it might just make us look intelligent.

The BBC documentary series, Time was all about how the human body measures and perceives time, and it was presented by Japanese-American theoretical physicist Dr Michio Kaku - co-founder of what clever people like to refer to as string field theory. In the first of the series, however, Dr Kaku wanted to talk about comedy. Comic timing to be precise.

Michio came to London and filmed one of our workshops at Downstairs at The Kings Head in Crouch End, and the item kicked off with Georgina and me having a stab at an old music hall joke.

BRIAN: I say, I say, I say, what is the secret of good comedy?

GEORGINA: I don't know, what is the secret of....

BRIAN: Timing.

A dreadful old gag - and one for which Georgina and I actually needed to do three takes before we got it right - but for Dr Kaku it perfectly illustrated an important point about comedy. It's all about time. Who'd have thought a world famous theoretical physicist would be interested in analyzing a crap old joke told by Georgina and me.

Next, I stood in front of a flipchart and drew a graph with a big fat marker. The horizontal axis had a scale which measured "Time", and the vertical axis had a scale representing "Funny". It was more than a little tongue in cheek, but the producer seemed to go along with it.

Then one of our students Aaron Rice stood up on stage and did five minutes of material - culminating with what we thought was by far his best joke:

"I used to go out with an agoraphobic," he said. "Well, I say *out...*"

This got a big laugh from the assembled students and the crew, and Aaron was picked by the BBC's production team to repeat his act again during a real gig at the club that night. I think we were more nervous than Aaron as he walked out in front of the TV cameras that evening. And then something quite extraordinary happened when he got to his favourite gag:

"I used to go out with an agoraphobic..." he said. But before he had a chance to deliver the punchline at just the right moment, someone in the audience said something. A quiet heckle that would not have disturbed a more experienced comedian, but which stopped poor Aaron timing that punchline correctly. "Well, I say *out...*" he muttered. But it was too late. The gag was lost.

The cameras cut to the audience, including Georgina and me, who were sitting in uncomfortable silence.
"They don't even know that they are doing it," said Dr Kaku, "But the audience are *timing* this comedian."

In an interview after the gig we told Dr Kaku that the difference between timing a gag correctly and getting it wrong could be measured in *nano-seconds*. With our help, Michio and his team had got exactly what they came for, and this little film demonstrates perfectly the thin line a comedian walks between success and failure. Time has now been repeated about 6 times on BBC3, and we're told its destined for BBC2. Meanwhile, our little comedy workshops have never been busier.

GETTING PERSONAL

But our podcasts weren't just about formula laughs. They were primarily about a relationship, and we suspect that it was the listeners' sense of eavesdropping on our personal lives that may have kept us in the iTunes charts for so long. Other podcasts came and went, but we hung on in there. The shows got more and more personal as we became ever more comfortable standing in front of those microphones. One of the best illustrations of this was a regular item we introduced called Are You Happy Now? This feature focused on one particular thing, usually quite trivial, that I'd done in the preceding week, to try and make Georgina happy. After much discussion, and often quite lively argument, the item would always end with me asking the question, "So, are you happy now?" Georgina would invariably reply, "No."

A shrink would have a field day with this kind of material. Sure, the item was designed to be funny, but it was also drawing on the type of everyday goings-on in a relationship which would normally only be shared on a psychiatrist's couch.

When Georgina and I ran our workshops, we did an exercise in which we got attendees to reveal to the group something they wouldn't tell their mother, and in this way we extracted the kind of genuinely confessional comic material we were looking for. So, maybe our podcasts were a form of self analysis. Is it possible they performed the same function as a weekly visit to a relationship counsellor?

There are hundreds of stand-ups on the circuit who will never make it as top-of-the-bill comedians. And most of them know it. But that's not why they're doing it. They're doing it because they *need* to do it. Sharing their lives with a handful of comedy fans once or twice a week is how they stay sane.

Chapter 15
Going for a Curry

In March 2007, Georgina and I attended a podcasting conference in London called PodcastCon, an event which turned out to be rather aptly named. Because it was there that we first came face to face with Adam Curry – the ex-DJ from Guildford who once claimed to have virtually invented podcasting single-handed.

[Note: Legend has it that Adam actually doctored the Wiki history of podcasting, adding his name several times and deleting the names of numerous others who had been involved in the creation of the technology. He has since apologised for this cyber-tampering, and offered a fairly lame explanation of why he did it.]

On that day in Exmouth Market, the self-styled Podfather was suave and charming, if a little cheesy, and Georgina managed to pin him in a corner, over a warm glass of Chardonnay, and talk to him about The Big Squeeze. Meanwhile, I stood chatting with one of Adam's UK executives, Neil.

Neil was pumped up about Podshow's hot new UK talent signing. Apparently, he was funny, versatile, and sexy, and Curry's Podshow Network were planning to make him into a big star!
"What's his name?" I asked.
"Dr Cockney," said Neil.

Georgina and I had met Neil before. He'd been instrumental in getting us involved in the Mobipod project, which had briefly enabled us to distribute our podcasts via mobile phones, and earned us a little beer money a couple of months before. His brain still swimming from the heady success of signing Dr. Cockney to the Podshow Network, Neil invited us to a meeting at Adam Curry's London headquarters. These "headquarters" turned out to be a small flat over a wine bar in Old Street, but we were undeterred. This, after all, was our big break.

Neil made us a cup of tea in the kitchen, which also doubled as the meeting room and a TV studio, and he began to pitch to us all the amazing things that Podshow could do for our podcasting careers. Neil said he could get our podcast onto the prestigious online radio station Sirius. He said he could promote our show as a key product on Podshow's Network. Most importantly, he could hook us up with a sponsor who "would enable us to be podcasting full time within a year." In short, he'd make Georgina and I podcasting superstars.

To be fair to Georgina, I have to say that she was dubious about Neil, and the whole Podshow thing, right from the start. But, ever the optimist, I persuaded her that Podshow were the biggest podcasting network in the world, and that we were better off working with them than remaining as independents. Without getting a media lawyer to check it over for us, we signed one of Podshow's standard promotional contracts, and were now a part of Adam's worldwide podcasting family.

A couple of weeks later, we set about creating a brand new weekly series, exclusively for Podshow. We came up with new items, recorded new jingles, and threw ourselves headlong into the whole Podshow experience. The Big Squeeze became The Sowerby and Luff Show.

We had already syndicated six Sowerby and Luff Shows before the promised sponsorship finally came through, several weeks later. The partner that Podshow lined up for us was a web domain marketing company called GoDaddy.
"So, how much are GoDaddy going to pay us?" I asked Neil.
"A hundred pounds," said Neil.
"A hundred pounds per show isn't very much," I grimaced.
"Not a hundred pounds per show," said Neil. "A hundred pounds a month."
I laughed.
"No, seriously," I said. "How much are they going to pay us?"

The deal was that our sponsorship income would come from driving traffic to GoDaddy's website, and if any of our listeners bought a domain name from the company, we'd be paid an impressive £1.50.

Even a year before we'd been earning more from product endorsement than this, so the figures were a little disappointing to say the least.

"Don't worry," said Neil. There are podcasts in America making thousands from this sponsor. Just be patient.

OK, I was prepared to give Podshow the benefit of the doubt on the sponsorship front, as long as our audience began to build. But it didn't. It fell. Not only did it fall, but it dropped almost out of sight. Podshow had promised Sowerby and Luff prominent promotion on their network, but day after day, week after week, all we saw heavily promoted on the Podshow UK network were our main U.S. competitors Dawn and Drew.

"Why are you promoting U.S. podcasts on your UK network?" we asked.

"Where's all the PR and promotion you promised for the Sowerby and Luff Show?" All we received in return was corporate bullshit. It was becoming increasingly obvious that Adam and his huge network cared little about Brian and Georgina. In the meantime we were losing the loyal listenership it had taken us almost 2 years to build. We started to get numerous emails from our audience saying that Podshow's website was so confusing to use and slow to operate that they simply didn't have time to subscribe to our new series. Life was too short.

Georgina and I had a crisis meeting. Before we lost anymore of our audience, we had to take action. We decided to distribute our podcast through both Podshow and our old feed Comedy 365. This feed was still running repeats of The Big Squeeze, and still had many thousands of existing Sowerby and Luff listeners, so we reasoned that this was probably the only way of re-building our audience before it was too late.

"You can't do that," said Neil at Podshow. "We have the exclusive right to syndicate your show on our network."

"Neil," I said. "We're earning less from our show than we were before, and our audience is falling by the minute. What possible incentive do we have to not use our own feed to reach our own audience?"

"You'll be in breach of contract," said Neil.

"But that doesn't *mean* anything," I ranted "if we're not benefitting from being in a relationship with Podshow."

Neil dug in his heels. "Those are the terms of your contract," he said.

"Neil," I said, through gritted teeth, "If you were paying us a fair fee to produce the show for you, then you'd have the right to control its distribution. As it is, you're having your cake and eating it. You're getting virtually free content, and benefitting from exclusivity. You can't have it both ways!"

"I'll speak with the guys in the States," he said. It was something he was going to say to us many, many times over the next few weeks. Meanwhile, we began to do some serious digging into the whole subject of Podshow contracts. What we found on the internet was alarming to say the least.

Our fellow podcasters in New York, Keith and the Girl, had taken a rather closer look at their Podshow contract, and had refused to sign it in the first place – going on to dedicate the whole of one of their shows to warning other podcasters about entering into partnerships with Podshow.

We even found a Facebook group for people who had quit Podshow in disgust. It looked like Georgina's gut feeling might have been right in the first place.

SAVED BY A RUSSIAN GENERAL

The whole Podshow fiasco came to a head at the end of that week, when we received a provisional offer of programme sponsorship from a company called Kalashnikov Vodka.

Kalashnikov had been founded by a British entrepreneur called John Florey, who had bumped into the infamous Soviet general Mikhail Kalashnikov at a tradeshow in Russia. During a fairly heavy drinking session with the 84 year old general, John had suggested that Kalashnikov would be a great brand name for Russian vodka, and the general had agreed.

After being wounded in World War II, old Mikhail had invented the world famous AK47 assault rifle. But having created it for the Soviet people, he had been paid bugger all for his idea. The old feller was therefore relatively penniless, so the notion of co-creating a product for which he would actually receive royalties appealed to him.

Having swiftly hired a distillery to make the stuff in St Petersburg, a few short months later John was proudly presenting the general's new liquor in London. From gun-toting to vodka-tasting – General Kalashnikov was certainly moving up market – and best of all, no-one was getting shot in the process.

During the media-crammed launch for Kalashnikov Vodka, the general was quoted as saying that he was delighted that this new brand of 82% proof spirit was continuing "the good name of his gun".

We met with John Florey in a rather smart gentlemen's club in Mayfair. He was already a fan of our podcast, and when we talked to him about the promotional work we'd once done for Malibu Rum, he was particularly impressed. John immediately understood the potentially excellent brand match between alcohol and comedy, and was excited by the prospect of Kalashnikov having its very own podcast. By the time the dessert course arrived, we were shaking hands with a brand new sponsor for The Sowerby and Luff Show.

When we came out of the club we danced around Mayfair like Fred Astaire and Ginger Rogers on uppers. It was by far the most exciting moment so far in our podcasting adventure. Breathlessly, I rang Neil Dixon at Podshow.
"Great news!" I said. We've found a sponsor for The Sowerby and Luff Show."
Neil was in no mood to join the party. "You can't do that," he said.
"What?"
"Only Podshow's marketing people can find sponsors for your show," he explained.
"But this is 10 times more money than we're earning from GoDaddy!" I winced. "Surely you can't be serious!"

I even suggested that Georgina and I would be prepared to agree to a percentage from the Kalashnikov deal, if Podshow, in return, stepped up their level of promotion for The Sowerby and Luff Show. In the face of everything everyone else was telling me, I really was still trying to cut a realistic deal with Podshow. It was as if I had been brainwashed.

"Here's how it works," said Neil. "You put us in contact with Kalashnikov, we do a deal with them, then we distribute their sponsorship money across a number of UK podcasts, including yourselves."

"You are fucking joking," I said.

"I can validate your anger!" said Neil.

"Neil," I said, "I am going to start running Kalashnikov endorsements in programme 15. That's in three weeks time. Would you be kind enough to remove the GoDaddy branding from our show by then?"

"I'll talk to the guys in the States," he said.

When Georgina and I launched the first Kalashnikov-sponsored programme three weeks later, Podshow were still stubbornly inserting GoDaddy sponsorship stings into the beginning of every new Sowerby and Luff Show. They obviously knew this would jeopardize our valuable new partnership with Kalashnikov. But they clearly didn't care.

BYE BYE PODSHOW

We signed a termination of contract letter the following week, and I faxed it to Podshow. But the GoDaddy branding stayed in place. I rang Neil.

"Will you please remove the GoDaddy promos from our podcast," I pleaded.

"I'm afraid I'm not able to do that," said Neil. He was slowly turning into an annoying computer, like the one in 2001: A Space Odyssey.

Neil had started out as a podcaster himself. He had built a reputation for promoting good UK podcasts with his own excellent website Britcaster. But now he had clearly gone over to the dark side. I became so incensed when the GoDaddy promos continued to jam our Kalashnikov podcasts the following week that I rang Neil, on his private mobile number, on a Saturday afternoon. My language was so colourful on that occasion, that he was prompted to immediately email his boss Joe in the States. When Joe replied, he accidentally sent the reply to me, instead of to Neil, and when Georgina and I read the tone of that email, we finally realised what a thoroughly unpleasant bunch of characters the Podshow executives were.

Joe had telephoned me at home only a couple of weeks before and had gone to extraordinary lengths to tell me how much he "valued our talent", and how "committed" he and his colleagues in the United States were to furthering our careers. But the arrogant and dismissive email he sent to us by accident that day proved that neither he nor his network appeared to give a damn about any of their UK talent.

We were clearly nothing more than a disposable resource. If one lot of podcasters were unhappy, the strategy was to just get rid of them as quickly as possible and sign another bunch of mugs. Of course, Georgina didn't trust Podshow from the start. "Validating our anger," and asking us to "Play as part of the bigger picture," was never going to impress her. Child-like mid-Atlantic jargon like that has always made a little bit of sick creep up in the back of Georgina's throat.

We were both desperately disappointed at the way Podshow treated us and the way in which the company so blatantly and cynically failed to keep their promises to us, then did everything they could to damage our chances with our own sponsors. We felt stupid, we felt ridiculously naïve, and we were deeply, deeply hurt. But we were also extremely angry, and absolutely certain that no-one would ever take advantage of Sowerby and Luff in the same way again.

Chapter 16
Fear and Loathing at the BBC

Georgina and I were fast achieving minor-celebrity status within the fast-growing podcasting industry, and around this time we were offered an opportunity to write our first regular column in *Podcast User* magazine. It's probably worth reproducing the whole of that first article, because it's also an intriguing little anecdote about the changing face of radio broadcasting.

> Georgina and I were recently invited to talk about comedy in a live interview for a drivetime show on local radio. The BBC doesn't expect anyone from London to actually travel to any of its more far-flung outposts of broadcasting, so we were instructed to go to Television Centre in Shepherd's Bush, where our programme contribution was to be linked down the line to a local radio studio.
>
> When we arrived at Television Centre, the receptionist at the Stage Door took us to what looked like a cupboard in the basement. She punched a 4 digit code into a security lock, opened the door, pushed us inside, and scurried away like a sewer rat. We were greeted by a darkened, empty room with a microphone in the middle. On the wall was a sign. "Welcome to the BBC's Unattended Studio," it said. "Please follow these simple instructions."
>
> No studio engineer. No production assistant. No runner to bring us a nice cup of tea. Just a piece of faded A4 paper, gaffer-taped to the wall.
>
> "First, switch on the power at the big switch next to the door," it advised. Georgina hunted around, found the switch and activated it. A faint fluorescent light flickered on.
> "Switch on the microphone using the big red button in the middle of the desk." I located the button. It had a Post-It note stuck on it which read, "Yes, this one."

"Now, call the studio at the other end, and announce your presence." Georgina picked up the phone. No dialing tone. She looked at her mobile, and I looked at mine. No signal on either handset. We were in the basement after all. Like Batman and Robin on a case, we dashed up to the first floor, and called the local radio studio on Georgina's mobile.

"Are you there already?" said the programme assistant. "The interview's not for another 2 minutes!" God help us, we've always been over-eager.

"Just go back to the studio and wait," she said. We legged it downstairs, but when we got back to the unattended studio we couldn't remember the entry code to the door.

"Can you let us into the Unattended Studio in the basement?", I asked the receptionist. She looked up from searching for jobs on Google. "Didn't I just let you in?" she sighed. We explained.

A minute later, we were back in the Unattended Studio, headphones on, waiting to go on the air, but we hadn't had a second to go over what we were going to talk about, being too busy doing the jobs of a couple BBC studio engineers.

Georgina said she needed a glass of water. We looked around the room for something to drink. All we could find was a ten week old cup of coffee with something sinister and smelly incubating inside. G dashed upstairs to the coffee bar, but there was a long queue. She looked at her watch. We were on the air in thirty seconds. No time for liquid refreshment.

She dashed back downstairs, and threw her headphones back on. Only the right channel was working. She gave the headphones a thump, and the left channel went off as well. I couldn't hear a bloody thing either. I fiddled with the phono socket, on which was another Post-It note which read "Do not touch."

Suddenly, the headphones spurted into life, at three times the original volume, taking out my right eardrum, and we heard the booming voice of a local radio presenter welcoming us to his show.

There was one final item on the checklist of stuff to do on the wall. It said "Make your programme contribution into the microphone". So we did. Fifteen minutes later we were walking towards White City tube, wondering if we'd managed to say anything mildly intelligent on the radio, and understanding completely why it used to be such a good idea to have BBC staff working in BBC studios.

The Beeb are in the process of laying off thousands of staff at the moment, in order to make the corporation a more lean machine. Judging by this experience, we'd say they're pretty damned lean already.

GOING MULTIPLATFORM

Impressed by my apparent expertise on the subject of podcasting and "user generated content", I was contracted to manage the BBC's online comedy team in the spring of 2007, so I was back at the Beeb faster than I'd anticipated. This time, Georgina and I planned carefully how we were going to balance producing our podcast with me working at Television Centre, and I was determined not to experience the frustrations I'd suffered at Endemol the previous year.

One of my briefs during this temporary contract was to add more audio and video content to the BBC comedy website and I threw myself into the project with my usual smiley enthusiasm at being back at the home of British broadcasting. I have a love-hate relationship with the BBC, intensely disliking the way the corporation is run in the twenty first century, but at the same time having a deep fondness for Auntie the way she used to be.

One of my very first jobs after leaving school was working in the video tape library at TV Centre, and in those days it was an exciting, almost magical place. Many of the Beeb's most famous comedy shows were being recorded at that time -The Good Life, Till

Death Us Do Part, Some Mothers Do 'Ave 'Em - all those shows were rotating around the studios while I was there. I once stepped into a lift with Morecambe and Wise, and all that went through my mind was that Eric Morecambe wasn't as tall as I thought he'd be. Nowadays when I walk around those evocative circular corridors, I can literally feel the ghosts of those great performers, and I wonder if the BBC will ever again return to such glory days.

Georgina says I view my spells at the BBC as a sign of defeat – an admittance that I'm not clever enough to earn a full-time living as a comedy writer or broadcaster in my own right. I hope she's wrong about that. My problem is I have an extremely low tolerance of static situations - sitting in the same claustrophobic office day after day drives me insane. Taking the same crowded tube train to work. Having to deal on a daily basis with completely institutionalized staff. To me, all of these things are like a prison cell.

NO BUDGET

On the exact day I started my contract in BBC online comedy, the whole department, along with the rest of the BBC, was completely re-structured, with the effect that nobody in the entire place knew what the fuck they were supposed to be doing. The online department suddenly appeared to be called "The Vision Multiplatform Studio".

"Can I see my production budget?" I asked on my first morning.
"You don't have a budget," replied the Interactive Executive.
"How can I manage a website if I don't know what's in my budget?" I said.
"I don't know," said the Exec.
"Do you have a budget?" I asked.
"I'm not sure," he said.

I rang Georgina. "How can you manage a website if you don't know what's in your budget?" she said.
"I don't know," I said.
"What do you want for dinner," she said.
"Kalashnikov and tonic," I replied.

I spent the next couple of days familiarising myself with the BBC comedy site for which I was now responsible, and was delighted to discover that I myself was listed as a scriptwriter within the pages of its vast online Comedy Guide.

"That's me!" I said to the web producer sitting next to me.

"You've got one of my Channel Five writing credits on your site. Great!"

"I've been meaning to talk to you about that," she said.

"Oh?"

"We're cutting costs on the Comedy Guide."

"Costs?"

"So one of your main jobs while you're here will be to oversee the removal of all the non-BBC credits."

"Including mine?" I asked.

"Starting with yours," she said.

ANIMATING THE BOOSH

The BBC is a fantastically frustrating place to work. Even jobs which *sound* exciting can fast turn into experiences in which you might consider taking your own life. Let me give you an example. I was charged with the task of creating a fully animated, interactive website for The Mighty Boosh - one of the BBC's flagship comedy shows. In other words, the kind of project your average media student would chew off their right arm to undertake.

I set about visiting some vibrant young web design agencies in the West End of London, and within a few days found an agency I thought would do a great job.

"You can't do that," said a BBC Jobsworth.

"What?"

"You can't just go and talk to people."

"I don't understand," I said. How am I going to find the right web design agency for The Boosh if I don't go and talk to people?"

"Because that's not fair," said the BBC Jobsworth. "If you go and talk to people you might give one agency an advantage over another."

I was lost for words. "So what *do* I do?" I asked.

"You use the BBC's Online Commissioning System," he said proudly.

"And how does that work?" I enquired.

"It's simple. I'll give you a username and a password…"

My heart sank. "Then you login and the system will give you a long list of all the skills you think your agency might need to build a nice website for *The Mighty Boosh*."

"Right…"

"Next to each useful skill on the list is a little tick box."

I had died and gone to Hell.

"You place a tick in the box next to the skills you need, and the Online Commissioning System will cleverly give you a list of all the web agencies in the world who might be able to do the job for you."

I felt myself slowly sinking down into my BBC chair. "Then what do I do?" I asked.

"You make a long shortlist of the ten or twelve agencies who get the highest points on your scoresheet."

"Can I talk to them then?" I ventured.

"Of course not," said Jobsworth. "That would be unfair. First, you have to fill out a 30 page Request for Proposal form, and email it to each agency."

"Where do I get the form from?"

"I'll give you a username and a password," he said.

Sigh.

"When you've received official pitches for the work from all of the agencies on the long shortlist, you can go ahead and make a short shortlist."

"How short should it be?" I asked.

"Ooh, I don't know, seven or eight agencies is usually a good number."

"And then I can talk to them?"

"Absolutely not," he snapped. "Then it's their job to come in here and pitch to the BBC for the work."

"Seven agencies?" I squeaked

"All on the same day, yes," he added.

"Why does it have to be on the same day?" I asked. But I guessed before he could answer.

"Don't tell me," I said. "If the pitches for work are not all delivered to the BBC on the same day, some of the agencies might have more time to prepare than others."

"I can see you're getting the hang of this," he said.

I rang Georgina.

"How long does all this take?" she asked.

"He says they can usually rush the procedure through in about two years," I said.

"I thought you said the programme's on the air in six weeks!"

"It is," I said.

"Well you should have started sooner," said Georgina helpfully.

CROWNGATE

Every time I go and work at the BBC the corporation seems to be hit by some kind of major crisis. I'm pretty sure none of these incidents have been my fault, but it is rather an odd coincidence.

During my previous contract, Greg Dyke had been hounded out of his post as Director General following the Hutton Report, and on this occasion it was the crisis that became known as "Crowngate". During a press launch for the BBC Autumn Season, the Controller of BBC1, Peter Fincham had shown the press a clip of what appeared to be the Queen angrily storming out of a room.

It later transpired that scenes had been deliberately re-edited to make the sequence appear more interesting and controversial, and that the Queen had actually been storming *into* the room at that moment. Of course, no-one at the press launch really gave a toss which way the Queen was storming, but Buckingham Palace kicked up a stink and heads began to roll.

Then, only a few weeks later, the BBC's flagship childrens' programme Blue Peter admitted that it had deliberately fixed the result of a viewer competition. The effect of both of these unrelated scandals - one after the other – was that the BBC's general trustworthiness was called into question, and the corporation went into total panic-mode, issuing apologies for everything it had ever done and sacking staff left, right and centre.

That week *all* competitions were banned on *all* BBC programmes, and staff were marched into Nazi-like briefing sessions, me included. We were instructed to blow the whistle on any fellow staff we knew to have deceived viewers in any way. There would be an "amnesty", they said.

No-one would be punished, they said. So, like idiots, dozens of BBC staff routinely shopped their colleagues for any minor deceptions they could think of. A few days later, equally routinely, most of those named and shamed by their colleagues were disciplined or sacked. They're lucky they weren't put up against a wall and stoned.

The result of all this, was that most BBC staff were afraid of their own shadows. We were running a page on the BBC comedy website with an interactive game called Numberwang – based on a ridiculous non-existent gameshow in a sketch series called Mitchell and Webb.

I actually received a call from the Managing Editor of BBC Online, saying that the Editorial Policy department had asked for the page to be removed, because it was clearly a competition.
"Have you ever seen the Mitchell and Webb Show?" I asked him.
"No," he replied.
"There is no such game as Numberwang. How could there be a game called Numberwang? It's a sketch. A comedy sketch."
"Just checking," he said, and quietly put the phone down.

But I wasn't going to get involved in this witch-hunt, was I? It was simply my job to put more video onto the BBC comedy website. So, off I went to the Edinburgh Fringe to direct some comedy clips. Co-financed by BBC New Talent, the idea was to talent-spot some up-and-coming comedians, and give them a showcase online.

To my amazement, even during production of this innocent little web project, the corporation's astonishing paranoia kicked in.

I was warned by EdPol (the BBC's equivalent of the SS) that they might have to pull the plug on our shoot because showcasing new talent might imply a potential offer of future work by the BBC, and that might, in turn, be construed, by some viewers, as a sort of prize, which meant that what we were doing could be considered a form of competition.

Which was no longer allowed at the BBC. There seemed no escape, even in Edinburgh, from the utter lunacy that was the BBC following "Crowngate".

Techincal Superviser Bennsy (left) and Forbes Collins.

The Svendborg Comedy Festival.

Sketch Club, Downstairs at the Kings Head.

Keeping warm in Lanzerote.

Sowerby & Luff's Sex Guide. Official Press Picture.

Lord Kibble (left) with Brian in Hong Kong.

The little Fertility Statue we bought in New York.

Hey, Manhattan.

Georgina at 30 Rock, Brian at the Ed Sullivan Theater on Broadway.

The Cranberry Bog in Rockefeller Plaza.

Georgina with Emily Gordon in the East Village.

Georgina at the New York Marathon.

Downtown Singapore.

Posing with the doorman at Raffles.

On the Avenue of Stars in Kowloon.

In the freezer room in Hong Kong.

Ying Ying not eating bamboo at Ocean Park.

Presenting the fertility statue to Suzanne Gendron.

Doctor Rabbit and Nursey Lamb host the very first Fluffy TV.

In the Studio, May 2006.

Chapter 17
Scissors, Paper, AK47

My BBC contract finished at the end of September 2007, and I breathed a sigh of relief as I strode out of Television Centre in Wood Lane.

The lovely people at Kalashnikov were still sponsoring T*he Sowerby and Luff Show*, and we were becoming ever more professional about how we planned and produced the shows. We even began to run competitions. Hey, just because the BBC had banned them, it didn't mean we couldn't give away the odd bottle of vodka.

Of course, as soon as you begin to give out prizes, particularly alcohol, there's a long list of disclaimers you have to read out in order to stay inside the law. Some of those early Kalashnikov podcasts had more damned terms and conditions in them than they had programme content.

In order to win a bottle of the stuff, listeners had to play a game called Celebrity Russian Roulette, in which we gave out the names of six B-list celebrities, and they had to guess which one of them was dead. A little tasteless perhaps, but generally OK as long as we stuck to people who hadn't only just kicked the bucket.

The rest of the show also began to take on something of a Russian theme, and we were delighted when Kalashnikov hooked us up with a great little musical combo called The Kremlinaires. These lunatics branded themselves as the Commissars of Cool, and with their help we begin to sprinkle our podcasts with some delightful touches of "Soviet Swing" and "Bolshevik Boogie". Our favourite was a Russian comedy song (if there is such a thing) called Fat Vlad from Volgagrad.

Fat Vlad arrived in The Sowerby and Luff Show as something of a coincidence, since a couple of weeks before we had

begun one of our infamous running features by innocently telling a dreadful joke.
"What do you call a vampire with asthma?" I'd asked Georgina.
"I don't know, what do you call a vampire with asthma?"
"Vlad the Inhaler."
It was the shittest joke Georgina and I had ever told, but the emails began to flood in. "Simon" suggested that a vampire antelope might be called Vlad the Impala. Our old mate Jacob from Illinois came up with an internet spam guru called Vlad the E-Mailer, a porn star called Vlad the Stud-Nailer, and a shopper in Manhattan called Vlad the Taxi-Hailer. Then it got completely out of hand:

Captain Ahab – Vlad the Whaler.
A promiscuous person who doesn't use prophylactics: Vlad the STD Test Failer.
A guy hemming your pants, who says "Nice Package": Vlad the Inappropriate Tailor.
A UPS or Fedex employee – Vlad the Airmailer.
Someone who is drowning – Vlad the Desperate Flailer.
A merchant who buys items in bulk, then sells them for a profit – Vlad the Wholesaler
A man who writes books for the blind – Vlad the Brailler.

By this time, a small core group of regular listeners were single-handedly writing the show for us - not only sending in follow-up emails from our talking bollocks sections, but proactively inventing features, competitions and brain-teasers for us to play.

From: "Logan"
Subject: New game to try

I was wondering if you'd like to play a game of my invention on the new show. It's called "Rock, Paper, Anything". The game is like "Rock, Paper Scissors", except that you can pick anything in the universe instead of scissors. The only rule is that what you choose has to be something you can argue about. The random pairings that come up can be very amusing. I'll provide an example from a game I had with one of my friends a while ago: It was Shakespeare v Time. The playwright won, because he transcends Time. Hope this game brings you joy in some small way.

Ever keen to keep Kalashnikov happy, we renamed Logan's game Scissors, Paper, AK47, and launched it in the next show with: Darth Maul v Harry Potter.

From: "Chris"
Subject: Scissors, Paper

While Darth's laser sabre would clearly have the advantage in close combat, Harry's wand has the ability to cast spells from a distance. So he could easily disarm Maul with a simple *sabrus expulsious* or some such *faux latin*. Brian's argument that "it depends who is holding the sabre" is spurious, since both the sabre and the wand are agnostic towards good or evil. ie. Obi Wan and Dumbledore are examples of "good" users, while Darth Vader and Voldemort represent evil. Of course, given the fact that both of the good guys got their arses handed to them, maybe it does depend on who's using the weapons.

With Scissors, Paper, AK47 we'd clearly stumbled upon a winner. But like a couple of idiots, we failed to mention who had invented the game in the previous show.

From: "Logan"
Subject: Paper, scissors, plagiarism

I must say that I'm quite upset with you, as you stole the game of my invention (Rock, Paper, Anything), renamed it Paper, Scissors, AK47, then passed it off as simply something that was "going around". While I do appreciate that you enjoy my game, and have now made it much more popular, all I wanted was for my name to be mentioned. The game is essentially my intellectual property, as I came up with it, Beta tested it, and nurtured the concept until it became viable. Hurtfully yours, Logan.

Oh boy. Sounded like the kid had a lawyer. We were going to have to be a bit more careful when we used ideas sent in by listeners. Every time we played the game after that we went to great lengths to credit Logan. Another brilliant listener suggestion for that game was Red Tape v Health and Safety.

PERSONAL INJURY

Of course, The Sowerby and Luff Show was not subject to Heath and Safety regulations and, as a result, there continued to be a steady stream of those worrying emails in which our listeners appeared to have suffered personal injury as an indirect result of listening to us. This one came from as far afield as Australia.

From "Daniel"
Subject: More Sowerby and Luff related injuries

You guys have injured *another* two people here in Australia. The other day my sister and I were waiting for my mother at a coffee shop.

While we were waiting, I got bored of my sister's conversation, so I started listening to your podcast. Being the klutz that I am, I accidentally laughed so hard I kicked the table leg, knocking hot coffee into my sister's handbag, ruining everything in it, and also scalding her leg.

This caused my sister to hit me on the side of the head, giving me a lump which was still there two days later.

Maybe we should have read out a disclaimer before every show. But back to those games: My own personal favourite was What the Fuck? Georgina would simply think of anything in the universe, and I would try and guess what was in her mind.

A fairly uninspired premise you might think, except that the closer I got to guessing the answer, the closer Georgina would appear to get to achieving orgasm. Our favourite suggestion for WTF was this one:

From: "Simon"
Subject: What the Fuck?

How about "Yvette Fielding's guilt at perpetrating the shameful hoax that is 'Most Haunted' upon the viewing public."

Believe it or not, I guessed that one correctly, giving Georgina a climax to rival Meg Ryan in When Harry Met Sally.

A PLACE WHERE DREAMS LIVE

The Kalashnikov shows were going down well, and there was particularly good feedback for our mad Russian house band the Kremlinaires. In addition to their Bolshevik Boogie, Georgina and I went to a great deal of effort to find strong, original music tracks around which to build the segments of our programmes.

We spent hours on the internet ploughing through hundreds of music tracks which had been cleared by the composers for free use in podcasts. Eventually we stumbled upon an inspired song which we thought completely captured the vibe of Sowerby and Luff.

There is a place where dreams live
Nothing there is relative…

Dreams of Piccadilly was recorded by a student band from Vancouver called Curiosity Shop. The group had since split up, but we like to think we gave their sound a new lease of life in our podcasts I set about cutting the track up into a series of short themes, bumpers and underscores.

And it's got me so excited about the possibilities,
It's not silly, Dreams of Piccadilly,
The weather's kind of chilly, on the porch at Piccadilly

The track skipped along with a kind of sixties pop feel - with rhythmic clapping throughout and the lyrics seemed to exactly capture the way we always imagined our American listeners might visualise the chilly streets of old London Town. We trawled the web for contact details for the band, and for weeks we were unable to track them down. Then we were delighted to get this email.

> From: "Thomas"
> Subject: Curiosity Shop
>
> I was in the band. By all means, use Dreams of Piccadilly. That would be cool. It's really old stuff - twelve years to be exact. Thanks for the interest.

We had no idea the track was so ancient, but we'd fallen in love with it and our listeners soon took it to their hearts as the theme music for The Sowerby and Luff Show.

DEAD PENGUIN

We also discovered another massively underrated British band. Three Blind Mice reminded us a little of Squeeze from the 1980s, and we began to create more musical elements for the show from their album Good Grief.

We soon got regular emails from the band, and after a few weeks, we met up with them for a drink in The Gay Legs. The group's lead guitarist and co-composer, Lindon had actually toured with Squeeze, and we spent a great evening talking about the pop business, and how much the online music industry might change the fortunes of bands like theirs.

Three Blind Mice's brilliant multi-layered tracks Dead Penguin and Your Face Is not Enough also became an important part of the sound of Sowerby and Luff, and along with music written and produced by Richard Cray and Hywel Luff (no relation), in the band Dogs Must be Carried, our podcasts were beginning to develop a quite unique musical feel.

SIGNING TONY'S FRIDGE

We love meeting up with other podcasters, comedians and musicians, partly because it's a damned good excuse to go to the pub, but also because it gives us an opportunity to drop the names of famous people into our podcasts. When writer and broadcaster Tony Hawks was thinking of producing a podcast of his own, we were introduced by a mutual friend, and spent a very pleasant evening with Tony talking about podcasting, comedy writing and some of the ridiculous adventures he's undertaken in the name of humour.

Tony's played tennis against the entire Moldavian soccer team and he's had a number one hit in Albania with ageing comedian Norman Wisdom, but he's probably best known for lugging a fridge around the entire perimeter of Ireland in order to win a bet.

The bet was a mere £100, and in fact the fridge cost him more than that. But that was the whole point. There was no point. Except that the adventure ended up making a splendid book. Chatting with Tony that evening gave Georgina and me much food for thought. Maybe we too should set out on some pointless adventure and then write a book about it.

It certainly seemed to have worked for Tony. A couple of weeks later he invited us to a charity event at the National Geographical Society, where he was to re-tell his famous Irish adventure in front of a specially invited audience. By this time, Georgina and I were becoming more and more convinced that we should consider setting off on some daft quest of our own, so we were delighted to attend.

We loved the live version of Round Ireland With a Fridge, and after the gig we hovered in the bar so that Georgina could get Tony to sign our own paperback copy of the book. While we were waiting I glanced inside the front cover.
 "This book's already been signed by Tony Hawks," I laughed.
  "What? Show me!" grumbled Georgina.
  "There," I said. "To Jim, from Tony Hawks."
  "Who's Jim?" demanded Georgina.
I looked at the battered book again, and suddenly realised that it was in fact a copy I'd borrowed several years before from a friend. As it turned out, that friend had borrowed it from a friend of his called Jim, who neither Georgina nor I had ever met.
  "I'll get him to sign it anyway," said Georgina.

"You can't do that!" I said. "That would be very rude. You can't ask an author to sign the same book twice!"

"Wouldn't it make the book terribly valuable?" said Georgina. "It would be the only copy to be signed twice. We could take it to the Antiques Roadshow."

Georgina can be very stubborn at times. I tried a different tack.

"Look, it's probably not good book-signing etiquette to ask someone to autograph an *old* copy of a book. Surely the idea is that you buy a nice *new* copy of the book, and get that signed."

Georgina dug in her heels. "But we've *got* a copy of the book," she said.

When Tony's not explaining to Americans that he's not the famous skateboarding star, he writes travel books which make a very close connection with his readers. You really get the sense that you're going with him on his mad little trips – which is exactly the kind of intimate journey Georgina and I want our listeners to experience.

"We should go on a trip like that," I said to Georgina.

"But what are we going to use as a fridge?" she asked.

"We'll think of something," I said. "In fact, I'm guessing our listeners will think of something for us!"

FRIENDS AND NEIGHBOURS

Podcasting is a far more emotive and personal medium than broadcast radio, and many of the audience make a very close connection with the presenters. This can prove to be something of a responsibility, particularly when you actually get asked for advice. Georgina has been cast in the role of Agony Aunt on numerous occasions – being asked her opinion on everything from fashion sense to unreliable boyfriends.

From: "Sally"
Subject: Whatever should I do?

Dear Georgina, I trust your judgment, so I'm going to ask your advice on what to do about my boyfriend. I've just recently found out that he's a compulsive liar. Should I stay with him and work through it with a counsellor, or should I leave him?

My own view was that it wasn't a good idea to offer advice to someone on the other side of the planet, but Georgina took messages like that very seriously. Her view was that ignoring such an email could do more harm than good, so she believed she had little choice but to offer a few cautious words of advice.

The point at which our real life stopped and the podcast began was becoming more and more blurred, and some of our listeners probably remember certain things that happened to us back then better than we do. Like our ongoing battle with our noisy neighbours. Our flat is on the first floor, and our bedroom backs directly onto the garden of the downstairs flat.

Throughout the summer, and often even on freezing cold nights in the winter, our neighbours sit outside smoking and drinking and talking in extremely loud voices until the early hours. This sometimes makes it virtually impossible for us to sleep in our own bedroom, and we're often forced to retreat to the tiny bedroom next door – the one that's also crammed with recording equipment.

One particularly noisy night we decided that since we couldn't sleep with so much racket going on, we'd record a podcast in the bedroom there and then - against the audio backdrop of the racket downstairs. We placed a microphone on the window sill, to be sure of recording as much of the neighbour's noise as possible, then vainly attempted to record an episode.

e were forced to give up after only about five minutes, but the section of that recording that we did play caused a flood of supportive emails from our listeners – some offering suggestions as to how we might silence our downstairs neighbours. The following week an acquaintance who knows both us and the couple downstairs, mentioned to our neighbours that their drunken rantings had featured in one of our podcasts. It may be my imagination, but I'm pretty sure that the sound levels from the garden have lowered considerably since. Social action through the medium of iTunes? Who knows?

At the other end of the day, our slumbers are frequently interrupted by a gentleman who lives in the large house next door. We actually don't know his name, but we have christened him Noisy Dad. Every morning at around 7.00am, Noisy Dad sings nursery rhymes to his baby.

MARY HAD A LITTLE *LAMB!*

He has such a deep and booming voice that the foundations of our house actually tremble.

ITS FLEECE WAS WHITE AS *SNOW!!!*

Noisy Dad's voice is like a cross between three sounds; the voice of Mr Bean, the voice of former Prime Minister John Major and the foghorn on the Isle of Wight ferry. It wasn't long before my hastily-cobbled-together impression of our over-amplified neighbour became a regular feature in the podcast.

> From: "Jacob"
> Subject: Noisy Dad
>
> I just spat coffee out when Noisy Dad started shouting "Mary Had A Little Lamb." Precious

Chapter 18
Sex and the Single Sheep

We had a regular section in the podcast called Sex and the Single Sheep, in which Georgina would read out fascinating and absurd facts about animals. One week she stumbled upon a wealth of hilarious information about pandas. Who could have guessed that that this innocent little item would ultimately lead us to a rendezvous on the other side of the world.

As everyone already knew, Giant Pandas only eat bamboo. But what people don't tend to realise is that there is virtually no nutritional value at all in bamboo, rendering the pandas permanently weak and lethargic.

"No wonder they're so fucking lazy," I quipped. "Why don't they just change their diets?"

"Maybe they can't," reasoned Georgina.

"Let's get to the bottom of this," I said. "Where do pandas live?"

"Half way up mountains," said Georgina.

"Why?" I asked.

"Because that's where the bamboo is."

"Is there any food at the bottom of the mountain?" I asked.

"Yes," said Georgina. "Loads of it. Lots of nice green, thick, luscious vegetation."

"So, why don't the pandas come down the mountain and eat something that's better for them?" I asked.

"They're too lazy," said Georgina.

"It's *downhill!*" I screamed. "How hard could it be?"

So began our ongoing rant against the pandas. Of course they were dying out. They couldn't be bothered to look for any food other than bamboo, and that was bad for them. Of course they couldn't be bothered to mate - they were too damned weak from all that bamboo. The emails flooded in. Some in support of the pandas, but mostly climbing onto Sowerby and Luff's anti-panda bandwagon. But more often than not, it was the pandas' sex lives that people were the most interested in. This email was from Emily in New York, who by this point was one of the most regular contributors to The Sowerby and Luff Show.

Subject: Fat Pandas.

A male Giant Panda at a zoo in the Far East has been placed on a month-long diet to avoid squashing his partner during sex. "Chuang Chuang is gaining weight too fast, and we found Lin Hui is no longer comfortable with having sex with him," said the zoo's chief veterinarian. As a result, zoo authorities are cutting out bamboo shoots in the daily meal for Chuang Chuang and giving the obese bear only bamboo leaves. This diet plan is the latest in an unsuccessful and often strange campaign by zoo officials to get the two bears to mate. They have held a mock wedding, announced plans to separate the two to spark a little romance and even talked of introducing panda porn - videos of other pandas mating — to get the pair in the mood.

Now pandas were overweight? In the space of a few programmes we'd gone from weak, hungry pandas to obese ones. But it was the notion of panda *porn* that really caught the imagination of our listeners. A bit more research quickly taught us that Panda Porn appeared to be a fast-growing industry in the Far East. It was apparently quite common for the creatures to be shown videos of other pandas shagging.

In Kalashnikov Show 34, we finally began to feel a little guilty about our vendetta against these gentle creatures, and I mentioned, quite in passing, that maybe Sowerby and Luff should offer some sex tips for pandas. Maybe send them a gift or some sort?
"What kind of gift?" Georgina asked.
"How about some kind of fertility symbol," I said off the top of my head. "To bring them luck while they're trying to mate."
"I'll look it up on the internet," said Georgina.

The following day, Georgina Googled "Fertility Gods", and found a beautiful little statue in a posh new age shop in the East

Village in New York City. The shop didn't appear to have online shopping, so Georgina rang them up.

"I'm interested in the fertility statue on your website," she said.

"Is it for you?" said a long-distance voice.

"No, it's for a panda," said Georgina.

There was a pause, followed by a click and a dialling tone.

We laughed until we cried. Coincidentally, when Georgina next checked our emails there was a message from the United States.

"Emily is inviting us to come and stay with her in New York," screamed Georgina excitedly. "I've never been to New York. Let's go, let's go!"

"I've never been either," I said. "So, maybe we should take her up on her offer. And while we're there, we can go and buy that fertility statue in that shop in the East Village."

This was by far the most ridiculous idea we'd had so far. Were we really going to climb onto a plane to America, just to go into a new age shop in New York and buy a twenty dollar ornament?

"Emily says we can stay in her apartment, and she'll show us around New York while we're there," said Georgina. "And we can record some podcasts too."

Kalashnikov loved the idea when we suggested it to them, so it appeared that the Sowerby-Luffs were going to New York.

FACING FACEBOOK

In the late summer of 2007, social networking on the internet reached new heights of popularity, and people began to spend half their lives staring at a web phenomenon called Facebook. We were increasingly told by our listeners that we should have a Facebook page, so I started to do a little research.

One of the first things I discovered was that over a third of BBC employees had pages on Facebook. No wonder it took so bloody long to get anything done at the BBC. The license-payers were essentially paying 10,000 staff to spend all day updating their Facebook profiles and network with their friends.

As self-styled Head of Social Networking in our own little corporation Georgina threw herself into building a splendid Facebook page for Sowerby and Luff. Since Facebook is not designed for double-acts, we had to call ourselves Sowerby AndLuff – the rather irritating AndLuff effectively being our collective Facebook surname.

It wasn't long before Georgina was spending every waking hour on Sowerby AndLuff's Facebook page, and our group of friends was accelerating nicely. Georgina put so much hard work into that page. So many hours. So much creativity. Then one weekend I thought I'd have a go on it. While Georgina was out, I logged into Sowerby AndLuff, and had a little rummage around.

"I'm sure I can get us more friends than this," I thought, and I began to start nicking the friends of some other well-known podcasters on Facebook.
"If they like that podcast," I reasoned, "They're gonna love Sowerby AndLuff."
How very wrong I was. That Monday morning Georgina attempted to login to our Facebook page, and was greeted by this sinister message:

Your account has been disabled by an administrator. If you have any questions or concerns, you can visit our FAQ page here.

Oh fuck. What had I done? Georgina grabbed me by the ear and led me red-faced towards her laptop.
"What does this mean?" she screamed. Somehow, a part of her knew that this was my fault. I clicked on the FAQ link and read sheepishly.

"Your account was disabled because you violated Facebook's Terms of Use, to which you agreed when you first registered for an account on the site. Accounts can either be disabled for repeat offenses or for one, particularly egregious violation."

What is God's name was an "egregious violation"? What were these bastards accusing me of?

> "Facebook does not allow users to register with fake names, to impersonate any person or entity, or to falsely state or otherwise misrepresent themselves or their affiliations."

Had Facebook considered "AndLuff" to be a fake name? Or were they concerned about my awful impersonations?

> "We do not allow users to send unsolicited or harassing messages to people they don't know, and we remove posts that advertise a product, service, website, or opportunity."

To this day I can only assume that Facebook has some kind of top secret software in place that can detect if one podcaster is trying to nick listeners from another. It's hardly Watergate though, is it?

> "Our Code of Conduct includes any obscene, pornographic, or sexually explicit photos, as well as any photos that depict graphic violence. We also remove content that threatens, intimidates, harasses, or brings unwanted attention or embarrassment to an individual or group of people."

For the life of me I couldn't remember threatening or harassing anyone, and when we asked to be shown the infringement for which we had been so unceremoniously "disabled" we were told that this was not technically possible. The bottom line was that Georgina has wasted hundreds of hours building a network which Facebook had subsequently deleted in a nano-second with a single touch of the delete key. She was never going to forgive them for it. Or me.

In order to make amends, I immediately set about building a new Facebook group called Sowerby and Luff's Fully Optimized Social Media Network – a name which I felt went some way towards expressing my view that social networking was turning out to be rather more cynical than its inventors had intended. I'd been adding the names of all the Sowerby and Luff listeners we'd had emails from over the past year or so, but I was frankly starting to get pretty sick of all the hype surrounding Facebook. Then I got this message posted on our page.

Thank you for the invite
Between You and "Bradley". Today at 12:56am

I was quite surprised when I saw the friend invite for your profile when I logged in. The thing is, I've been going through a divorce, and I was sad to discover how loyal my so called friends were while I was divorcing. You're the first person to send me an invite on Facebook, and the first invite for anything, anywhere for that matter in over a year. So it meant a lot to me, even though you don't really know who I am. I also wanted to let you know that your many shows have done a lot for me. I've been listening to the podcast since the Big Squeeze started, and have enjoyed hours of conversation and comedy. Comedy 365 also introduced me to John Dredge, who has become one of my all time favorite comedians. Through this past couple of years I have had only to turn on my iPod to be able to cheer up and laugh during the hardest time in my life. I know that I do not truly know who you all are, but the comedy that you've provided has helped more then you can ever know. I'll keep a copy of your podcasts on my computer for a long time to come, as means to bring a smile and remember the best times in my worst.

This letter is as much to Georgina as to anyone else at Comedy 365, including all those behind it. I hope you will extend my sentiments to all of them for me. Thank You.

When I read that message to Georgina it made her cry. Perhaps I'd been a little hasty in dismissing the usefulness of Facebook.

ANOTHER INVITATION

Meanwhile, on the other side of the world, David Kibble was listening to programme 34 in his office in Singapore. David was immediately taken with the idea of Sowerby and Luff sending a fertility statue to a panda, so he picked up his Blackberry and telephoned a zoo in Hong Kong.
  Georgina and I were in the middle of packing our bags for New York, when we stopped for a moment to check our emails. There was a message from David inviting us to go to China.

"What?" I screamed.
"He's perfectly serious," said Georgina.

Having only just got used to the idea that our podcast was capable of taking us to America, we now had an opportunity to fly right around the world.

"I have a flat in Hong Kong," explained David, "So you can stay there. And I've spoken with Ocean Park Zoo in Hong Kong, and told them that you'd like to meet with the pandas."
Clearly, our listeners were becoming as crazy as we were, and the Sowerby and Luff podcast was beginning to gain momentum on a global scale, at a quite alarming rate.

"How far is it to Hong Kong?" Georgina asked.
"Six thousand miles," I said.
"This is mad," she frowned. Then she laughed.
"Hey, how hard could it be?" I said. "We pop over to America, pick up a statue, fly to Hong Kong and give it to a panda."
"Why?" asked Georgina quizzically.
"Because," I reminded her, "That's *our* fridge. The pandas are our next ghost in the cave."
"It's not very green is it? said Georgina. "Flying half way around the world to do something so daft. What about our carbon footprint?"
"Oh, we'll sort that out when we get back!", I said. "We'll offset our emissions or something."
"What's does that mean?" asked Georgina.
"I have no idea," I said. "But I promise I'll find out."

We didn't sleep very much that night. For us The Sowerby and Luff Show had been about simply strolling into the spare bedroom once a week and talking bollocks into a couple of old microphones. Now, the podcast appeared to be changing our lives. It was a scary thought.

"But I don't even like flying," said Georgina, as we chatted about the whole globe-trotting thing a couple of podcasts later. We immediately had an email suggesting something that might help.

From: "Doug "
Subject: Fear of Flying

I tried balloon therapy for my fear of flying. I was taken up in an airplane and the therapist blew up three big red balloons and had me write "I am not afraid to fly," on them. I was then instructed to pop the balloons to rid me of my fear. Unfortunately, it did not work. I am still afraid to fly and to make matters worse, I am now terrified of fucking balloons.

Of course if you popped a balloon on a transatlantic flight these days, you'd probably be wrestled to the floor by a couple of sky marshals.

A week before we had to leave for America, I decided it might be a good idea to get myself fit for what I was certain was going to be some pretty exhausting travelling over the next month or so. So, I'd taken the extraordinary step of doing some exercise. Walking mainly. In fact, in the space of about three days, I put on my big boots and walked for about twenty miles.

"Why are you limping?" asked Georgina.
"Because," I replied "I have been getting myself into shape."
"What?"
"I'm like a coiled spring," I said, "A finely tuned athlete, ready to explore the Brave New World. There's only one problem."
"What's that?"
"I can't walk."

I'd made this mistake before. Rather than exercise slowly over a period of months, I would suddenly undertake a furious regime of exercise in about 48 hours, and completely cripple myself for the following week.

"How are you going to explore New York without being able to walk? asked Georgina.
"I don't know," I said. "In a wheelchair?"
"You'll be fine," she said."I'm not joking," I said, "I think I've sprained my foot. Unless it gets better pretty damned quick we're going to have to cancel the whole New York trip."

"You idiot!" ranted Georgina. "How could you be so bloody stupid as to risk our trip to America for the sake of a bit of exercise?"

"I only went for a walk!" I said.

"For TWENTY MILES???" screamed Georgina.

With just a couple of days to go before we set off for the States, I was still slumped on the sofa with my leg propped up on a cushion - my foot swollen to the size of a basketball.

"You'll have to go alone," I said. "I won't be able to get to the airport, let alone to New York."

"I'm not going on my own," said Georgina sadly. "I suppose we'll have to ring up the airline and cancel the whole thing."

Chapter 19
Fear of Flying

The next 48 hours were a white knuckle ride for Sowerby and Luff. We piled ice onto my ankle. I took painkillers. I drank whisky to numb the pain. When we woke up on the morning of the flight I gingerly slid out of bed and put weight onto my right foot.
"I think it feels a little better," I said.
"Get dressed," snapped Georgina. "We're going to America."

As I hobbled inch by inch towards the check-in desk for flight AA142 from London Heathrow to JFK, I kept my fingers tightly crossed that my buggered foot would not spoil our New York adventure. Meanwhile, Georgina chewed her way through half a packet of Valerian, in preparation for the flight. Valerian is some kind of herbal valium, and it was the only thing that would get Georgina anywhere near an aeroplane. She'd also had a couple of sleeping pills as well, so it looked like the flight to America was going to be a fairly subdued affair.

Georgina's desperate fear of flying is something we just had to grin and bear, but optimistically she'd only had one of her gruesome "plane dreams" during the week before this flight, so all seemed to be well. Her dread of flying was, she admitted herself, a completely nonsensical whim, which she thought she had only developed due to her sister's panic attacks whilst on aeroplanes. On the day of that flight, however, she was so far calm and well behaved, with only minor fluctuations of mood before we set off.

"But I wanted a window seat," I grumbled, as I limped from the check-in desk towards security.
"Well, you can't have a window seat," said Georgina.
"But I *always* have a window seat" I said. "I want a window seat."
"There were no window seats," she snapped. "Get over it!"
"Maybe I could swap," I said.
"Oh for God's sake," said Georgina. "It doesn't matter. You won't be able to see anything anyway. It's night time."

"It won't be night time when we get there, will it?" I ranted.

"It'll be daytime. I want a damned window seat!"

"You are so fucking selfish!!!", Georgina suddenly yelled. I was momentarily taken aback. "What?"

"Why can't you just relax and enjoy yourself! Who cares what fucking seat you sit in?"

"I was only joking," I said. "It was just a bit of banter -to pass the time? And my foot hurts."

"Can we please just have ten fucking minutes without banter!" Georgina screamed.

I grinned, but for once in her life Georgina did not grin back. The thought of what lay ahead over the next few weeks was finally manifesting itself as stress. Up until that moment, the idea of gallivanting around the world on a fairly pointless and tenuous premise seemed like fun.

Now, it suddenly felt like we were flying into the unknown. Who knew what our listeners would think of us when they actually met us face to face? Who knew whether we'd be able to record radio programmes away from the security of our own little spare room. Podcasting's pioneers were about to become podcasting's intrepid explorers. And it was a little scary. I gave Georgina a hug and she hugged me back.

"Sorry," she said.

"I'm sorry too," I replied. "But I still want a window seat."

As we approached security I was horrified to note that some passengers were being asked to remove their footwear and feed them separately through an X-ray machine.

"I hate taking off my shoes in public," I grumbled. "Why do I have to take off my shoes?"

"Just do it," said Georgina.

As I sat and removed my boots, so that they could be screened for high explosives, I noticed that the swelling on my foot was slowly going down.

"You should elevate that ankle," said an American woman sitting next to me.

"Thanks," I said.

THE FLYING RABBI

As we settled into our central aisle seats on the plane, our attention was immediately grabbed by the blustering arrival of a large, elderly Rabbi. He was staring at his boarding pass in a completely bewildered fashion, and he seemed to be in great distress.

After wandering up and down the aisle for about 5 minutes, he finally showed his boarding pass to a woman sitting in an aisle seat. She undid her safety belt and got up, so that he could sit down in his window seat. But he refused to sit. So she got back into her seat again, and put her safety belt back on.

The Rabbi wandered up to the end of the plane, turned around, came back and once again stood next to the woman in the aisle seat. As before, she removed her seat belt and stood up to allow him to sit down.

"What's he doing?" I whispered to Georgina.
"He can't find his seat," she replied.
"He should use the seat number on his boarding pass as a guide," I said.

Meanwhile, the Rabbi had again refused to sit down, and the woman in the aisle seat had yet again, very patiently, re-seated herself and put her seat belt back on.
At this point, two American Airlines staff appeared, and after much huffing and puffing and tutting and muttering it transpired that the Rabbi *did not want to sit in a window seat.*

"Is he crazy?" I whispered. "Everyone wants to sit in a window seat. That's the best place to sit!"
"Sssshhh," went Georgina.
"I could have his window seat, and he could sit here with you," I suggested.
"I am not sitting next to a fat elderly Rabbi all the way to New York," said Georgina.
"It might be fun," I said.
"No fucking way!" she said.

"How could he not want a window seat," I mumbled.
"Oh shut up," hissed Georgina.

As our plane rattled down the runway, Georgina held my hand.
"Don't squeeze," I said.
"I won't squeeze," she promised.

Every time we'd flown together before, the flight had begun with Georgina grabbing hold of my hand and crushing the bones into a fine powder. It was her way of dealing with the stress of take-off.
"You're squeezing," I said.
"I am not squeezing," she said.
"Don't squeeze!" I pleaded.

But it was too late. As our plane rotated at the end of the runway and began its ascent, my left hand was being crushed like a Christmas walnut in a nutcracker.
"Ahhh!" I screamed under my breath.
"Is everything all right?" asked the lady in a shell suit sitting next to me.
"Fine," I said.
"Are you a nervous flyer?" she inquired.
"No," I replied, "My partner is."
The lady in the shell suit seemed confused.

As well as the ritualistic squeezing of the hand, other passengers were also treated to Georgina's detailed running commentary of the sights and sounds on an aircraft that make her nervous. The noise of the wheels being clunked back up into the fuselage, the gentle shaking of the wings on take-off, the retracting of the flaps.

We were at 23,000 feet before Georgina finally let go her vice-like grip on my fingers. At least the pain in my hand had taken my mind off the throbbing in my foot.
"Are you OK?" I whispered. But she was fast asleep.
As I tucked into my cardboard American Airlines omelette, complete with minute cardboard vegetables, I couldn't help wishing that I was over in that window seat, while Georgina snoozed gently

on the shoulder of the elderly Jew, who would now of course be nursing four severely crushed and bruised fingers. Before take-off, the Rabbi had finally agreed to swap seats with a gentleman in the very middle of the centre aisle, which meant that every time he needed to empty his bladder, which was about every ten minutes, two passengers would have to unclip their seat belts, place their trays in the upright position, and stand in the aisle for fifteen minutes while they waited for him to come back.

The flight to New York passed very quickly for both Georgina and me. She snoozed most of the way, and I was kept almost continually entertained by the amazing Flying Rabbi. On every flight there always seems to be one person who is the centre of attention, and I thanked God that on this one it wasn't Georgina, scrabbling to try and escape out of one of the exits.

We touched down in New York City in late afternoon twilight.
"Please remain in your seats," said the pilot.
Everyone stood up immediately and reached for the overhead lockers.
"Why is that stewardess wearing little devil's horns on her head?" I asked Georgina as she carefully lowered her duty free.
"Because it's Halloween," she said.
"Oh, God, I forgot," I said. "They take that pretty seriously here, don't they?".
We filed out of the plane, past a flight deck on which the pilot was wearing a witch's hat, and the first officer was sporting a pair of vampire's teeth.

WELCOME TO AMERICA

"Were you a member of the Nazi Party between 1933 and 1945?" asked the immigration officer at JFK Airport.
"What should I tick?" I asked Georgina.
"Well, *were* you a member of the Nazi Party between 1933 and 1945?" she said.
"Not as far as I remember," I replied.
"So, tick the box that says NO," she said.

"How about espionage?" I asked
"Industrial or international?" inquired Georgina
"It doesn't say. Shall I write don't know?"
"I wouldn't," said Georgina.
"Have we ever been involved in genocide?" I asked.
"You're not serious," she said.
"It's the second question on the immigration form."
"If I had been involved in the systematic mass murder of tens of thousands of people," she said, "I think I'd probably remember."
"Any Ethnic cleansing?" I asked.
"No."
"Final answer?"
"Final answer," said Georgina.

We slowly worked our way through the rest of the customs and immigration forms, also assuring the United States that we were not seeking political asylum and that we did not have any hand grenades or throwing stars in our hand luggage.
"What do you do?" asked the immigration officer as we offered our hands up for fingerprinting.
"We're writers," we said in unison.
"What do you write?" he asked.
"Comedy, mostly," said Georgina.
"Got anything in print?" he asked.

I don't think Georgina and I were ready for the United States to take such a deep interest in our writing careers. Perhaps they were going to offer us some freelance work. I thought about telling the security guy that we were in New York primarily to buy a fertility statue for a couple of pandas in China, but I didn't want to risk spending the next six hours in an interrogation room with his finger up my arse. Instead I replied politely.
"Print, internet, a little television," I said. "Anything really."
"Why are you limping?" he asked.
"It's part of my keep fit regime," I said.
The officer pointed his little digital camera at Georgina, and she frowned back at him. "Hey, smile" he said, "You're on vacation!"

As we struggled out of the arrivals hall with our cases, we were filled with a heady mixture of excitement and trepidation.

Never having been to New York before, and not knowing our way around, it was just possible that we would be little more than lambs to the slaughter.

"How's your foot?" asked Georgina.

"I'd forgotten all about it," I said. "But thanks for reminding me."

While we were waiting for a taxi at JFK, the first thing we saw was a famous comedian with a moustache jump into a Yellow Cab.

"Hey!" said a loud New Yorker in a baseball cap queuing next to us, "It's that famous comedian with a moustache." He tapped Georgina on the shoulder, and pointed. "Hey, it's that famous comedian with a moustache!"

It was indeed an extremely famous comedian, but neither Georgina nor I could remember his name, or indeed the name of his moustache. But it was good to see someone famous within a few minutes of arriving in the Big Apple. The famous comedian with a moustache waved back to the New Yorker in a baseball cap, and sped off towards Manhattan in the back of his cab.

"I'll look him up on the internet," said Georgina

"How can you Google a face?" I asked, and Georgina said she'd try Googling "Famous comedian with a moustache."

HAPPY HALLOWEEN

The first distant sighting of the Empire State Building, as you drive towards the city, is extraordinary. The Art Deco skyscraper looks as imposing and spectacular as it must have done when it was first built in the thirties, and it still stands proud and tall in the centre of midtown. Georgina and I bounced up and down like a couple of over-excited school kids when we first caught a glimpse of it.

"I can't believe we're actually here," gushed Georgina.

"The podcast that ate New York," I said.

"Let's hope New York doesn't eat us," she replied.

We arrived in Brooklyn just after dark, which on Halloween proved to be one of the most surreal, exciting and at the same time alarming experiences of our entire trip. We'd arranged to pick up the keys to Emily's apartment at a diner called Aldo's, and the cab driver took us around Williamsburg at least three times before we finally asked him to set us down, so that we could locate the diner on foot.

Brooklyn is not difficult to navigate. Like everywhere else in the USA the roads are numbered in a very obvious way, so how anyone could possibly get lost I can't imagine. Was this the only cab driver in New York who didn't know his way around the city? As we clambered out of the cab with our bags, we were both pretty apprehensive.

Brooklyn, night falling, and we didn't know where we were. It's fair to say our relief was palpable when we crossed the street and immediately found the diner. The cab had pulled up right opposite it. Entirely by accident. Aldo's was closed, but we peeped through the iron bars and shutter and a lady called Lina welcomed us to New York with a huge smile and gave us our keys, along with a note from Emily explaining how and where to use them. All we had to do now was find the apartment.

The unfamiliar noises of Brooklyn filled our heads. The streets were crawling with zombies, monsters and white-faced ghouls, all of whom were screaming out for candy, and some of whom, slightly more worryingly, were asking for cash.

"I hate to admit it," I said to Georgina, "But I'm a bit scared."

"Just don't make eye contact," she said, and she fixed her eyes firmly on the sidewalk.

Williamsburg is one of those up-an-coming New York neighbourhoods we hear so much about. The area is filled with trendy bars and restaurants, and populated by thousands of creative types wearing expensive designer glasses. But at the same time, it retains some very run down and shamefully dilapidated apartment blocks.

"Trick or treat," coming from a child on Halloween is a familiar cry, but as we walked along South 3rd Street, with our expensive iPods and digital cameras, it made us feel more than a little uncomfortable to also hear the words "Help the poor," from the kids.

Emily's apartment building was old and extremely well worn. Paint flaked off the walls everywhere, and the downstairs lobby had signs which read "No Loitering" and rows and rows of metal-fronted post boxes for each tenant in the building. We wrestled with the keys for a while in the hallway, and finally fell exhausted through the front door into Emily's kitchen. Straight away the little apartment reminded us of our own flat in Crouch End. Books, magazines and paraphernalia filled every available inch, and we could immediately see why Georgina had struck up such a close friendship with Emily, even though the pair were on opposite sides of the Atlantic.

We dropped our bags on the floor and bravely decided to head out into the night towards the nearest bar. Williamsburg has its own style, each shop, each diner, each restaurant separates itself with its own quirky idea. But in many ways, the area didn't look like it had changed much since the 1950's. We walked down Havemeyer past quaint little drug stores and corner markets.

In America, Halloween is indeed a far bigger deal than it is in the UK, and we were amazed to see that almost everyone in Williamsburg was in fancy dress. Adults of all ages, teenagers and children were all dressed in the most incredible variety of hired costumes. Vampires, cowboys and cartoon characters hurried everywhere.
"I feel a little out of place," I said to Georgina.
"How so?"
"Because I'm not dressed as a Telly Tubby," I said.
"You *are* a Telly Tubby," she replied. And that made me feel a lot better.

We sat in a bar called The Lodge on the corner of South 3rd Street and Grand, and we drank our first beers in the USA – served in jam-jars and accompanied by bread with olive oil and balsamic vinegar, which we didn't order but ate anyway. Right across the street we recognised the little internet café where Emily had told us in emails she often listened to our podcast. A man dressed as a baby came in and ordered a burger. A girl dressed as a bunny rabbit waited for her boyfriend. It was a bizarre, yet strangely appropriate way for Sowerby and Luff to spend our first evening together in New York. The bar was a lot better prepared for Halloween than we were, with a bowl of candy the size of an elephant by the door.

MEETING EMILY

Georgina took out her handset and dialled Emily's mobile number and, as she did so, something rather odd occurred to me. Emily had listened to our voices on podcasts for over two years and Georgina had exchanged hundreds of emails with Emily. But, even though our luggage was now sitting in the middle of Emily's kitchen, this was the first time Georgina was actually going to hear her voice. Such was the power of podcasting. Remote and yet intimate.
"Hello?" said Georgina, without introducing herself.
"Hello Georgina!" said Emily, as if she'd been chatting with her only a moment earlier.
Twenty minutes later Emily walked through the door, and we recognised her instantly - that blurry little photograph on MySpace had somehow captured her essence perfectly. She and Georgina hugged and jumped up and down in the middle of the bar. It was a very special moment, and I think Georgina and I both wiped away a tear.

The connection between Georgina and Emily in that little Brooklyn bar seemed to make flesh the connection we'd made with unseen thousands of listeners during the previous two years. I had a lump in my throat for about half an hour.
"Did you see the kids collecting candy for Halloween?" asked Emily.
"Notice them?" we said. "We've done well not to get trampled in the stampede!"

"You know what's really strange," said Emily "is that you two are in my brain."
"What do you mean?" asked Georgina.
"After two hundred or so programmes, I have your speech patterns so clearly in my mind that I can conjure your voices saying

almost anything. But now I don't need to do that, because you're sitting right in front of me, in 3D."
We weren't exactly sure what Emily meant, but we all agreed that it must be pretty weird seeing two people effectively climb out of her MP3 player.

A typically flamboyant New York waiter sat down at our table and took our order while at the same time delivering 10 minutes of stand-up material. Georgina went for mussels and fries, Emily ordered a steak and I had the Halloween special, which I think was duck and parsnips. Or maybe pumpkin.

You could tell straight away that Emily was a journalist. Over dinner she grilled us about how we met, and why we did the podcast, although it soon became apparent that she knew more about Sowerby and Luff than we did. Which was weird.

As the evening went on, Bugs Bunny, President Reagan and Spiderman came in and sat at adjoining tables, and we chatted late into the night with Emily. When it was finally time to leave, Georgina gave the waiter our bank card. A few moments later he came back to the table. "Your card has expired," he said.

Mortified with embarrassment, Georgina grabbed the card and carefully studied the expiry date.
"No it hasn't," she insisted. "Look, 31st October 2007. Halloween night. That's tonight."
"It may be tonight in New York," said the waiter. "But it's tomorrow morning in London. You're from London, right?"
It could only happen to us. Our plastic was valid in New York, but out of date in London. Which was, unfortunately, where our bank was located.
"I've got another credit card somewhere," I said limply, rummaging in my pockets.
The waiter laughed. "And which time zone is that in?" he said.

After dinner, Emily took us on a whistle stop tour of the neighbourhood, pointing out street names, shops, bars and restaurants, and finally the L Train, which could whisk us into the heart of Manhattan in twenty minutes. Even at 11.30 at night, the streets were still noisy and heaving with people. Still open was the old municipal swimming pool, and the huge bouncer on the door invited us in. He proudly told us the history of the place, including the fact that on Thursday nights the pool was packed with Hasidic women, because someone had had the bright idea of curtaining off one of the swimming lanes, so that they could swim without being seen.

The old swimming pool was by far Georgina's favourite building in Williamsburg.

When you first arrive in New York it's as though you've known it all your life, having seen its streets and buildings so many times in movies and on TV. Three and a half thousand miles from London, you feel at home. We weren't even surprised when we saw a fat police officer sitting in an NYPD squad car smoking a huge cigar and eating a pizza.

Chapter 20
Hey, Manhattan

Wherever we go in the world, Georgina and I are always rudely awakened by road works at about 7.00am. Even if we're staying in a remote part of North Cornwall, miles from anywhere, a van load of council workers will invariably appear just before dawn, as if from nowhere, and begin to connect a dozen or so pneumatic drills to a generator.

In Brooklyn there were no road works. Instead, we were awakened at 6.30am by what sounded like some kind of automatic weapon.
"What the hell is that?" I muttered, pulling my pillow over my head.
"A machine gun?" said Georgina.
"That's what I thought," I said, thinking nothing of it. As far as I was concerned, everyone in Brooklyn owned an AK47. I just didn't want to hear it before seven in the morning.

I looked out of the bedroom window. On the roof of the apartment block opposite, two builders in yellow hard hats were fitting a new roof with a couple of industrial-sized nail guns.
"What's going on?" asked Georgina.
"Urban redevelopment," I said. "Let's get some breakfast."

While we were staying in Emily's apartment in Brooklyn, she was looking after someone else's larger apartment in Manhattan. We liked to think that the owner of that apartment was, in turn, staying somewhere even grander, leading to a long chain of apartment-sitters, with a person at the end of the chain who was looking after the White House for a few days.

Emily left various notes for us, attached to the fridge by colourful magnets, but the most prominent one of all said simply "FEED THE CAT."

"Cat? What fucking cat?" I screamed to Georgina on the first morning. My reaction may have seemed a little over the top, but the truth is, I am violently allergic to cats.

"It must be in the other room," said Georgina, and she crept into Emily's bedroom to discover an angry-looking black and ginger tom sitting on the bed, staring at her.

"Open the window and kick it out," I said to Georgina.

"We can't do that," she said, "It's an apartment cat. It isn't allowed out."

"That's just plain cruel" I said. "Let's liberate it. Give the poor thing its freedom!"

"We can't do that," said Georgina. "We have to feed it."

"But I'm allergic," I whimpered.

"Then you'll just have to keep out of its way," she said. "Have you sneezed once since you've been in the apartment?"

"No," I said.

"There," grinned Georgina.

"But that's only because I didn't know it was here."

"I rest my case," said Georgina, and she poured something smelly out of a tin and pushed it in front of the cat. It snarled and looked up at me with pure hatred.

Another note on the fridge door said "GO TO ALDO'S FOR BREAKFAST. TRUST ME." It was the place we'd picked up the apartment keys from the night before, but it was also Emily's favourite diner.

"Let's go," I said.

Half an hour later we were each tucking into six rashers of bacon, two eggs over easy, and a pile of pancakes as tall as the Chrysler Building. All covered with maple syrup.

"Do you think Americans eat like this every morning?" I asked Georgina.

"Only the very large ones," she said.

Aldo's is a great diner, perched on the corner of South 5th and Havemeyer - right underneath the ramp onto the Williamsburg Bridge. It's a perfect example of how they like to eat in the Big Apple, and an excellent place to listen to the unique way that New Yorkers order their food - both rude and funny at the same time.

"Hey, I ordered a bacon cheeseburger, here!"
"You want bacon? You didn't order bacon."
"I ordered bacon!"
"You want eggs?"
"No eggs. I wanna cheeseburger, bacon, fries on the side, no eggs. You think you can manage that?"
"Coming right up!"
"An' gimme a coffee."

NATIVE NEW YORKERS

We could have sat in Aldo's all day, but hey, we had a fertility statue to buy for a Chinese panda. So we finished our breakfast, and jumped into a Yellow Cab on the corner of Havemeyer.

We got our first real close-up look at Manhattan as we drove across the Williamsburg Bridge that morning. It was a misty, overcast day, and the top of the Empire State Building was shrouded in low-lying cloud. Over to our left we caught our first view of the Manhattan Bridge, stretching its way across the East River.

"Now, there's something you don't see every day," I said.
"You do if you live in New York," said Georgina.
It was a totally joyous moment. What is it about the Manhattan Bridge that is so damned sexy?

[There's transcript of part of our first podcast from New York City at the end of this book.]

Between Brooklyn and the East Village every single street seemed to be being dug up, and a combination of huge bumps in the road, holes in the tarmac, and fierce braking, meant that we were both suffering mild whiplash by the time we jumped out of the cab on 2nd Avenue.

"Have you got that piece of paper with the name of the shop on it?" asked Georgina.
"Paper?"
"I gave you a piece of paper with the address of the shop in the East Village?"
"Did you?"

"Oh, Brian…"
"Don't worry, we'll just walk around until we find it. What's the name of the shop?"
"I can't remember," said Georgina. "That's why I wrote it down."
"Are you telling me we've come all the way to New York to go to a shop, and you can't remember the name of it?"
"It's you that's lost the address," said Georgina.
"Can't we Google it?" I suggested.
"Google what? I can't remember the name."
And then we started to laugh. We didn't have a hope in hell of finding that damned new age shop in New York City.

We set off eastwards, and after fifteen minutes or so, we'd crossed Avenue B and Avenue C and were getting close to the East River. The streets suddenly began to feel less safe. Groups of kids were hanging around on street corners, and the smart shops had become thrift shops and bargain stores. We went into a drug store and supermarket to buy a couple of cokes, and as we left through the checkout two security guards wrestled a junkie to the ground and held him down, kicking and screaming.

"Something tells me it's time to head back towards Broadway," said Georgina.
"I'm right with you," I said.
Around 3rd Avenue we felt more comfortable with our surroundings, and we went into an internet café, in search of inspiration. Even our listeners were beginning to email us ideas for panda gifts.

From: "Douglas"
Subject: For the pandas

Hello, luvs, I'd like to suggest that perhaps the most appropriate gift we could send with you to Hong Kong would be a photo of Charles Darwin. Maybe a subtle reminder of the pandas' numbered days would motivate them toward procreation.

We rather liked that idea, but felt that it might offend, or even confuse the people at Ocean Park Zoo. What we needed was a fertility statue.
"Let's go to the Metropolitan Museum," said Georgina. "We might be able to pick up something in the gift shop. Something Egyptian, maybe? The Egyptians were into fertility charms, weren't they?"

MYSTERY TOUR

It may not have been the greatest idea, but even we could locate the Metropolitan Museum of Art, and Georgina had been hankering to go there for years anyway. A quick look at the map told us it was only a few miles away, so we went to the corner of Bowery and hailed another Yellow Cab.
"The Metropolitan Museum of Art, please," said Georgina. The cabbie peered back at us from beneath a bright purple turban.
"Which way you wanna go?"
"Whichever way you think?" I said. "We're not native New Yorkers, so we'll leave the route up to you." This was probably the most stupid thing I said to anyone during our entire stay in America.

The Metropolitan Museum was roughly half way up the east side of Central Park, on 5th Avenue, exactly 4 and a half miles to our north, so I was more than a little surprised as the Yellow Cab headed due *south* towards the Lower East Side. Before long we were speeding past the Brooklyn Bridge, and heading for the Financial District at the furthest southern tip of Manhattan Island.
"Why are we driving south?" I asked the driver.
His reply was both reassuring and cryptic.
"5th Avenue is one way," he said. "You can only drive down it from the north."
This was clearly going be an unscheduled Magical Mystery Tour of the whole of Manhattan.

Twenty minutes later we were sitting in a completely stationary traffic jam in Battery Park, at least two miles further away from the Metropolitan Museum than when we had got into the cab. Annoyed and frustrated, we glanced over to the right hand side of the road, and noticed a busy building site, surrounded by tall buildings. It wasn't until Georgina pointed out a giant American flag flying at the far side of the site, that we suddenly realised we'd arrived, completely by accident, at Ground Zero. Georgina put her hand over her mouth. It gives you a very strange feeling in the pit of your stomach to see Ground Zero with your own eyes. The destruction of the World Trade Centre was a global catastrophe on a vast scale, and the events of that day - even though they changed the lives of everyone on this planet - seemed to most people remote and distant.

Unreal, even. Like watching a movie. To find oneself, unexpectedly, just a few feet from the scene of such an event is oddly surreal, and it's actually quite hard to feel any emotion at all. Being at Ground Zero makes you feel numb - the history and horror of the place simply too great to take in. Too terrible to put into words. By the time the traffic got moving again, we'd almost forgotten why we were in the cab in the first place, and neither of us said anything for a quite a while.

Ten minutes later we were hammering up West Street, the Hudson River on our left, and weaving in and out of traffic at about sixty miles an hour.

"This driver is insane," I whispered to Georgina, as he threw the cab into a sharp right turn and headed northwards again, up through the West Village. It was around here that I think he sensed that Georgina and I were not entirely happy with the route he was taking, so he slammed his foot down flat on the gas, accelerating along 9th Avenue like a Boeing 777 going along the runway on take-off.

Another glance at the map told us that we were now drawing level with the Metropolitan Museum, but it was still on the opposite side of Central Park. As the meter ticked furiously past forty dollars, we decided that this was probably the moment for a timely intervention.

"Excuse me" I said. "Are you now planning to drive all the way around the north of Central Park to get to the other side?"

"5th Avenue is one way," he repeated like a mantra. "You can only drive down it southwards."

"Tell you what," said Georgina. "Why don't you drop us here. We'll walk across the park."

The driver seemed momentarily confused.

"You want to get *out*?"

"Oh, yes please," we said. "I think we both feel fairly strongly that we can get to the Metropolitan Museum from here without spending the next twenty five minutes driving around Harlem."

"OK," he said. I gave him forty five dollars.

"Why are you giving him a tip?" snapped Georgina.

"I don't really know," I said, and we headed off towards Central Park.

LOOKING FOR REMBRANDT

We arrived outside the Metropolitan Museum of Art, to discover a vast cheering crowd on the front steps watching a couple of break dancers spin around on the pavement. At the end of the performance they collected at least 200 bucks from the punters, thus proving that worldwide the tourist dollar is as likely to end up in the pockets of street performers as it is in the wallets of Equity members.

The Metropolitan probably has the largest collection of Egyptian artifacts in the world, and they don't do things by halves. The entire Temple of Dendur has been transported from Egypt and rebuilt, brick by brick in a large room, partially surrounded by a reflecting pool and illuminated by a slanting wall of glass which opens onto Central Park. The whole thing looks like a set for an early James Bond movie.

"Any ideas for the pandas?" I said.

"What about one of those Egyptian fertility goddesses," suggested Georgina.

"How are we going to get it out of the case?" I replied.

On the next floor we came upon the Age of Rembrandt Exhibition, which was absolutely packing in the tourists. But after walking around for several minutes we were unable to find any paintings by Rembrandt.

"Where are the Rembrandts?" I asked Georgina.

"I'm guessing there aren't actually any Rembrandts in the exhibition," she replied.

"Why not?" I said.

"Because this is the *age* of Rembrandt," she grinned. "It's all the other painters that were alive at the time."

"What, all the shit ones who weren't quite as good as Rembrandt?"

"Yes," said Georgina.

"What a completely brilliant idea for an exhibition," I said, and I sat down in front of a de Hooch, a de Booch and a de Gooch to rest my throbbing ankle.

Georgina's favourite painting at the Met was a giant canvas, completely covered by solid black paint.

"What's it called?" she asked.

I glanced at the information card. "Untitled," I said. "So, not only could this artist not be bothered to put anything into the painting, he also couldn't be arsed to think of a name for it."

"What's the name of the artist?" asked Georgina.

"I can't be bothered to find out," I said.

Before leaving the Met, we had a good rummage about in the museum shop, in the hope of picking up some kind of fertility-connected gift for the pandas, but all we came away with was a souvenir postcard of a painting by a Dutch artist other than Rembrandt.

Chapter 21
Take the L Train

On our second day in New York we were awakened at precisely 7.28 am by what sounded like a chainsaw and a steam hammer, which of course made us feel right at home. Before we left for the States, Richard Cray had assured us that the best way to see Manhattan was from a boat on the Hudson River, so we once again set off early for bacon and pancakes at Aldo's, then grabbed a Yellow Cab into town.
"Pier 83, please!" said Georgina.
"You wanna tell me where that is?" asked the cabbie.
"It's on the West Side," I explained.
"You wanna give me directions?" said the driver.
"Not really," I said.

Many New York cabs actually have satellite navigation systems in them. But surprisingly, they're not in the driver's cab. They're in the back seat, so that the passengers can work out where the fuck they are. After yet another uncomfortable, confusing and frankly dangerous white-knuckle ride into Manhattan, we decided that from now on we would use the New York subway to get around the city.

The cab finally dropped us off at Pier 83 and we bought a couple of tickets for what New Yorkers call the semi-circular tour of Manhattan. While we were waiting for the boat to depart, we sat by the side of the Hudson and recorded our first podcast in New York. Recording technology has come a long way since the days of portable tape recorders or even mini-disc machines. Georgina and I are now able to record broadcast quality audio anywhere, in stereo, on a tiny pocket MP3 recorder no bigger than an electric razor. Our own little recorder is called an Edirol R-09 24 bit, but we just call it Roland for short.

Our first USA special was a 40 minute podcast, recorded entirely on location in New York City, and edited on my laptop in Emily's flat. As soon as it was finished we went and sat in an internet cafe and uploaded it to the internet. It was on the air while we were still in America.

While we were on the semi-circular tour of Manhattan, Georgina took a picture of me in front of the Statue of Liberty, and I took a picture of her. But sometimes it's more important to look at things than it is to take pictures of them. One of my best friends Max, who has been all over the world, says he never takes a camera anywhere. He says he'd rather spend the time looking at things and remembering them in his mind's eye. Then he goes and buys a postcard.
"The best pictures are on the postcards anyway," he says. As we chugged close to the Statue of Liberty, Max's words popped into my mind and I put the camera in my pocket. Now I just wanted to look at it.

Sadly you can't climb to the top of the statue anymore, but the National Park Service claims it's not shut because of any terrorist threat, simply because of a long list of boring fire regulations and inadequate evacuation procedures. Fucking Health and Safety. It removes our liberties all over the world, but you'd think it would give us a break here, at the world's greatest symbol of escape from oppression.

REGARDS TO BROADWAY

We got off the boat and walked eastwards, along 42nd Street. It really is quite amazing how many street addresses and locations in New York City are also the names of songs. We persuaded a couple of fellow Brits to take a picture of us in the middle of Time Square and, we in turn, took a picture of them. Then someone else asked us to take a picture for them. We were only in that place for about ten minutes, and I'm guessing we took at least ten photographs with other people's cameras. No wonder it costs so much to advertise in Time Square. It's also a great place to steal a camera.

"Are you Jewish?" came a voice from the kerbside.
"No, we're not," I said politely, and I smiled at the man who had asked us the question, quite out of the blue.

He and an associate were standing in front of a large luxury camper van, on which were printed the words "The Mitzvah Mobile."
He approached a businessman who was walking along behind us.
"Are you Jewish?" he asked.

A little research in a nearby cyber café revealed that these Mitzvah Mobiles (or Mitzvah Tanks as some New Yorkers call them) were started by Brooklyn's Lubavitch sect of Orthodox Jews in the mid seventies, and they comb the streets searching for lapsed Jews. Mitzvah means good deed and these vehicles apparently act as impromptu mini-synagogues in high-density areas.
"Do I look Jewish?" I asked Georgina.
"You are Jewish," she said.
"I am one eighth Jewish," I said.
"Get in the van. Read the damned Torah," he said. "It might do you good!"

Experiencing exactly one eighth Jewish guilt, I followed Georgina along Broadway and northwards through the theatre district, and before long we found ourselves chatting with a few of the guys and girls promoting Manhattan comedy clubs in the street.

We stood and interviewed one up-and-coming comedian for the podcast, a guy called Harry Katz who was just starting out in the business, and who was happy to chat at length about the comedy scene in New York.

There are far fewer stand-up clubs in the Big Apple than there are in London, and many only employ comedians who have already appeared on one of the four major TV networks. You need to do gigs to appear on TV, and you can't get gigs unless you've been on TV. How stupid is that?

When we got to West 53rd, we stopped and took a snap of the famous old Ed Sullivan Theatre, where they nightly record the Late Show with David Letterman.
"Hey, we should go and have a sandwich in Rupert's Deli," I said.

Rupert's is a sandwich shop which has become famous on the Letterman Show. Dave regularly sends live TV cameras into the deli, and involves the owner Rupert Jee in a variety of strange activities involving members of the public.

Rupert was born in the USA, but his parents were from China. Ever since he was a kid he always dreamed of owning his own deli, but he never imagined it would end up on TV almost every night of the week. Rupert's now one of the most famous faces on Broadway.

"So, where is Rupert's?" I said, and we set off to find it. After walking around in circles for about fifteen minutes, we got too hungry to continue, and went and sat in MacDonalds, opposite the Paramount Plaza.
"Maybe we should have asked someone?" said Georgina.
"We don't need to ask someone," I insisted stubbornly.
"Rupert's is right next door to the Ed Sullivan Theatre. I've seen it on TV."
"So, why couldn't we find it?" asked Georgina, tucking into a Big Mac.
I couldn't think of an answer, so I fell back on a trusty old excuse.
"My foot hurts," I said.

The following day, in Emily's favourite internet café in Brooklyn, I looked up Rupert's Deli on Google.
"Damn!" I shouted, and everyone turned around and looked at me.
"What?" asked Georgina.
"It's not called Rupert's Deli. It's called the Hello Deli, and it's right next door to the Ed Sullivan Theatre. Right where we were looking."
"Oh, I saw that," said Georgina. "Didn't I ask you if that was the place?"
"No."
"I'm sure I did," said Georgina, and then she started to laugh.
"Oh, shut up," I said.

STRAWBERRY FIELDS

We came out of MacDonalds and headed north along Broadway towards the south west corner of Centre Park. That morning I'd splashed out on a new pair of boots, and my foot was finally starting to feel a little better, so I suggested we walk up as far as the Dakota Building.

"Why would I want to go to a place just because someone was shot there?" asked Georgina.
"Did you like John Lennon?" I asked.
"Yes."
"Well, why wouldn't you want to go to the place where he was shot?" I said.
"Because he was shot there," she said.
I think I understood what Georgina meant, but headed, in any case, towards the Dakota Building.

When we got to the corner of Central Park, there were grandstands and crowd barriers erected everywhere, and since it was still only a couple of nights after Halloween, we reckoned these had been used for spectators to view some sort of parade. We walked into the park and followed West Drive northwards. The grandstands became larger and ever more tightly packed.
"Are you sure this is for Halloween?" said Georgina. "It must have been a pretty big parade."

A little further along the road there were TV crews and photographers everywhere, and it wasn't until we walked through a big blue archway with the word "FINISH" on it, that we realised that we'd just wandered very slowly along the final 500 metres of the course for the New York Marathon.
"When's the race?" Georgina asked an official.
"This Sunday," he said.
We picked up a newspaper, and were delighted to discover that the route of the race ran right past the top of our road in Williamsburg, so we immediately decided that we must record a Sowerby and Luff Show at the New York Marathon that Sunday morning.

Only a few hundred metres further along West Drive, we found Strawberry Fields, the garden of remembrance for John Lennon. It's a small circular mosaic, with the word "Imagine" in the centre, surrounded by park benches. Its simplicity makes it very touching, and it's probably the only location in New York where the place is named after a song, and not the other way around.

The memorial was created by Yoko Ono, with the support of the city of New York. Over a hundred countries contributed to the garden with native plants and stones, and a small plaque lists all the countries who contributed. John and Yoko loved to walk in Central Park and one of their favourite spots is precisely where Strawberry Fields now lays.

While we were there, the sombre atmosphere was slightly offset by the fact that the mosaic was covered in pumpkins, candles and Halloween party props - John's fans obviously feel their hero would want to be a part of the celebrations for this holiday. In the same way, I imagine that Strawberry Fields is probably adorned with tinsel and holly at Christmas. I'll bet it looks great in the snow.

There were about ten people sitting on the benches around John's memorial, all of them, as far as we could see, either drunk or stoned. One elderly tramp had a cardboard begging sign which made us laugh out loud. It simply said "Why lie? I need a beer!"
We sat on a bench between Strawberry Fields and the Dakota, and recorded a short chat for the second of our New York podcasts. Then we crossed Central Park West and went and stood in the exact place where Lennon was shot.

John and Yoko bought several apartments in the Dakota building, and Yoko still lives there. The place was built in the late 1800's, and it's part of a series of spectacular gothic buildings which overlook the park – one of which featured in the movie Ghostbusters.

Access to The Dakota is restricted and the entrance is guarded by a fairly eccentric doorman who stands permanently outside, posing for photographs and filling in the tourists on any gory details they care to enquire about. John was shot right in front of the main entrance on December 8th 1980, when he was returning from a recording session for his final album Double Fantasy, accompanied by Yoko.

"I really don't want to be here," said Georgina. So I resisted the temptation to try and interview the doorman, and we headed back towards Broadway.

"What was the name of the guy who shot Lennon?" asked Georgina.

"I can't remember," I said.

UPRIGHT CITIZENS

We couldn't go to NYC without seeing some live comedy, and as much as we enjoy watching stand-up, we wanted to see a gig that was similar to our own show Sketch Club. So, we jumped on the L train from Brooklyn and headed towards Chelsea on the West Side.

The buskers on the New York subway are so good that people don't hurry past them like they do in London, they actually stop to listen to them. Then they stand and applaud afterwards. You see entire horn sections, string sections and the occasional drum kit. You see PA systems, microphone stands, and mixing desks. If someone asks you how to get to Carnegie Hall, tell them not to bother. Just go down the New York Subway.

We'd heard good things about a sketch show and character comedy night in Chelsea, so we showed up at the Upright Citizens Brigade Theatre at West 26th Street, and booked to see the 7 o'clock show Shameless, which featured a female character comedian called Eliza Skinner. We caught up with Eliza at the bar afterwards, and she described it as "a show about people you don't like, but have to love."

Eliza puts raw, repellent desperation front and centre, both in her scriptwriting and in her performance - wrenching humour from awkward circumstances, and cringe-inducing comments. We asked her if it was more difficult to break through with a character show, as opposed to a stand-up act, and she told us that there are now more and more clubs in New York which cater for that style of comedy.

The Upright Citizens Brigade Theatre, apart from being a name which is almost impossible to remember, presents four or five shows a night, with a different audience coming in for each show. You can buy a ticket for the whole evening, or you can just pay around $10 to see one of the shows. There's nothing like that on the London comedy circuit, but it's how venues operate at the Edinburgh Festival, so it was something Georgina and I were very familiar with. The UCB runs like the Edinburgh Fringe all year round, seven nights a week, and that's something we found really exciting.

We interviewed Eliza for our podcast, then we went back into the theatre to watch the second gig of the night – a one-man show featuring an LA comedy actor called Will Franken. This lanky, long-haired comedian's genius resides in his excellent sense of the absurd, and a total disdain for any kind of political correctness. Will is devastating as he skewers liberals and bigoted right wing fanatics in equal measure. He plays activists, Christians and homophobes, and often walks a precarious tightrope between good and bad taste.

Will finished his show with a scene about a terrorist with a bomb, who inadvertently finds himself on a plane that is going to crash anyway, due to engine problems. It was a very strange experience, sitting not four miles from Ground Zero, and watching a sketch about a terrorist on a plane with an audience of New Yorkers.

"He's performed that sketch many times in Los Angeles," one of the audience said to us afterwards. "But I think he may need to tone it down a little for New York."
We loved Will's show, and he has since become a regular contributor to our podcast.

THE BAR WITH NO NAME

On our way back to the apartment, we hooked up with Emily in a late night drinking joint in Brooklyn, which we immediately dubbed The Bar with No Name, as there was no sign above the door, and no lights on the outside to tell you that there was any kind of bar there at all. Inside, everything was lit by candlelight, and everywhere smelt of beer, garlic and lemongrass.

The only customers seemed to be those who'd been introduced by someone who'd been there before. The late night crowd were *uber cool* and very European, and the whole place was dripping with understated Bohemian style. Every surface was distressed, in that very New York kind of way – woodwork being carefully painted, then quickly rubbed off with paint stripper until it looked like shit. Nothing was allowed to appear new. Or too clean. How uncool would that be?

"This place reminds me of Prague," I said out loud. The guy standing next to me patted me on the back.
"Where you from?" he said.
"London," I said. "Where are you from?"
"Prague," he said.

"How long you been coming here?" Georgina asked Emily.
"About five years," she said. "What do you two want to drink?"
Georgina asked for a coke and I ordered a Jack Daniels.
"They don't have Jack Daniels," said Emily.
"What do they have?" I asked.
"Have a Guinness," said Emily. "And Georgina should have a Guinness too."

Sometimes we'd forget that Emily had been listening to Sowerby and Luff for over two years.
"OK," we said. "We'll have a Guinness." I think Emily would have been a little disappointed if we'd drunk anything else. After all, this little bar was her very own Gay Legs.

Chapter 22
Bogs Across America

For some reason that we were unable to fathom, while we were in New York we were invited to cover a press event called Bogs Across America. Not even knowing what this meant, it was an invitation so insanely odd that we felt right from the off that it had Sowerby and Luff written all over it. Obviously "bog" does not have the same connotations in the U.S. as it does in Britain, and the hundred foot tall "Bogs" placard that greeted us at the Rockefeller Center was testament to this.

    Let's face it, whatever the reason, 30 Rockefeller Plaza is a pretty cool address to show up at. The Crossroads of the World is how some Americans describe it. There's even a TV show called 30 Rock. We had an hour to kill before we could enter the Bogs event with our press passes, so we wandered around the brightly lit Plaza. As she looked up at the 70 story Rockefeller building, Georgina sighed aloud and announced that this was the first time she'd actually felt dizzy at the sheer size and scale of Manhattan.

    Everything was floodlit in a soft peach-coloured hue, and tens of thousands of twinkly fairy lights adorned every tree in the square. Giant American flags fluttered outside all of the surrounding buildings, and the spectacular ice-rink - complete with lavish waterfall and huge golden statue - was being prepared for the evening.

    At the designated time we strolled back to 30 Rock, and entered the huge Art Deco lobby of the building. We asked the receptionist about the Bogs event, but he hadn't even heard of it. I think it may have been his first day on the job. So, we wandered back outside, this time stumbling upon a tennis court-sized pit, filled to the brim with cranberries.
"How did we miss this before?" I said.
"We weren't looking," Georgina replied. To be fair, how often do you go looking for a tennis court-sized pit filled with cranberries?

We were, of course, on the guest list, and gained immediate access to the Ocean Spray Bog, where we were handed a couple of alcohol-free, cranberry juice cocktails. I took Roland the MP3 recorder out of my pocket and we recorded a quick link for the podcast.

"I'm guessing that Bogs Across America is something to do with cranberries," I said, as Georgina and I described the strange scene for our listeners. Nearby, was a woman standing knee-deep in cranberries and giving an interview to a man with a microphone. Georgina started to laugh.

"Look who's doing the first interview," she said, and to our amazement it was Podshow. What were the chances of us running into them in a cranberry bog?

We waited our turn, then took Roland over to meet the lady in the bog. It was an odd sight - the centre of the plaza completely taken over by a huge pit filled with 20,000 lbs of fruit.

"Why are we at the Rockefeller Centre talking about cranberries?" I asked the lady, who turned out to be called Irene Sorensen.

"Because this is the Crossroads of the World," she said.

"What is a bog?" I asked her.

"A bog is the name we give to the place where we grow cranberries," she said. "It's actually a wetland."

"And why are we here now?" I asked.

"We're celebrating the cranberry harvest," she said "on the eve of Thanksgiving and Christmas."

Most of the people around the bog seemed to be involved with Ocean Spray in some way, or actually worked for them, but there was a marked absence of media people or journalists. In fact, the only media we could identify was Podshow and Sowerby and Luff. The Rockefeller Bog wasn't exactly hitting the headlines.

Irene was generous and funny with her interview for our podcast, even though she didn't have the faintest idea who we were. We finished by telling her that we'd never again eat Cranberry Sauce without thinking of her standing in that bog in Rockefeller Plaza. And we probably won't.

At the mention of alcoholic cocktails some thirty minutes later, there was a veritable stampede of guests towards the Brasserie Ruhlmann on 50th Street. Some people moved so quickly that the PR lady had to hold back the crowd outside the revolving doors of the restaurant.

"You can't go in," she said to us. "It's too crowded. It could become dangerous in there."

Once inside we picked up our press badges and followed our well-trained PR noses toward the unmistakable smell of Moet and Chandon. We were handed two tall glasses of champagne, with dried cranberries floating around inside, and were surprised to see that the cranberries floated up to the surface, then down again. Up, and then down again.

It was very entertaining, and strangely hypnotic. But it completely ruined the taste of the champagne.

"Do you have any bubbly without cranberries in?" I asked one of the waiters. But he just frowned, and walked away.

Surrounded by Armani suits and designer dresses we felt a little under-dressed in our grubby jeans, but we downed as many glasses of fizz as we could, while watching a desperately dreary presentation about cranberries.

"What's that?" I asked another waiter as he sped past with a silver platter covered in delicious looking, but tiny appetisers. "This is French toast, with spicy lamb, on a bed of cranberries" he said. The nibbles may have been small but they were perfectly formed. A bit like Georgina.

"What's that one?" Georgina asked.
"That's garlic bread with a little Roquefort cheese on a bed of cranberries," he replied.
"Oh I get it," I whispered to Georgina, "Everything here is made out of cranberries."

That press bash at Rockefeller Plaza must have cost a small fortune. Let's hope for the sake of Ocean Spray that there were one or two real journalists there as well.

WEIGH MY MEAT

Our heads spinning from Moet, and desperate for something substantial to eat that didn't involve cranberries, we headed off into the night, and ended up in a Texan restaurant in Chelsea. This seemed to be a place where New Yorkers went when they wanted to pretend to be Texans, and the whole restaurant was based on the idea of an indoor barbecue. Hickory wood was piled high next to the kitchen, and you ordered your meat by the pound. God, the Americans love their meat.

"Half a pound of lean brisket," you'd say to the chef, and he'd grab it off the hickory grill and slap it on the scales. In order to further duplicate the experience of eating at a real Texan barbecue, the meat was then served not on a plate, but in brown paper, out of which you were also expected to eat it.

"I'd like a quarter of a pound of moist brisket, please," I said meekly, and it was quickly weighed and slapped into my brown paper with little ceremony. As the meat was wrapped for me to take to the table, the fat quickly soaked through, and dripped appetizingly onto the floor.
"You want sides?" asked the chef?
"What are sides?" I whispered to Georgina, and she pointed towards another serving hatch, at which a number of mashed-up vegetables bubbled on a hob.

"I'll have some of that, and some of that," I said politely, not really knowing what it was I was ordering. The sides were scooped into big paper cups, and placed on my tray. I think I ordered corn on the cob and sweet potato, but both had been liquidised beyond recognition. It was like eating food that had been specially prepared for an old person with no teeth.

Georgina ordered about a half a pound of lean brisket and some sides that were a slightly different colour and texture to mine, and we took our trays and sat down at a table.

An authentic Country and Western band were playing somewhere, but the restaurant was so big we couldn't actually see them.

"How's your moist brisket?" Georgina asked.

"Very moist," I said. "I particularly like all the little bits of brown paper mixed with the meat."

"That's what makes it authentic," Georgina said.

"Fancy another half a pound of brisket?" I asked.

"I'm good," she said.

PORNOGRAPHY AND SANDWICHES

Next day we were awakened as usual by the sound of heavy machinery, and made our way via pancakes at Aldo's to the Museum of Sex on 5th Avenue.

"You simply *have* to go to this place," Emily had advised, in yet another urgent Post-It note, stuck to the door of the fridge.

The Museum of Sex opened in New York in 2002 and, despite its provocative title, claims to offer a studied, historical look at the history of sex in our culture. We put fresh batteries into Roland and took him along, so we could make audio notes as we went.

Sex and the Moving Image seemed to be the main exhibit. It claimed to trace the way sex and sexual imagery have impacted film, television and advertising through the ages. In reality, it was a big dark room filled with TV screens showing hard core pornography. There's nothing quite like watching Paris Hilton performing felatio, while surrounded by elderly Japanese tourists eating sandwiches.

It's funny how people are prepared to watch or listen to sexual content, as long as it's not actually wrapped up as porn. Our podcast has always been labelled "Explicit" on iTunes, and tens of thousands of respectable people, who would never dream of going into a shop and buying porn, download it every week and listen to us swearing like a couple of troopers and talking about everything from nipple clamps to anal sex.

But because we're packaged as comedy, it doesn't really count as filth. Talking dirty is ideal content for an iPod. After all, no-one else knows what you're listening to.

We moved onwards into the sex museum's Geography of the Erotic Imagination exhibition, featuring pony play, furries, peeing and sploshing – a truly eye-opening tour of various sexual fantasies from around the world.

"Would you like to dress up like a pony for me?" I asked Georgina.

"Nay," she said.

"How about a furry? I could get one of those Bugs Bunny suits for you."

"If you're so keen, *you* dress as a rabbit," she said.

"Sploshing" is shorthand for various wet and messy fetishes whereby participants become aroused when substances are deliberately and generously applied to their naked skin. "Messy" substances can include whipped cream, mud, shaving foam, custard, pudding, chocolate sauce, or simply "gunge". Tiswas has a lot to answer for.

This area also included the activity of directing high pressure water jets at the genitalia.

"We could try that," I suggested.

"I suppose it would save you having to bathe," said Georgina.

"Perhaps we could call the New York Fire Department to give us a hand," I said.

The erotic roadmap continued on the next floor with odours, textures, and sensations. We were invited to feel a piece of latex, followed by a piece of rubber, and then had an opportunity to touch the breasts and nether regions of a very expensive, life-sized sex doll.

"Oh, for heavens sake, Brian, leave it alone," said Georgina. "You've been there for twenty minutes!"

Macrophilia was next – a bizarre exhibit which went to great lengths to tell the story of a man whose fantasy was to be captured and forced into sex by a giant, 50 foot tall women. There were numerous images of a tiny little man being crushed underfoot by a huge female, and I couldn't help wondering how he could ever satisfy her, in that his entire body was barely the size of her vagina.

Georgina's favourite exhibit was the sex machines. Huge, industrial-sized devices, run by electric motors, designed for mechanical pleasure.

"Do you think it's one of those that's been waking us up every morning?" asked Georgina.

Feeders and Gainers was the last thing we looked at in the museum, a section dedicated to people who deliberately fatten up their partners, before having sex with them. Georgina stood looking at this exhibit for a very long time.

"Lets go eat," I said.

Moments later, we found ourselves in a pizza restaurant in the Flatiron District. Pizza is a very different animal in New York City. They seem to be prepared to put anything on top of one. Georgina stared at a spectacular, two foot diameter thin crust in the window that appeared to have on it every kind of meat known to modern man.

This was a pizza with beef, fish, pepperoni, ham, pork, seafood, sausage, bacon, hot dogs, lamb chops and what looked like an entire portion of Kentucky Fried Chicken.

"We'll have that one," said Georgina.

An hour later we were still trying to get through the second slice, and when we asked for the rest to be put in a box to take it away, we found that the whole thing was too heavy to carry out of the restaurant.

We headed back to Brooklyn. That afternoon, still musing about the tiny man and the 50 foot woman, I fell into a deep sleep, and dreamt that Georgina had clawed her way to the top of the Empire State Building, and spent the entire day swatting aircraft with a giant slice of pizza.

PRESSING THE FLESH

One of our most loyal and fanatical listeners was a guy who lived about a hundred miles north of New York City called Gary. "Bozo", as he liked to be known, had been emailing us with programme ideas and daft stories for around two years, and he was keen to hook up with us while we were in town. Bozo sent us directions to a small bar called The White Rabbit on the Lower East Side, so we once again jumped on the L Train and headed off down there to meet him. We sat in the White Rabbit sipping beers at around 7pm. The place was deserted.

"Are you sure this is the place?" whispered Georgina.
"Absolutely sure," I said. "I'm sure he'll be here in a minute."
"What if he's a complete maniac?" said Georgina.
"He must be to listen to us," I smiled.
Minutes past, then half an hour.
"He's not coming, is he?" said Georgina, and we both began to feel pretty daft. Who would drive a hundred miles to meet a couple of complete strangers. Who were we kidding? About an hour later, we finished up our drinks, and Georgina put on her coat. I tipped the waiter and we climbed off our stools. Suddenly, I spotted a guy peering through the front window and into the bar. I tapped Georgina on the shoulder.

Gary and his wife walked in a moment later, looking slightly shy and bemused. Bozo looked exactly like his picture on MySpace, and his wife arrived with a huge friendly grin on her face.

He was as thrilled to meet us as we were to meet him, and there was genuine electricity in the air as he offered to buy us a beer.
"It's Gary's birthday, you know," Bozo's wife whispered to Georgina. "I asked him what he wanted to do as a special treat, and he said he'd like to drive into Manhattan and meet you guys!"
"Wow!" I said, That's quite a compliment."
"Well, he has been listening to your show for over two years," she smiled.

Unlike his often lively and provocative emails, Gary was quiet and unassuming in the flesh. His wife explained that he was really a rather shy and introverted person, and that listening to our weekly shows was his equivalent of going to a bar and talking bollocks with his friends over a beer.
"You two are Gary's bar!" she said.

Bozo came and sat next to me and we chinked our bottles of Bud together.

"I'm sorry about that email I sent you," he said.

"What email?" I asked.

"I think I made you pretty mad," he said sheepishly. "The email about the advertising in your podcast?"

Then I remembered. When Sowerby and Luff had first signed up with a sponsor and started running advertising jingles, one of our listeners in the States had been outraged, and had sent us a message telling us angrily that we were selling out. I'd fired off a pretty bad tempered reply, saying that we had to pay our damned mortgage like everyone else, and that if he didn't like it he could piss off. Or words to that effect.

"Oh, was that *you*?" I asked.

"I'd like to apologise," he said.

"Forget it," I said.

I think Gary had been worrying about that email for almost two years. Meanwhile, I hadn't even noticed who it was from. That might even have been one of the reasons he wanted to come and meet up with us in New York. So that he could apologise in person.

We introduced Gary to Emily, and the pair chatted as if they'd known each other for years. They had, after all, been listening to us reading out their emails for two years, so knew as much about each other as we knew about them. Emily, in turn, then introduced us to another couple of New Yorkers who had become listeners through knowing her. One was a cartoonist and one was a comedian. This was indeed social networking on a global scale. The comedian was a guy called Liam McEneaney.

"I'm going to London in three weeks to do some gigs," he said. "Let's hook up."

"We'll be in Hong Kong," said Georgina. She really was getting the hang of all this showbiz stuff. Meanwhile, the world was becoming smaller by the second. It turned out that Liam was a friend of Richard Cray's. The first comedian we're introduced to in New York City, and he knows someone we know in London.

Now that we actually had more than one Sowerby and Luff listener in a single place, it was clearly time to record the next section of our New York podcast. But there was a slight problem. The background music was now so loud we couldn't hear ourselves think.

"Could you possibly turn the music off for a while," I said to the barman.

"What?" he said.

"I said, *could you possibly turn the music off for a while!*"

"I can't hear you," said the barman in a strong Bronx accent. I tried again. First by scribbling it on a piece of paper, then by using elaborate sign language, and finally though the medium of dance.

"The customers wouldn't like it if I turned da music off," he said.

"But we're the only customers in here," I reasoned politely.

"What you want da music off for?" he asked.

"I want to record a podcast," I said.

He looked at me long and hard. He obviously didn't know what a podcast was, but he wasn't going to admit that to anyone. After all, this was a classy place. He looked over at the strange little group huddled around a table in the corner.

"How long you want da music off for?" he said.

"Half an hour?" I asked.

"You can have ten minutes," he said.

"Fifteen?" I haggled.

"You can have ten minutes," he said again. You don't argue with a barman in New York City.

"Thanks a million," I said, and I hurried back over to the table with the record light on Roland already flashing red in the semi-darkness.

"Where's Georgina?" I asked.

"She's outside having a cigarette," said Emily.

"Oh, for bollock's sake," I yelped, "We've only got 10 minutes to record!" I ran outside and shouted into the darkness."

"I'm just finishing my cigarette," said Georgina.

"You heard what the lady said," growled a bouncer.

Not only was Georgina smoking, but she was being looked after by security while she was doing it. This guy was built like a heavyweight boxer, four times Georgina's size.

"Enjoy," I said with a squeaky voice, and I trotted back into the bar.

The barman actually allowed us around twenty minutes to record in The White Rabbit, and then we sat and chatted above the music until the early hours.

SPORTING HISTORY

Next day, when I opened my mouth to speak, I discovered that I'd completely lost my voice. It was obviously a combination of having a head cold and yelling at the top of my voice for five hours.

"What do you mean, you've lost your voice?" said Georgina.

"We're supposed to be recording at the New York Marathon this morning".

I held up a piece of paper. "Fuck," it said.

It was a bright, crisp morning, and as we walked along 3rd towards Bedford, we heard the unmistakable sounds of a huge crowd cheering a sporting event. As we turned the corner, we were greeted by a spectacular scene. The leading runners were sprinting through a water station, set up at the top of our street, and on either side of the road there were thousands of New Yorkers screaming encouragement for the runners.

Only a few seconds before we arrived at the corner of Bedford - roughly the halfway mark in the race - the world famous British runner Paula Radcliffe had sprinted past, en route to her second New York Marathon win. She was running in her first marathon for over two years, and bravely fought off her great Ethiopian rival Wami to finish in an amazing 2 hours 23 mins and 9 secs. A piece of British sporting history. If we hadn't stopped for breakfast on the way, we'd have seen it with our own eyes. But hey, those pancakes at Aldo's…

The New York Marathon starts on Staten Island, then goes through Brooklyn and Queens before crossing the Queensborough Bridge into Manhattan, where it makes its way up to the Bronx and then south again to the finish at Central Park, through which we had walked ourselves just a couple of days earlier.

We stayed at Bedford Avenue until every single one of the 39,000 runners had flowed past us towards McCarren Park. The cheers from the locals were incredibly supportive of the competitors, and strangely moving.

In fact we both got quite tearful at one point.
Calls like "stay strong" and "you can do it" could be heard all along the street, as spectators joined in the spirit of the day, whether they knew anyone in the race or not. Georgina quickly got caught up in the excitement, and was soon shouting encouragement to all the runners with names printed on the front of their shirts.

"Go Bob!" she'd shout.
"Go Barney!"
Of course, not having a voice, I was unable to join in with this ritual, but I'd occasionally give the runners a wave or even high-five them as they went past.

Many spectators wore matching shirts and hand-painted signs to show extra-special support for their friends or favourite runners. There was a girl standing opposite us holding up a big sign which read "Go Sue!". As soon as Sue had run past, the girl turned the sign over, and on the back it read "Go Carol!"

In Williamsburg, former marathon runner Luis had been standing watching the runners from this exact spot for almost 20 years. "It's never disappointing," he said. "The energy is fantastic."
"It sure is," said Georgina.
Someone once said that if New York is a human being, then the marathon is its heart.

I think Georgina and I would both agree that's very well put. Roland captured the atmosphere of the race brilliantly, and Georgina did a little commentary for the podcast. I recorded my own thoughts a few days later, after my voice had returned, and we edited the whole thing together for Show 39.

THE WEST VILLAGE

Next morning we headed off towards Greenwich Village, determined to track down a fertility statue for the pandas in Hong Kong. We took the L Train to Union Square, then made our way to the southern end of 5th Avenue, where, as we sat and drank coffee in the cool autumn sunshine, we were delighted to encounter our very first authentic New York Crazies.

Crazy Number One was a grubby, tanned man in his mid thirties, who stood shaking his fist at passers-by, whilst routinely taking his morning shower in the ornate water fountain in the centre of Washington Square, and shouting at the top of his voice in Spanish. Crazy Number Two was a girl in her early twenties, who chose to skillfully interpret Crazy Number One's loud rantings by dancing in ever decreasing circles with a large wooden hoop. These two were the perfect double act.
"Should we give them some money?" I croaked to Georgina.
"I think we should give them as wide a berth as possible," Georgina smiled.

We crossed the street and strolled past number one, Fifth Avenue, which we guessed was probably the most exclusive address in Manhattan. Right opposite was an estate agent.
"Shall we take a look at the property prices?" quipped Georgina.
"I think we should," I replied.
As we stood with our noses pressed against the glass, I suddenly felt a little like Tiny Tim in A Christmas Carol.
"Would you like to buy my apartment?" asked a smartly dressed old lady as she came out of the estate agent's front door.
"I've just put it on the market this morning."
"Really?" replied Georgina. "How much is it?"
"It's seven million dollars," she smiled.
I whispered in Georgina's ear. "Ask her if she'll accept six and a half."

Finally deciding that number one, Fifth Avenue was a little out of our league, we turned left, and headed towards the West Village. We'd been assured by New Yorkers that it was now extremely uncool to refer to Greenwich Village as Greenwich Village, so we were careful to call it simply The West Village, even while talking amongst ourselves. We walked past a School of the Performing Arts. Then another one.

"There seem to be more drama schools in New York than there are supermarkets," I said. "There's one on every corner."
"Where else will they train the next generation of Crazies for Washington Square?" Georgina replied, as she peered into a boutique window featuring a Vivian Westwood body stocking printed all over with fake tattoos.

We crossed to the other side of West 8th Street and noticed a cluttered little thrift shop. I think it reminded Georgina of her favourite Cancer Research Shop in Crouch End Broadway, so we ventured inside.

The shop was packed with all manner of old furniture and discarded electrical equipment, as well as thousands of paperback books, vinyl records and cassette tapes. At the back of the shop, close to the stairs, and in semi-darkness, was a small wooden shelf, covered in vases, and small ornaments.

One of the ornaments was partly wrapped in brown paper. Georgina picked it up and unwrapped it carefully.
It was a little statue, about six inches tall.
"Look at this," said Georgina.
"What is it?" I asked.

Georgina uncrumpled the brown paper, which appeared to have some handwriting on it.
"Statue of the Rice Mother," it said. "An ancient Earth Fertility Goddess."
"Well, would you believe it," I said. "How much is it?"
"The same price as everything else seems to be in New York. Five bucks."
"Where's it from?" I asked.
"Thailand," said Georgina.

"So we've come to New York, to buy something from Thailand, and take it all the way back to China."

"Looks like it," she said.

Georgina read a little more. "When the Rice Mother becomes pregnant, when rice flowers bloom, she delights in the scented powder received from the stamen, and swells with its fertilization, much like a pregnant woman."

"This is just what we've been looking for," I said.

Georgina read on:

"The Rice Mother's offspring is the rice itself, each grain of which contains its own soul that must be ritually gathered along with the harvest. From the realm of spirit, which is fiery, the power passes through the watery astral realm to the physical world."

"If that doesn't get the pandas shagging, nothing will," I said.

"Gimme five dollars," said Georgina.

Chapter 23:
Singapore Slings

Having arrived in New York on Halloween Night, we flew back into London on 5th November, which is Bonfire Night in the UK. Fireworks flashed and banged around the airport as we touched down at Heathrow.

"Please remain in your seats," said the pilot.

Everyone immediately stood up and reached for the overhead lockers.

"I didn't expect a reception committee," I said to Georgina as she grabbed her duty free.

"I think the fireworks are probably for Guy Fawkes," she said.

"Does he have a podcast?" I grinned.

American Airlines managed to lose our suitcases at JFK, and when they arrived back in Crouch End, two days after we did, we barely had time to unpack them before we were once again stuffing them with un-ironed clothes, in preparation for our trip to China. On the morning we set off, we received a very official looking email from the press office at the zoo in Hong Kong.

From: "Gillian"
Subject: Re: Ocean Park

Dear Brain *(sic)*, Here is the itinerary for your visit:

10:10 Brian and Georgina arrive and walk to Giant Panda Habitat.

10:15 Visit GPH and watching panda feeding in the guest area.

(Some info: For the feeding process, the panda keeper will first let the pandas go to the back of house, then they will place the food for panda in their habitat. The panda will be released to the habitat to enjoy their food afterwards.)

215

10:25 Suzanne Gendron (our Executive Director of Zoological Operations and Education) arrives in GPH and meet Brian and Georgina.

10:30 Taking pictures with Brian, Georgina and Suzanne in GPH (by photographer of Brian).

10:35 Walk back to meeting room to conduct interview with Suzanne.

11:30 Interview finishes

The pandas we were going to meet were apparently quite famous, and their names were Ying Ying and Le Le. And by the look of that email, it appeared that our visit was going to be an official one. We were actually accredited press. When we explained that we also wanted to present Ying Ying and Le Le with a fertility statue, Gillian quickly sent back a rather concerned-sounding email.

From: "Gillian"
Subject: Re: Visit to Ocean Park

Dear Brain *(sic),* Could we know the outlook of the statue? Any photos of it can be seen first?

"They obviously think we're going to turn up with one of those fertility ornaments with a giant penis," I said to Georgina.
"Maybe we should send them a photo to set their minds at rest."
"Nah, let's keep them guessing," said Georgina.

David Kibble had arranged virtually everything for our trip to Asia, including a three day stopover to record a podcast in Singapore.
"Isn't it rather hot in Singapore?" I said to Georgina.
She opened up Google Earth and clicked a few buttons.
"It's right on the Equator," she said, "Just a few miles from the Malaysian jungle."

She opened up Wikipaedia: "Singapore has a tropical rainforest climate with no distinctive seasons, so it's usually around 93°F with 90 percent humidity in the morning and 60 percent in the afternoon. During prolonged heavy rain, relative humidity often reaches 100 percent. The monsoon season is November to December."

"So, the answer is...?"

"It'll be hotter than the sun," she said.

INCREDIBLE CHINESE SINGING MAN

As we took off from Heathrow, I tucked my hands deep into my pockets, and Georgina was forced to climb to 37,000 feet without crushing any of my bones. In fact, overall, Georgina was a lot more blasé about this flight, even forgetting to take her placebo chill pills. Which had to be a good thing.

The Boeing 747 had just been re-fitted, and had that yummy smell of new car, which seemed to placate Georgina even more - her good mood only tempered by a man sitting to her right who had recently been a finalist in The World's Boniest Elbow competition.

It was our third long haul flight that month, so we quickly turned to comparing breakfast omelettes, which now seem to be an obligatory in-flight meal, no matter where you're travelling to. You may be interested to learn that Cathay Pacific's breakfast omelettes piss on American Airlines' breakfast omelettes - the former being light and cheesy, the latter being made from a concentrated mixture of latex rubber and corrugated polystyrene.

A couple of hours into the flight, night-time was unceremoniously forced upon us by the cabin crew - window shutters slammed shut, cabin lights switched off. We're constantly amazed that people can sleep on airplanes, but everyone seemed to doze off within seconds. Everyone, that was, except for us, and Incredible Chinese Singing Man.

Incredible Chinese Singing Man sat just three seats away from us, and began knocking back the beers almost as soon as the aircraft had raised its landing gear. He got drunk very quickly indeed, which on its own might not have been a problem, except that

Incredible Chinese Singing Man was a bit of a karaoke fan. He placed his headphones on his ears, tuned to one of the pop music channels, and immediately began to sing along. At the very top of his extremely high pitched voice. In Chinese.

"Yeeeeeeeeeeeeeeee….. aaaaahhhhhhhhhhhhh…… kaaaaaaaaaaaaa… nooooooooooooo…. Waaaaaaaaaaaaaa…"

Remarkably, since most of the other passengers were fast asleep, no-one complained. And those that could hear him seemed to quite enjoy the live entertainment. After about an hour, one of the stewardesses walked over and politely told Incredible Chinese Singing Man to "Sssh". He smiled benignly and ordered another beer, which the stewardess dutifully scurried off to get him.

A strong tail wind meant that our Cathay Pacific flight was mercifully short at ten and a half hours, and luckily it perfectly suits Georgina's nature to watch television for ten hours on the trot. We actually had enough time to watch all six episodes of the 5th season of Curb Your Enthusiasm. All six episodes, that is, except for the last thirty seconds of episode six.

"Can I have your headphones, please, sir," said the stewardess.
"It's almost finished," I said. "Just one more minute."
"I'm sorry sir, I have to take them now."
"It's just a minute," I said.
"I'm sorry, sir."
"Look, I've watched six episodes, and there's only a few seconds left. I want to see how it ends. Can't you pick up the headphones on your way back?"
"I'm not coming back," she said.
"Don't make a fuss," whispered Georgina.
"It's just a few seconds!" I screamed.

Ironically, it was exactly the kind of thing that happens to Larry David all the time in 'Curb'. I'd obviously been watching that show for way too long, and was actually beginning to metamorphosise into its hero. The stewardess collected my

headphones, and I angrily crossed my arms and tried to lip-read the final punchline to the six part series.
"You can watch it on the way back" said Georgina.
"It was just a few seconds," I said.

After the loss of our baggage on the return flight from JFK, we nervously watched the carousel at Singapore Airport spew cases past us. The tension built to a crescendo. We glanced nervously at our watches, and at each other. But to our amazement, after just a few short minutes, both suitcases rolled majestically into view. Our relief was palpable. Our luggage had defied all the laws of physics and international air travel, and had arrived safely in Singapore.

FEELING HOT HOT HOT

The Republic of Singapore is a tiny island nation located at the very southern tip of the Malay Peninsula, and it's actually 85 miles north of the Equator. The heat hit us like a wall. Even Wikipaedia cannot prepare you for the barrage of such heat. Just a few hours before, Crouch End had just experienced its first snow of the year, and we alighted from Singapore Airport into 94°F.

Our jeans stuck to our pants and our pants stuck to our bottoms within a nano second. We'd missed a full night's sleep and the humidity weighed heavy upon us - our eyes red and puffy, our limbs heavy.

Of course, everyone in Singapore spends their entire lives huddled in freezing cold, air-conditioned apartments, offices and cars, so exposure to the country's extreme climate rarely lasts more than a few seconds. Most of the time you're indoors, blowing on your hands to keep them warm, and wearing a polo-necked sweater.

We Brits, in the form of the East India Company, first established a trading post on Singapore in 1819, and for years we used the place as a strategic trading post, until it was occupied by the Japanese during World War II. When peace broke out in 1945 it reverted back to British rule, and in 1965 became independent. Now it's the 17th wealthiest country in the world, despite having a tiny population of less than 5 million.

We took a taxi from the airport into the centre of Singapore, where you can almost *smell* the money as you walk around in the financial district. The city centre is crammed with glinting silver skyscrapers, and everything looks as if it's just been vacuumed, waxed and polished. In fact, Singapore is so clean and well kept it's like the entire city suffers from some kind of Obsessive Compulsive Disorder.

    We got the feeling that if you dropped a piece of litter it would be swooped upon by a cleaner before it even reached the ground. The whole place seemed to embody extreme anal retentiveness.

    "This is the cleanest place I've ever seen," I said, as we strolled through the Downtown Core.
    "It's even cleaner than *Svendborg*!" said Georgina. "In fact, there's something almost sinister about it. As if someone has just tidied up after a crime."
    "Oh, there's no crime in Singapore," I said.
    "Why not?" she asked.
    "Because virtually everything is punishable by execution," I said. "I'd be careful where you put that cigarette butt if I were you. You'll find yourself on Death Row."

    Georgina and I were genuinely dumbfounded by the list of fines for doing almost anything in Singapore; smoking, littering, sneezing, walking, not walking, or just simply *being* in the place. The locals call it a "Fine City". Of course, the bonus side to all of this is that you feel extremely safe everywhere. Even walking around in a park at 11 pm at night, there is no sense whatsoever of personal danger.

    There are 63 islands in Singapore, and the government are busy trying to join them all together into one big land mass. Everywhere you look they're digging up earth and pouring it into the sea to create some new real estate. In Singapore, the tide doesn't come in, the beach goes out.

LORD KIBBLE OF KIBBLE

After so many long-distance messages and emails, it was incredibly exciting to finally meet David Kibble face to face for the first time during our inaugural evening in Asia. Georgina jumped up and down and hugged poor David until he was blue in the face, and more than a few tears were shed. Just as Emily had so kindly done in New York,

David actually gave up his bed for us on our first night in Singapore. Throughout the writing of this book, Georgina and I have been staggered by the kindness we've been shown by our listeners during our travels, and we'll never be able to thank them enough for their contributions to our podcasting adventures.

An IT manager for a large international company, Lord Kibble, as we decided to call him, has apartments in both Singapore and Hong Kong, and he flits back and forth between these two cities like most people catch a bus down to the shops. He thinks nothing of jumping on a plane and flying 1,500 miles to attend a ten minute meeting.

We dumped our bags on the floor in his apartment, and within minutes we were sleeping off our long haul flight in his big double bed. When we awoke the next morning (or was it afternoon?), Lord Kibble had gone to work, and left a note which simply read "I'll meet you later at Raffles."

We didn't know much about Singapore, but we'd certainly heard of the world-famous Raffles Hotel. We got out of bed and took a shower. Then we had some coffee, took a shower, had breakfast, took a shower and jumped into a taxi outside the apartment.
"The world-famous Raffles Hotel, please," we said.
"Can you give me directions?" asked the taxi driver.
"No," we replied confidently.

Had it been practical to take a shower in the cab on the way to Raffles we would have done so. But sadly it wasn't possible. The cab finally pulled onto the crunchy gravel drive at the front of Raffles, and the door was held open for us by a bearded man in a turban and a smart white uniform. Raffles was declared a national monument in 1987, and the hotel is seen as the Jewel in the Crown of Singapore's tourist industry. When it opened in 1887 it was nothing but a rather sombre-looking old bungalow known as the Beach House, but it's now a splendid white wedding cake of a building.

MAD DOGS AND ENGLISHMEN

Raffles has welcomed innumerable celebrities, including Rudyard Kipling, W. Somerset Maugham, Charlie Chaplin and even Michael Jackson. But it's most famous guest was undoubtedly Noel Coward, who must surely have been thinking of Singapore when he wrote Mad Dogs and Englishmen Go Out in the Midday Sun.

Raffles' latest pair of C-list celebrity visitors, Georgina and I, were shown into the Billiard Room, and we ordered Earl Grey tea and a tray full of cakes and sandwiches.
"Do you think they have showers here?" I whispered.
"Ssshh!" hissed Georgina.

We pressed the record button on Roland. "I keep expecting to see Denholm Elliot come bumbling in," I said "wearing a sweat-stained white linen suit and sipping a Singapore Sling."
"That's it!" screamed Georgina. "That's what we should be ordering. You can't come to Raffles without having a Singapore Sling!"

The Singapore Sling was created in the Long Bar at Raffles at the turn of the 20th century by a Chinese bartender called Ngiam Tong Boon, and it was so exclusive they used to keep the recipe in a wall safe. It was originally designed as a woman's drink, hence its rather attractive pink colour, but today it's enjoyed by everyone - even a couple of oiks like myself and Georgina.
"Two Singapore Slings, please," I said to the waiter.
"Make that three," said a voice.
It was Lord Kibble.

"What's in this cocktail?" I asked His Lordship, as Georgina and I sipped our Slings a few minutes later.
"I have no idea," he said. "But I shall find out for you."

It turned out to be gin, Cherry Brandy, pineapple juice, lime juice, Cointreau, Benedictine, Grenadine and a dash of Angostura Bitters. The whole thing was garnished with a slice of pineapple and a cherry on the top.

"I'm not sure it needs the cherry," I said.

"Just neck it," said Georgina.

"Do you want to hear something strange?" said Lord Kibble.

"Last night, I went to the gym and I was listening on my iPod to one of your podcasts from New York."

"OK..." I said.

"As you and Georgina were chatting away in my headphones, I suddenly thought to myself, 'Those two are at home in my bed.'"

"That must have been pretty surreal" I said. We've said all along that podcasting's probably the most intimate form of entertainment ever invented, but I don't think we ever expected it to become quite as intimate as that.

Lord Kibble was joined at Raffles by a friend of his from Hong Kong, and fellow listener, called Kate.

"Kate's my dog's reflexologist," he said.

"I'm sorry, I thought you said that Kate is your *dog's* reflexologist," I said.

"That is what I said," replied David.

He'd been listening to our shows since the start, and he knew that this kind of material was bread and butter for Sowerby and Luff. So we immediately reached for Roland, and within seconds Georgina and I were interviewing Kate for the podcast.

"Yes, I perform reflexology on dogs," said Kate, "And I have to say it's been extremely beneficial for David's Labrador."

"Tell us more," Georgina probed.

"Well, at first the dog was a little suspicious of the whole thing, but now he's really taken to it," she said. "I use the pads on the dog's paw like the human hand or foot. I do the first pad as the brain, the ball of the paw for the intestines, then the other pads for the pituitary gland and the hypothalamus."

I looked at Georgina. Even in Raffles Hotel in Singapore we could not escape the extraordinary world of Talking Bollocks.

"He used to pull his paw away," Kate went on. "But now he pushes his paw towards me as if to say, hey, come on, it's reflexology time!"

"Can you see a change in the dog?" I asked.

"Well, he looks a lot calmer," said Kate. "And it's completely cured his epilepsy."

As we left Raffles, Lord Kibble took a photograph of us standing either side of the smart uniformed doorman, and then we jumped into another cab and headed for the Botanical Gardens.

"The world-famous Botanical Gardens, please" we said to the driver.

"Where's that?" he said.

The gardens were huge, and packed with giant jungle plant life. They also had the noisiest fucking insects you've ever heard in your life.

"What do you think of Singapore so far?" asked Georgina.

"Pardon?" I said.

Gasping for breath in the stifling heat, we strolled into the Orchid Garden, which was full of tourists. We sat and watched one group of Japanese orchid enthusiasts take it in turns to stand in front of a particular species of orchid, take a photograph, then move on to the next species of orchid. When they'd done this about fifteen times, I turned to Georgina.

"How many species of orchid do they have in here?" I asked. She consulted the guidebook.

"Three thousand," she said.

We wandered from tree to unrecognisable tree and recorded the introduction to our Singapore programme. Past Swan Lake, through fountains and pagodas, and into formally planted areas of quiet solace, filled with Bonsai trees. After 20 minutes we were knackered.

"I need to take shower," said Georgina.

"Pass me the oxygen," I said.

CHRISTMAS IN CHINATOWN

Keen to let Lord Kibble have his bed back, we checked into the Orchard Grand Court, a serviced apartment building with air conditioning so bitterly cold that the place could be used for breeding penguins in captivity. We scrambled into the lift with our suitcases, and Georgina pressed the button for the fourth floor. The doors closed and then reopened. Georgina gamely tried again. No response.

We moved across the foyer and into another lift and repeated the procedure. Still no luck. The lift stubbornly refused to budge. In turn, we tried all four of the lifts in the foyer before sidling up to the receptionist to tell her that all of the elevators in the building were broken. With a slightly too rueful smile, she condescendingly informed us that before selecting our floor, we must slide our little plastic room card into a slot in the control panel. "For your security," she said.
"I've never seen that before", I said to the receptionist with a thin smile.
"Oh," she said, as if I had just crawled out from under a rock.

We staggered once more into the lift, and inserted the room card in its slot. The lift made a sighing noise, as if to say "Who are these people?", and we headed for the fourth floor - the mirrored doors serving only to double our embarrassment.
Georgina switched on the bathroom light. Nothing happened.
"We really are going to have to read the manual for this apartment," I said.

She tried the switch again. On, off, on, off. Nothing. It wasn't until the following morning, when a grinning maid knocked on our door at 6.00am and demanded to clean the room, that we realised that the switch outside the bathroom silently illuminated the "Please Disturb Us Very Early in the Morning" sign outside the room.

"I clean room now?" said the maid.
"No, thank you," said a blurry eyed Georgina. "We've only just arrived, we don't need the room to be cleaned, thank you."
"OK," said the maid.

Georgina was about to close the door when the maid strode into the room, clutching a huge pile of white towels and sheets.

"Where are you going?" asked Georgina.

"I clean room now."

"No, we don't need the room cleaned." She closed the door on the maid. There was a moment's silence, followed by a loud knock. Georgina opened the door.

"I clean room now?"

We plugged the laptop into the apartment's broadband and emailed the photograph of us outside Raffles to our agent Peter.

"However did they allow Brian into Raffles dressed like that?" he replied almost immediately. Charming.

That night we were determined to struggle through our 8 hour jet-lag and stay up and watch our favourite football team Spurs in an important Premiership match in London. However, the game's 4pm kick-off meant that West Ham v Spurs would not be on in Singapore until after midnight.

We propped ourselves up in front of the TV, and determinedly waited for the match to begin, but we were fast asleep long before the teams walked onto the field, and by the time we awoke six hours later the game was long over.

Next morning we got up early, and jumped into a cab to Chinatown. To our amazement, on the dashboard of the taxi was a small Teddy Bear wearing a West Ham United shirt.

"Are you a Hammers fan?" I asked the driver.

"Did you see the game last night?" he said.

What were the chances of finding a West Ham supporter in the middle of Singapore?

"What was the score?" I asked keenly.

"One-one draw," he replied. "Spurs missed a penalty in the last minute!"

"Damn!" I said.

"Are you a Spurs fan?" he asked

"Yes."

"Oh dear," he said.

To our surprise, Chinatown was adorned with Christmas decorations. Neither Georgina nor I had ever been in a hot country during the run up to the festive season, and it was truly bizarre to see Santa Claus and his reindeer sweltering in the tropical heat, or Frosty the Snowman set up next to a golden statue of Buddha.

We weaved our way through the colourful shops and stalls.
"You want to buy a nice silk shirt for Christmas?" said a tailor.
"No thanks," I said determinedly.
"Come inside, I show you a nice shirt."
"I really don't want to buy a shirt, thank you," I emphasised. But it was too late. I was an English tourist in Chinatown, and it was my job to buy a shirt. It was my absolute destiny to buy a shirt. To fight it was pointless.
"This shirt suits you," he said, holding a shirt that didn't suit me up to my chest. "Forty Singapore dollar."
"No thank you." I repeated.
"How much would you pay for this shirt?" said the tailor.
"I don't know, twenty dollars?" I said. "Ten?"
"Sold," he said. "You want a nice tie to go with that?"

"Why are you wearing that horrible shirt?" asked Georgina, clearly concerned that she'd only left me for about three minutes, and I'd already started spending our money on random items.
"I just bought it for ten dollars," I said proudly.
"What was the other shirt like?" asked Georgina.
"Sorry?"
"Well, surely you must have got two shirts for that money!"

We decided to do the next section of the Singapore podcast while we were in Chinatown, but almost as soon as we began to record, the heavens opened and we experienced our first full-on tropical monsoon. Despite the weather, we kept going and the stereo sound of the rain beating down on the streets turned out to be one of the most dramatic recordings we made in Asia. At one point, while we were reading a listener's email, you can hear us both jump clean out of our skins at a mighty crack of thunder.

Our favourite yuletide decoration in Singapore was a spectacular walk-in Nativity scene in Orchard Road. At 8pm every evening, fake snow, in the form of what appeared to be bubble bath foam, spread up and over the Nativity, causing much excitement to anyone under ten, and much hilarity for anyone over. Of course, the fake snow melted within a couple of minutes, but no-one seemed to care.

"Isn't there something missing here?" I asked Georgina. She counted off on her fingers. "Er, shepherds, sheep, wise men, Mary, Joseph…"

"There's no baby Jesus," I said.

Sure enough, the crib contained no Saviour, but in place of the Holy Child was a life-sized model of Lassie the Wonder Dog. In this modern climate, no city council wants to offend anyone, and there is an annoying dismissal of anything that represents any specific religion above another.

"I suppose it's multi-denominational," I said. "A dog that rescued mankind is considered a suitable substitute for the Lord Our God".

"The Lord Our Dog," said Georgina.

"Bark The Herald Angels Sing!" I said.

We left it there. Georgina and I were still not ready to embrace the Christmas spirit, it being too fucking hot to walk more than five steps at a time.

ON SAFARI

That evening we decided to record a podcast segment at the world-famous Singapore Night Safari and, astonishingly, the taxi driver knew exactly where it was.

Since sunset in Singapore always takes place punctually at 7.30 pm, everyone always knows exactly when to show up at the Night Safari. We arrived promptly, in broad daylight, at 7.29 pm, and a minute later the sky was pitch black. I swear I heard a click as night fell. We ventured slowly into the darkness, and before long came upon a clearing in the jungle, in which was built a bar and a fast food restaurant called Bongo Burgers.

The Night Safari, though voted best tourist attraction in Singapore for the last three hundred years, was just that, very touristy. Drumbeats and fire lanterns welcomed the crowds, and you were almost immediately subjected to enforced photo opportunities with painted backgrounds, ranging from shadow puppets to wild animals. Gift shops selling African mammal-based trinkets lined the walkways.

Night Safari is the world's first wildlife park built solely for visits after dark - offering visitors "the unique experience of exploring wildlife in a tropical jungle at night". If you think about it, it's actually a very clever marketing idea, since around 90% of the animals in most zoos are nocturnal anyway, and are much more active after dusk.

We quickly made our way to the bar, where we sat and ordered a couple of tall glasses of Chang beer, which quickly lightened our mood, and it was with alcohol driven fervour that Georgina dared herself to go and touch a huge snake on the stage adjacent to the bar area.
"What type of snake is it?" she enquired of a keeper.
"Python, very dangerous," came the terse response.
"May I stroke it?" Georgina asked, with no small amount of trepidation.
"Five dollar," came the stock response.

Georgina came back to the bar. "I'm buggered if I'm spending thirty dollars to get in here, then another five dollars to do something I'm not convinced I want to do in the first place," she snapped.
She ordered another beer.
"Five dollar," said the barman.

We were told that before we set off on the safari, there was some kind of live performance, so we downed our Changs and, with pseudo African drums ringing in our ears, made our way towards the Creatures of the Night show.

We were astonished to discover in the next jungle clearing an entire open-air theatre, complete with auditorium, raked seating and a

powerful lighting grid. I hit the record button on Roland as the show began with a classic voiceover intro.
"When the sun goes down... it gets dark. It becomes wet. It's cold. It's time for the Creatures of the Night."

A blue spotlight faded up slowly on a rocky platform at the side of the stage, and a real-life wolf shuffled tentatively out of the wings. He sat for a while scratching himself, then attempted to make an early exit, at which point he was silently encouraged back onto his mark. There was no way that wolf was going to be allowed off that stage until he'd howled at the moon.

The wolf looked wistfully into the wings, then reluctantly lifted his head to the night sky and let out a half-hearted howl. He looked off stage again. Was that it? Could he go now? Nope, he was going to have to howl with a little more effort than that. He howled a bit louder, then coughed and trotted off for his meagre food reward. The audience applauded politely. Georgina got the giggles.

To be honest, that was the highlight of the show, and we said as much in our short review for the podcast as we filed out of the theatre 20 minutes later. We'd thought that the days of training animals to perform humiliating tricks for tourists were over. But we were wrong.

Now it was time for the safari. We piled into the back seat of the zebra-striped road train and waited for it to begin. It wasn't long before we heard the voice of our guide come echoing through the loudspeakers.

"It's a jungle *out there*," she began, in an accent and style that was unlike anything we'd ever heard before. Kimberly, as we later discovered was her name, had a knack of placing a kind of exaggerated slow motion emphasis on the last two words in each sentence, in such a way that it sounded like she was voicing a porn film.
"Take a look at the *rhino's... skin*," she purred like Marylyn Monroe. "It may seem very rough *and.. tough*, but the rhino is still *very... sensitive*."

I pointed Roland at the loudspeaker and the red record light flashed in the darkness. We had a feeling that sexy Kimberly was going to be one of the stars of our Singapore podcast.

"These pigs may look rather ugly *to ... you,*" she teased, "But the female pigs find them *rather... sexy.*"

"Do you think this is the only safari in Asia to feature a Happy Ending?" I whispered to Georgina. But she was laying face down on the back seat, sobbing with laughter.

MEET THE LADYBOYS

On the way back from the safari, we stopped off at another Singapore landmark that we were told was famous for its night time activities. During the day, Orchard Towers was a fairly innocent shopping centre featuring four levels of restaurants and shops, linked by escalators. After dark, it instantly transformed into what was known locally as Four Floors of Whores.

We were dropped right outside this den of iniquity and took the escalator upstairs. On every floor there were what could only be described as gentlemen's clubs, pumping with deafening dance music and peopled by the some of the sleaziest characters you'd be likely to meet anywhere in the world. On the second floor we went into what looked like the busiest bar in the place.

A couple of years before, Bennsy and I had been to Bangkok and Pattaya in Thailand to shoot a video about a scuba diving school, and not since that trip had I seen so many man-eaters, prostitutes and lap dancers in one place. But the best thing about Four Floors of Whores was that it was a perfect location for one of my favourite parlour games: Spot the Ladyboy.

"How can you tell which ones are the Ladyboys?" Georgina asked.

"It's simple," I shouted above the music. "They're the *best looking ones!*"

Since most Singaporean women are about 5 feet tall, with flat chests, you can be pretty certain that if you see a tall leggy woman with large breasts you're looking at a Ladyboy."

"But almost every woman in this bar is six feet tall with large breasts!" yelled Georgina.

"Then, almost every woman in this bar is a Ladyboy," I said.

Four Floors of Whores was obviously where European men came to get drunk and party hard with what they thought were women, and you couldn't really blame them. The Ladyboys were beautiful beings. Size zero, no hips, but with magnificently protruding fake breasts. Fake designer-labelled gowns flowed round us as we drank our beer and watched the dance floor's gyrating throng. There was a wonderfully bitchy atmosphere, with the waitresses in Burberry tartan mini-kilts, serving the men first and the real women second.

It was explained to us that most of Singapore's Ladyboys travel down by train from Bangkok, and one of their first destinations is Four Floors of Whores. Georgina was not at all shocked by this place, but revelled in its extreme, sexually charged atmosphere.

"Is this what it's like in Bangkok?" she asked.

"Yes," I replied, "Except that here they're wearing clothes." Georgina was eager to get up onto the dance floor, but after I explained to her that she'd probably not come back in one piece, she moped off towards the smoking room.

Singapore is obviously a lot more puritanical than its close neighbour Thailand, so you're unlikely to see ping-pong balls being launched out of front bottoms in Orchard Road. But Four Floors of Whores is as close as you're going to get in Singapore to X-rated action, and for that reason it's well worth a look if you're in town.

Our three days in Singapore passed very quickly, and before we knew it we were packing our bags once again and heading for the airport. After all, this steam-cleaned city was only a stopover on the way to Hong Kong for our most important visit of all. Breakfast with the pandas.

Chapter 24
The Podcast That Ate China

Just as the star of our flight to Singapore had been "Incredible Chinese Singing Man", so the star of our flight to Hong Kong was "Incredible Chinese Sneezing Man".
Yes, sitting in the seat right behind me, was a man with the ability to sneeze for China. Indeed, he could probably sneeze for Asia, in the final stages of the Intercontinental Sneezing Cup.

The effects on the sinuses of air conditioning and prolonged pressurisation are well documented. In other words, everyone has a right to sneeze on an aeroplane. But, frankly, this guy abused the privilege.
"Aaaaaaaaaaaaaahhhh... Chooooooooagghhh!" he went.
"Aaaaaaaaaaaaaaaaahhhh... ChooooooooooaAAAGGHHH!"

Having little better to do during the three hour flight, I timed Incredible Chinese Sneezing Man, and at one point he was sneezing at a rate of six per minute, which is a sneeze every ten seconds.
"Aaaaaaaaaaaaaaaaaaaahhhh... ChoooaaaaaaaaAAAGGGHHH!"
"Oh for fuck's sake," I whispered to Georgina.
"He can't help it," she said. "It must be some kind of allergy. He's probably allergic to air conditioning."
"They should put all the people who are allergic to air conditioning on a single flight," I said.
"Well, maybe they don't all want to travel at the same time," reasoned Georgina.
"Aaaaoooooaaaaaaaahhhh... Chooooaaa AAAGGGHHH!!!"
"Come back Incredible Chinese Singing Man," I said. "All is forgiven."

As we came in to land at Hong Kong Airport, we could immediately see the famous yellow smog of pollution which hangs permanently over the city.

"Isn't this one of the world's most dangerous airports?" asked Georgina.

"It used to be," I said. "But they moved the runway to somewhere safer."

"I hope they told this pilot where they've moved it to," said Georgina.

Once again, our luggage defied all laws of international air travel and arrived safely with us in Hong Kong, where we strolled delightedly into the fresh air outside the arrivals hall. A cool, spring-like breeze greeted us, and the temperature was a comfortable 70°F, with almost no humidity at all. There was oxygen in the air. We could actually breathe for ourselves without the use of any medical apparatus.

REACH FOR THE SKY

We jumped onto the Airport Express and after quickly passing through Tsing Li and Kowloon, arrived in the town centre twenty minutes later. We hailed a cab.

"L'hotel, Causeway Bay, please" we said to the taxi driver. He stared at us as if we were from the Planet Zob.

"L'hotel?"

He clearly didn't understand. We showed him our hotel booking form.

"Ah, L Hotel!" he said, and he shoved the cab into gear and headed across town.

French pronunciation appears to be frowned upon in Hong Kong, so L'hotel has always been known as L Hotel. How on earth could we possibly have known that? Had we not had that piece of paper, we might have been trying to locate L'hotel for days.

"Hong Kong is one of two special administrative regions of the People's Republic of China, the other being Macau. It lies on the eastern side of the Pearl River Delta, bordering Guangdong province in the north and facing the South China Sea in the east."

"Do you *have* to read that out loud?" snapped Georgina, as we headed towards Causeway Bay.

"I'm trying to educate myself," I said. And I stubbornly continued to read aloud from the guidebook.

"Hong Kong was a crown colony of the United Kingdom from 1842 until the transfer of its sovereignty to the People's Republic of China in 1997. China is still responsible for the territory's defence and foreign affairs, while Hong Kong maintains its own legal system, police force, monetary system, and immigration policy."

"Please tell me you have finished" said Georgina.
"But, I thought Hong Kong was now a *part* of China," I said.
"It turns out to only *partly* be a part of China."
"Does that matter?" asked Georgina.
"Well, it's just that for weeks I've been referring to this part of the trip as The Podcast That Ate China. I suppose that's not strictly true, is it?"
"I'm sure no-one will notice" smiled Georgina. "And it is a very snappy title."

The Podcast That Ate China arrived at L Hotel in the late afternoon of Monday 26th November 2007.
"Here's your room key, madam" said the receptionist to Georgina. "You are on the 26th floor."
Georgina went very pale. "Do you have any rooms lower down the building?" she asked. "Like, maybe, in the basement?"
"I'm sorry, madam," said the receptionist. "That's the only room we have available."

We hauled our bags over to the elevators. Nothing. We pressed the button again.
"Lifts very busy" said the man on the concierge desk.
"Thank you," we said. "We're not in a hurry."

About 15 minutes later one of the lifts arrived, and we pressed the button for the 26th floor. The lift lurched skywards, leaving our stomachs behind on the ground floor. Georgina gulped.
"You'll be fine" I said. "It could be worse. It could be the 27th floor."
Georgina said nothing.

"Wow, you have to come and take a look at this!" I said, as I pulled back the blackout curtains in the room.

Georgina swallowed hard. "I'd rather not" she said.

"I know you don't like heights, but you cannot stay in a hotel for a week and not look outside!" I said. "Look, solid glass. Double glazed glass. You cannot fall through it. You are safe. Perfectly safe. The bloody windows don't even open! Shall I call reception and ask for a parachute?"

Georgina slowly edged her way around the walls towards the large panoramic window.

"Oh fuck!" she said, as she took in the dizzying view for the first time. From 26 floors up we could see the whole of central Hong Kong and across the harbour, the whole of the centre of Kowloon.

"I think I'll have a little lie down," said Georgina and she slumped onto the large double bed, her hands pressed firmly over her eyes.

Even having so recently visited Manhattan, we were staggered by the height and scale of the buildings in Hong Kong. The city has quite literally been built vertically, with even ordinary apartment buildings towering to 50 or 60 floors. Of course, this means that most people spend their entire lives waiting for lifts.

Night was falling fast across a city which contains four of the tallest skyscrapers on the planet, and an extraordinary light show was flickering into life.

The room had an amazing view of the Bank of China Tower, which has attracted heated controversy in Hong Kong - its sharp angles said to cast "negative Feng Shui energy" into the heart of the financial district. We also overlooked the HSBC Building, which was built on the site of Hong Kong's first ever skyscraper.

"Two International Finance Centre" is the tallest building in Hong Kong and the 7th tallest in the world, and at 88 floors it's almost exactly the same height as the World Trade Center. They were actually half way through building this tower when 9/11 happened, which must have been a pretty traumatic time for the builders. We'd have had a terrific view of 2IFC from our hotel room, but someone had rather carelessly built a 50 story apartment block in the way.

SMOKE AND MIRRORS

I dragged myself away from the view, and shuffled slowly towards the bathroom in the twilight. Thud. I walked straight into a huge floor to ceiling mirror on the wall.

"Ow!" I yelped and went into the bathroom to study the bump on my nose.

"What are you doing?" called Georgina from the bed. There were a few seconds of silence, followed by another loud thud. Georgina came into the bathroom holding her forehead.

"Did you walk into the mirror too?" I asked.

"Yes," she said, and we both began to laugh.

My BBC Health and Safety training kicked in immediately. "That mirror is an accident waiting to happen!" I announced. "We must stick something on it!"

"Stick what on it?" said Georgina.

"I don't know," I said, "But we will find something."

Five minutes later, using L Hotel complimentary toothpaste as glue, we had attached six pieces of L Hotel notepaper to the mirror.

"That should do it!" I announced proudly. "We will never walk into that mirror again."

"I wonder what the cleaners will make of it," pondered Georgina.

"They must have seen it dozens of times before," I assured her.

"I need a cigarette" said Georgina.

"Well, you can't smoke in here!" I snapped. "You'll have to go outside."

"But that's 26 floors down!"

"Then it's an excellent time to give up smoking!" I said.

Georgina grabbed her duty free Marlboro and headed for the lift. 25 minutes later she came back.

"I can't get a lift" she said. "Can't I just have one cigarette in here?"

I pointed to the smoke alarms, and to the "No Smoking" sign which talked darkly of "severe penalties."

"Georgina, do you really want to spend the next 20 years in a Hong Kong jail?"
She headed back towards the lift. An hour later she came back into the room.
"Did you enjoy your cigarette?" I asked.
"I fancy another one now" she replied.
"See you in a couple of hours," I said.

THE MID-LEVELS

Following our Hong Kong tourist map carefully, we climbed up Lok Ku Road through the tumbledown "stone ladder" streets and markets of the "Mid-Levels". This part of Hong Kong appears to have been built almost entirely at a steep angle, and most of the shops and stalls seem to feature exotic sea creatures awaiting execution. Here you can choose your dinner based on how fast it can swim. We snapped many photos of Georgina giving the Last Rights to various lobsters, shrimp and crabs. After much semi-vertical walking, we gave up and climbed onto the Central-Mid-Levels escalator, arriving in the SoHo district moments later.

SoHo's crammed with restaurants, bars, nightclubs and art galleries, and the most famous street is probably Hollywood Road, which is where all the antique shops are. In the window of one antique shop in Hollywood Road was the largest and most intricately carved elephant's tusk we had ever seen.
"I thought it was illegal to sell ivory" said Georgina.
"Maybe what's why there's a sign in the window which reads "NO PHOTO" I said.

Georgina and I were disgusted at the amount of ivory that was on sale in Hollywood Road. You'd think that such a modern, civilized city as Hong Kong would take a more responsible view about what's sold in its antique shops.

For a while we tried following the "Sun Yat-Sen Historical Trail" through "Sixteen points of historical interest", but we quickly realised that most of the ancient sites on the tour have long been bulldozed and replaced by concrete skyscrapers. The architect who decided to build a multi-story residential complex alongside the Man Mo Temple should be put to death along with those lobsters.

PEAKING TOO EARLY

The most spectacular view of Hong Kong is from The Peak, and it's way too high to climb on foot, so we took the Peak Tram to the very top. The Trams originally used a steam engine to haul the cars but, thankfully, the whole thing was rebuilt 15 years ago, and it's now got a computerized control system.

"So it's perfectly safe?" asked Georgina, her eyes squeezed tightly shut.
"Yes," I said. "It carries 11,000 passengers a day, and most of them travel with their eyes open."
"I'll be fine as long as it doesn't stop, at a 45 degree angle, half way up the slope," she said.
10 minutes later, the Tram stopped, at a 45 degree angle, half way up the slope.
"Can I get off now?" asked Georgina.
"When we get to the top," I said.

It had been a while since we'd encountered any noisy road works or ear-splitting building work on our travels, so when we arrived at The Peak it was reassuring to hear the sound of pneumatic drills, electric saws and steam hammers. The normally quiet and tranquil gardens at the very top were being redeveloped, and the air was thick with dust, smoke and fumes.

My hands clamped over my ears, I approached a distinguished-looking Englishman, who looked like he could handle a camera.
"Lovely day!" I screamed at the top of my voice.
"Yes!" he shouted back.
"Would you mind taking a picture of us?" I yelled.
"I'd be delighted," he hollered back.
I handed him the camera. I had found my photographer. The hard bit was now going to be getting Georgina to stand anywhere near the edge of the viewing platform, so that we could get the best possible picture of us in Hong Kong.

"No way," she said. "I'm not going anywhere near that edge. That must be a thousand foot drop."
"But there's a handrail, and protective glass and everything" I said.
"I'm sorry, but no" she said.
"Just one," I said.
"No."
"You can keep your eyes closed," I said.
"No!"
"I'll give you five dollars."
"Excuse me!" said the distinguished-looking Englishman. "Would you like me to take this photograph or not?"

Using a combination of bribery, Valerian, and distorted perspective, we finally managed to take a photograph which made it look as if downtown Hong Kong and Sowerby and Luff were in roughly the same place at the same moment in history.

On the way back to street level, Georgina discovered that the only thing more alarming than the Peak Tram going uphill at 45 degrees, was the Peak Tram going downhill, backwards, at 45 degrees. Once again, she clamped her eyes firmly shut.
"Tell me when it's over," she said.

FREEZER JOLLY GOOD FELLOW

By the time we'd descended from The Peak, the clock had moved on to what we tend to refer to as "Beer o'clock". So we sought out a hostelry in which to spend Happy Hour. In D'Aguilar Street in SoHo, we stumbled upon the perfect place.

Balalaika is a Russian theme bar, complete with a huge bust of Lenin in the doorway, and lots of retro Soviet propaganda posters all over the wall. The centrepiece of the bar is a minus 20°C Siberian Vodka Room, for which they supply you with a huge warm fur coat.
"You want to drink a vodka at minus 20°C?" asked Georgina.
"That's cold," I said.
"That's the idea," she said.
"Can't we just have a nice cool beer out here?" I suggested.
"When in Rome..." said Georgina.

"But we're in Hong Kong," I said. "And this is a *Russian* bar!"

"Oh, you're such a wimp!" snapped Georgina, and she threw on one of the fur coats and strode into the freezer room. Never one to be outdone, I grabbed another fur coat and followed her.

"Bugger me, it's cold in here," Georgina said.

"Told you." I shivered.

"Let's just chuck down a couple of vodkas and go!" Shaking like a jellyfish, my ears bleeding from the cold, I shuffled over to the small serving hatch, where a frost-covered glass panel slid to one side.

"Yes?"

"Two v-v-odkas p-p-p-please" I said.

"What flavour you want?" said the barman.

"What f-f-f-flavour d-d-do you want?" I asked Georgina, who was shivering so much her face was becoming a blur.

"I d-d-d-on't c-c-c-care!" she said. "Just get the f-f-f-f-frigging drinks!"

I turned back to the serving hatch. The barman had slammed the glass shutter closed while I was talking to Georgina. It slid open again with a clunk.

"What f-f-flavours d-d-do you h-h-have?" I shivered.

"We have more than sixty flavours of vodka" he said. "You want me to read you the list?"

"No t-t-thank you," I said.

"Apricot vodka very nice," he said.

"Two apricot v-v-vodkas, p-p-p-please" I said. And then I discovered that my hand was too frozen to get it into my pocket and take out my wallet. The barman had clearly seen this phenomenon before.

"Pay outside," he said.

He placed two apricot vodka shots in the serving hatch, and as soon as I'd picked them up he slammed the shutter closed, sprinkling ice particles onto the floor. With trembling hands, we said

"Nastrovia!" and chucked our vodkas back in one. Georgina was now turning blue. "Let's get the fuck out of here!" she said.

"Very warm in Freezer Room today," said the barman as I paid for the drinks outside. "Only minus 14°C."

Next day, we took the Star Ferry across the harbour to Kowloon and recorded the next section of our Hong Kong podcast on the Avenue of Stars, which we stumbled upon purely by accident while looking for the ladies' toilets. Georgina's bladder is an extremely annoying beast. Even without any liquid intake whatsoever, it seems to require emptying about every 30 minutes, which can be very frustrating and leads to many silent moments of desperation.

The Avenue of Stars is on the Tsim Sha Tsui Promenade in Kowloon, and it's Hong Kong's equivalent of the Grauman's Chinese Theatre in Hollywood. The pavement's strewn with the names and concrete hand prints of China's top movie stars, and the whole place cost over 40 million Hong Kong Dollars to build.

"Wow, look at the names of all these movie stars!" I said to Georgina.
"Here's Lai Man Wai and Cheung Wood Yau !"
"That's nothing," said Georgina. "I've found the handprints of Wong Man Lei and Zhu Shi Lin."
"What was Wong Man Lei in again?" I asked.
"I can't remember," said Georgina. "But who could ever forget Tso Tat Wah and Kwan Tak Hing in the remake of Tang Wing Cheung."
"I thought Tso Tat Wah was dead" I said.
"No, that was Tso Tat Hing," said Georgina. Thus proving that even in this politically correct world, English people will never, ever grow tired of taking the piss out of Chinese names.

The sun was going down behind The Peak, so we decided to stay at the Avenue of Stars and watch the famous nightly performance of the Symphony of Lights, which claims to be the world's "largest permanent light and sound show".

Symphony of Lights creates "a stunning all-round vision of the coloured lights in Hong Kong, performing an unforgettable spectacle along the harbour front."

"Has it started yet?" I asked a fellow tourist with a video camera.
"Yes, five minutes ago" she said.
"I hadn't noticed" I said.

The light show claims to celebrate the energy, spirit and diversity of Hong Kong, but the truth is, they just flash the lights on and off on the buildings for 18 straight minutes. They even introduce each building individually, as their own lights join in the party.

"Ladies and gentlemen, please welcome The Sun Hung Kai Centre! Put your hands together for the Hong Kong Academy for Performing Arts! Give it up for the Hong Kong Convention and Exhibition Centre! Show your appreciation for the Chinese People's Liberation Army Forces Building!"

Our eyes were just beginning to glaze over as the announcer finally reached the end of his list about ten minutes later.
"And last but not least, a huge round of applause for the Standard Chartered Bank Building!"
It's fairly impressive when they use laser beams at the end of the show, but apart from that, the Symphony of Lights is a bit of a disappointment. Hong Kong itself is such a spectacular skyline after dark, that it really doesn't need event management to enhance it.

We jumped on the MRT subway at Tsim Sha Tsui, and headed back to the hotel.
"Only two days to the pandas," I said to Georgina, as we waited by the elevators in the foyer.
"Let's hope the lift arrives before then," she said.
"Lifts very busy," said the man on the concierge desk.

Chapter 25
Jockeys and pandas

The Royal Hong Kong Jockey Club is home to one of the most spectacular race courses in the world, and they have floodlit racing every Wednesday night.

"We simply have to go to the races," Georgina said over breakfast the following morning.

"But, we don't gamble," I said.

"For the *experience*," she said. "And anyway, I'm told there's a very nice Chinese restaurant with unlimited beer during the races."

"What time does it start?" I said.

That evening we got a cab to Happy Valley, and we were soon ensconced at a table overlooking the finish, with a delicious selection of authentic Peking dishes spread out in front of us.

"What do you fancy in the next race?" I asked.
Georgina studied the form. "I think I'm going to choose my horses based on the colours and designs of the jockeys' shirts," she said.

"How are you going to choose yours?"

"I might be a *little* more scientific than that," I said pompously, and I flicked through the Hong Kong evening paper until I found the names of the city's top racing tipsters.

"I'm going for Wong's Favourite," I said. "All the experts say it's going to romp it."

"I'm backing Natural Echo," said Georgina "because his jockey's wearing such a nice stripy red shirt."

"How much do you want to bet?" I said.

"20 dollars," said Georgina, and with a flourish she slapped a 20 dollar note on the table.

"That's only about £1.20," I said. "Surely you could be a bit more adventurous than that. It all goes to charity, you know."

"Charity?"

"Oh yes, it's not like in the UK. The Hong Kong Jockey Club is a non-profit, charitable organisation," I said. "Look, it says here in this leaflet: In 1955, the club formally decided to devote its surplus each year to charity and community projects."

"That's a great idea" said Georgina.
"The Club aims to bring a better quality of life to the people of Hong Kong," I read "and immediate relief to those most in need."
"Maybe they give some of it to the pandas!" said Georgina.
"So, how much are you going to bet? I asked.
"20 dollars," she said.

As we sat down at our table, we'd been given a leaflet, warning us about the evils of gambling, which seemed an odd thing to do at a race track.
"Gambling frequently leads to relationship problems, financial difficulties, and a range of emotional disorders," it said.
"You sure you want to risk it?" I asked Georgina.
"20 dollars," she said.

I read the last bit of the leaflet. It said that you should "Set and stick to a budget, only gamble what you can afford to lose, and that you should never borrow to gamble."
At that moment, I opened my wallet and discovered that I'd completely run out of Hong Kong Dollars.
"Can you lend me a few bucks, Georgina?" I asked.
"You should never borrow to gamble," she said.

We went and placed our paltry bets at the little window in the restaurant. Then we tucked into our bean sprouts and noodles, and waited for the first race to start.

"The winner is Natural Echo!" said the commentator a few minutes later. Georgina was magnanimous in victory.
"What happened to your horse?" she asked.
"Oh, my horse was that really *fast* horse that led all the way around the track and was passed in the last ten yards by Natural Fucking Echo!" I said.
"Nobody likes a bad loser," said Georgina.
"What are you backing in the next race?" I asked.
"I'm quitting while I'm ahead," said Georgina.
"After *one race*?" I squealed.
"You should set and stick to a budget," Georgina quoted back at me.
"And what was your budget?" I asked.

"20 dollars," smiled Georgina.

Determined not to be outdone, I scoured the newspaper, and discovered that all six tipsters were going for the same horse in the next race. I dashed over to the betting window and put twenty dollars on Lightning Speed. I've never backed a winning horse in my life, so the actual amount of the bet was immaterial. It was the winning that counted. More importantly, it was not being outdone by Georgina.

Georgina counted her winnings and we walked down the stairs to trackside to watch the next race. There was a whole lot more atmosphere outside in the open, and the place was packed with both tourists and serious local punters. We stood right next to the finishing post, where the floodlights gave the track an exciting, almost theatrical atmosphere.

As the second race started the noise from the massive crowd was deafening. Lightning Speed went into the lead almost immediately.
"Go on, number nine, go on my son!"
You simply would not believe how enthusiastic one man could get over a £1.20 bet.
"Go on, number nine, Go on, Lightning Speed!"

A huge roar went up as the horses flew past the winning post just yards away from us. We had absolutely no idea which one had triumphed.
"Did you see who won?" I asked a nearby Chinese punter who looked like he knew what he was doing.
"Number six," he said.
"Bugger," I said.

"You're supposed to tear up your betting slip and throw the little pieces up in the air," said Georgina. "It's traditional."
I rummaged around in my pocket and took out the betting slip. I held it up in the air and prepared to tear it to shreds.
"The winner of the second race is number 9, Lightning Speed," said the announcer.
"Yeeeeee haaahhhhh!" I screamed, and threw the ticket in the air.

"You'd better go and find that," said Georgina. "You don't want to go home without your winnings."

Georgina and I had only backed two horses in two races and, as if by magic, we'd both managed to get a winner in each. It really was that kind of a trip. The sights and sounds of the Hong Kong Jockey Club will stay with us both for years to come, and will definitely be one of our most vivid memories when we look back on our trip to the Far East. Tempting though it was to stay to the very end of the race meeting at Happy Valley, we really needed to get an early night. Tomorrow was the big day.

DUCK PORRIDGE

We awoke early and Georgina appeared at the breakfast table with some very odd looking cereal.
"What's that?" I asked.
"Duck Porridge," she said.
"Sounds like a Marx Brothers' movie," I said.

By the last few days of our travels, Georgina had gone completely native when it came to breakfast. While I tucked into my cornflakes, she was eating noodles. As I put ketchup on my bacon and eggs, she poured curry sauce over hers. I've always thought of myself as fairly cosmopolitan, but I just can't fancy Chinese food before lunchtime.

We hailed a cab outside the hotel and headed for Ocean Park. We knew we were on a very tight schedule, so we left plenty of time to get there. They weren't going to change the time of the pandas' breakfast for us, and this was our last day in Hong Kong, so we wouldn't get a second chance for our interview and photo opportunity. We also knew that Suzanne, one of the world's leading experts on pandas, could only spare us a few minutes from her extremely busy schedule.

"How far to Ocean Park?" I asked the taxi driver for about the third time.
"We be there very soon," he said. "Bout five minutes."
We were way ahead of schedule.

"Let's just check everything one last time," I said.

"Oh, for heavens sake," said Georgina. "Stop panicking. I've got everything in my bag."

"MP3 recorder and spare batteries?"

"Check."

"Digital camera?"

"Yes!!!"

"Fertility statue?"

Georgina laughed. "No, you've got that," she said. "You said you'd put it in your bag."

"Georgina, this is no time for jokes. You've got the statue, right?"

There was a long, agonising silence. I swear I could hear my heart thumping. Knowing that I hadn't put the fertility statue in my shoulder bag, I searched it. Knowing that she didn't have it either, Georgina emptied the entire contents of her handbag over the back seat of the cab.

"Please tell me that we have *not* forgotten the very thing we came to Hong Kong to give the pandas," said Georgina calmly.

"We *have* forgotten the very thing we came to Hong Kong to give the pandas," I replied. Then we both screamed. The taxi driver looked in his mirror.

"We have to go back!" we yelled. "We have to go BACK TO THE HOTEL!"

"But, we are arrive at Ocean Park," he said. "Very long way back to hotel."

"WE HAVE TO GO BACK!!!" we screamed.

The driver slammed his foot hard on the brakes, and spun the taxi into a U-turn.

"Georgina, we have come half way around the fucking world to do this. How could you have forgotten the fucking GIFT?"

"Don't blame me for forgetting it," screamed Georgina. "You're the one who's forgotten it!"

"How long back to the hotel?" I yelled at the driver.

"Maybe 20 minutes?" he said. He was beginning to look a little scared. I tried to calm him by explaining why we needed to return.

"We have forgotten our gift for the pandas," I said.
He looked even more scared, and stared at me, wide-eyed in the rear view mirror.
"Gift for panda," he said. "Very nice."

Georgina looked at her watch. Luckily we had set off pretty early in the first place.
"We might just make it," she said. "As long as we don't get stuck in traffic."
"But it's the MORNING RUSH HOUR," I said. "Of course we're going to get stuck in traffic!"
At that moment, the taxi ground to a halt. "We stuck in traffic" said the driver.

As if by some miracle, we arrived back at the hotel about 17 minutes later, and Georgina sprinted towards the elevators. She pressed the button, and stood waiting. Gentle, soothing music played in the lobby. I watched from the taxi outside as she looked at her watch.
"Lifts very busy" said the man on the concierge desk.

12 minutes later, Georgina came belting out of the hotel, and jumped into the cab.
"Have you got the fertility statue?" I asked.
"Very funny," she said.

"Go, go, go!" I screamed at the driver.
"Pardon me?"
"Could we please go back to Ocean Park, now?" I said politely.
"We go Ocean Park *again*?"
"Yes, please." I said. "We're very late."
"I go quickly," he said, and I suddenly had a rather nasty premonition of Georgina and me being pulled from a crumpled car wreck outside the Bank of China Tower.

The drive back to Ocean Park is something of a blur. It seemed to consist of a lot of red lights, a great deal of shouting and screaming, and numerous loud skidding noises. It reminded me of a car chase at the climax of some Cold War spy movie, or one of those

desperate dashes to the airport at the end of a Richard Curtis romance.
I didn't dare look at my watch. I just kept staring out of the window. How the hell could we have forgotten that fucking statue?

"Don't worry, we get there on time" said the cabbie. "You looking forward to riding on cable car?"
There was another deadly silence.
"Cable car?" said Georgina slowly. "What cable car?"
"You ride cable car to see panda house. Very high, very spectacular!"

Georgina turned green. At that exact moment we screeched to a halt outside the entrance to Ocean Park, and I looked at my watch. We were only four minutes late for our meeting.
"Come on!" I said and quickly paid the driver and jumped out of the cab.
"Good luck with panda!" he said.

Georgina sat transfixed in the back of the cab. She only had eyes for one thing: The cable car that soared high above our heads. The cable car that was taking visitors up a small mountain, around the edge of a five hundred foot sheer cliff, and down into Ocean Park.
"I can't do it!" said Georgina as she finally climbed out of the cab. "There is no way on Earth I can get into that thing. You'll have to go and see the pandas on your own."

"You'll be fine," I said to Georgina. "Look, we've come this far haven't we? You got over your fear of flying, so you can conquer your fear of heights!"
"No I can't!" said Georgina. "Look at me. I'm shaking just at the thought of it!"
"Just don't look down!" I pleaded.
"But look at the cable car," she whimpered. "It's completely made of glass. Even the floor of the car is made of fucking glass. It's my worst nightmare!"
"We've come half way around the world," I pleaded.
"That isn't helping," she said.

Georgina's sense of exasperation was very upsetting to see. Having braved flights, high-rise hotels and mountain peaks, her ultimate goal of meeting the pandas was now in real jeopardy. She couldn't disguise her disappointment and tears welled in her eyes. "I can't believe I've come all this way and I won't see them," she sighed.

VERTIGO

Ocean Park's PR assistant Gillian greeted us at the entrance.
"Do we *have* to go in that cable car to get to the panda house?" I asked.
"Not necessary," she said. "New panda habitat on this side of mountain. Quickly, we must go now."
Georgina heaved a sigh of relief that could be heard from space. I punched the air like I had just scored the winning goal in an FA Cup Final at Wembley Stadium.
"Thank God for that!" said Georgina.

I grabbed her arm and we ran after Gillian into the park. There, ahead of us, were two 50 foot tall concrete pandas on the roof of the brand new Giant Panda Habitat. Hong Kong sure knew how to hype its pandas.
"How's this huge place funded?" I asked Gillian.
"We have received big contribution from the Royal Hong Kong Jockey Club" she said.
"Well, would you believe it," smiled Georgina. "And I thought I was joking when I said that last night."

As we crept quietly into the panda habitat, Gillian slapped a couple of PRESS badges on us, and we were greeted with our first view of Ying Ying and Le Le.

"Ahhhhhhhhhhh," said Georgina. It was a genuinely fulfilling moment. We were finally stood there, face to face with two of the world's most famous Giant Pandas. Georgina was at once nervous, excited and joyous. Whispering into Roland the MP3 recorder she sounded professional, but couldn't disguise a tremor of jubilation. When you start on a journey like that, you never fully comprehand how the outcome will make you feel. It was truly overwhelming.

[There's full transcript of our podcast from the panda house at the end of this book.]

      Gillian handed us biogs of the pandas. Ying Ying was a two year old female, whose hobbies included climbing trees, playing with a PVC ball and "exploring new surroundings". It said she understood both English and Cantonese, but it didn't say how many words.

      Le Le was a two year old male, whose interests were listed as "playing with water, sleeping, and wrestling with Ying Ying. He also had what was described as a "signature move", which was "balancing off a branch with his leg, and swinging around". Le Le also claimed to understand two languages, but the biog was equally unspecific about the depth of his vocabulary.

      Both pandas were only two or three feet away on the other side of a huge piece of safety glass, and they were about to eat their breakfast.
Le Le made direct eye contact with Georgina as he took his first bite of bamboo. It was a very special moment for the Sowerby and Luff Show, and we recorded a running commentary of the whole thing.
      "Ahhhh," said Georgina.

      Ying Ying suddenly turned her back on us and headed back towards her tree.
      "Where's she going?" I asked Gillian.
      "She go back to bed now" she said.
      "Doesn't she want her breakfast?" I asked.
      "No" said Gillian.

      So we actually ended up having breakfast with just one panda instead of two. Ying Ying could at least have stayed and watched Le Le eating. Even if she wasn't hungry herself. Maybe had some fruit? We'd come a long way, after all.

THE INCREDIBLE BLEATING WOMAN

Exactly as the itinerary had promised, we were joined at exactly 10:25 by Suzanne. Once again, I hit the record button on Roland.

"We're here with Suzanne Gendron, Director of Zoological Operations and Education, here at Ocean Park" I said.

"*Executive* Director" said Suzanne in a clipped, corporate American accent.

"I was so close," I quipped.

"Suzanne, we've come from London to present Ying Ying and Le Le with this little statue of a fertility goddess," said Georgina.

"Have you?" replied Suzanne.

We were momentarily taken aback by this slightly cold and uninformed reply.

"Yes... it's to give them good fortune while they are trying to breed," I said.

"Well, that's very kind of you," said Suzanne, and from that moment she warmed up nicely, and became what journalists like to call "good value" for the rest of the interview.

"Have Ying Ying and Le Le attempted to mate yet?" Georgina asked.

"Oh no, they are much too *young*," said Suzanne. "They won't be capable of breeding for at least another 3 years."
Now she tells us.

"What about the other two pandas at Ocean Park?" I said.
"Are they likely to breed?"

"Oh, they're much too *old*" she said.
I was fast heading for a journalistic *cul-de-sac* here. Georgina stepped in quickly to help me out.

"So, how are Le Le and Ying Ying getting on with each other?" she asked.

"Well, not all pandas are compatible with each other," said Suzanne. "But we reckon they're getting on pretty well. They've even had a little *sexual play* as part of their repertoire."

"Do they flirt?" I asked.

"They *do* flirt" said Suzanne, flirtily.

"How can you tell when a panda's flirting?"

"Well, there's what we call *posturing* by the female," said Suzanne. "But the real challenge is that there's actually only 3 days every year when Ying Ying will be absolutely receptive to mating."

"That's a pretty fine line isn't it?" said Georgina. "Is there something that we, as humans, can do to help them? What sex tips can we offer to the pandas?"

"Oh, there are a number of things," said the Executive Director. "Tip Number One is good nutrition. That's probably the biggest bringer of success."

"Number Two?" I asked.

"The next thing is to keep them in separate enclosures," said Suzanne.

"Separate?".

"Oh yes, when pandas are sexually mature, being in separate enclosures makes them feel a lot more comfortable."

"So, we should keep them apart, in order to get them together?" said Georgina.

"Yes," said Suzanne, "We get Ying Ying and Le Le as far away from each other as possible in the run up to the mating season. The trick will then be knowing when to put them back together again."

"And how will we know that?" I asked.

"We'll watch their urinary hormones," she said. "We'll also be closely watching Ying Ying's behaviour. She'll begin by *scent marking*, then she'll start *bleating...*"

"Bleating?"

"Yes, she will make a noise like this…"

To our amazement, Suzanne pursed her lips at me, and began making a sound like a cat meowing.

"That's very good" I said cheekily. "Do that again!"

"Maybe later," said Suzanne, and then she realised what she'd said and blushed like a schoolgirl.

"Sex Tip Number 3 will be to put Ying Ying's hormones and urine on a piece of cloth and dangle it in front of Le Le."

"And that'll get his motor running, will it?" smiled Georgina.

"Absolutely!" said Suzanne.

I couldn't imagine getting Georgina's motor running by waving a piss-soaked cloth under her nose. But then, to be fair, I've never tried it.

Finally being face to face with one of the leading experts on pandas, we simply *had* to find out whether all that stuff about "panda porn" was true. Or was it just an urban myth?

"Oh yes, that's true," said Suzanne. "They used to show the pandas videos of other pandas mating. But it was totally unsuccessful, and it's no longer done. They were having so little success breeding pandas at one time that they were willing to try *anything*!"

"Is there competition between the zoos?" I asked. "To breed the most pandas?"
"We all have one goal," said Suzanne "for the pandas to survive. There are only 1,700 in the wild, you know."
"Well, this little fertility statue has now travelled from Thailand, to New York, and to Hong Kong, and it's been gathering luck along the way!" Georgina said.
"You know" said Suzanne, "It'd be an interesting study to see how the pandas are doing in all those places the statue has passed through."
That was a great idea. Georgina made a note of it in her little book.

"Well," I said in closing, "If Georgina and I hear in 3 years time that Ying Ying and Le Le have mated, we will, of course, take 100% of the credit."

I switched off the recorder, and Gillian used our camera to snap some shots of Georgina and me presenting the statue to Suzanne. When we'd finished and checked the pictures, Suzanne handed the statue back to me.
"No, you really can keep it!" I smiled.
"I can?" she said. "Well, that's great. That's really great."
"And good luck!" we said.
"Thank you," said Suzanne. "Thank you very, very much."

ELATED

As we walked away from the Giant Panda Habitat, we suddenly realised that we'd successfully completed our mission. The sun was shining brightly, and both Georgina and I felt completely elated. I punched the sky and jumped up and down like a gold medalist at the Beijing Olympics. Georgina slumped back onto the grass and kicked her legs in the air like a happy toddler.

"We did it!" she squealed joyfully. "We gave a present to a panda!"
We hugged and bounced and giggled, until we noticed a group of Japanese tourists staring at us in total bewilderment.
"We gave a present to a panda!" mumbled Georgina again, a little embarrassed this time. "We've come all the way from London to do it."
One of the tourists smiled and took a picture of her.

Moments later, as we melted back into the crowd outside the front entrance, we suddenly both felt an overwhelming sense of anti-climax. Our podcasting story was still only just beginning, but the panda chapter was now over.

We'd travelled 15,000 miles in a little over 4 weeks, and learned much about the inhabitants of New York and the mating habits of giant pandas. But if we were honest, we'd also learned rather a lot about ourselves.

"You want to take ride on cable car?" asked Gillian.
"No thanks," I said. "Georgina's afraid of heights."
Georgina stood very still, and looked up at the glass-bottomed cars, soaring hundreds of feet above our heads.
"Fuck it, let's go on the cable car!" she said.
"Are you sure?" I asked.
"Hey, what's life without a little adventure?" she said.

Chapter 26
Ordinary World

When we arrived back at Heathrow Airport, late on a Saturday afternoon at the beginning of December, it was dark, overcast and pouring with icy rain.
"I'm fucking freezing," I said.
"Oh, for heaven's sake," snapped Georgina. "For the past two weeks you've been complaining about how hot you are!"
Georgina's phone bleeped with an incoming text message. It was

    Lord Kibble of Kibble, checking to see if we'd arrived safely, and saying how much he was looking forward to listening to our Singapore and Hong Kong podcasts.
"Tell him I'm fucking freezing!" I said.
Georgina texted His Lordship back, thanking him once again for being such a fantastic and generous host to us while we were in Asia.

    We returned to our freezing flat to discover numerous emails from people in New York, Singapore and Hong Kong, saying that they'd love to hook up with us while we were in town. This, of course, is one of the main problems of presenting a "time shifted" programme. It can sometimes take a few weeks, or even months, for the message to get through. We even had an email from renowned New York podcasters Keith and the Girl, saying that they'd love to be interviewed for our show while we were in the Big Apple. Maybe on the next trip.

    An eight hour time difference between countries can take a lot of getting used to, but sometimes it can actually work in your favour. On Sunday morning I awoke at 4.00am, and before the sun had risen above the clock tower in Crouch End,

    I'd finished editing the Singapore programme and uploaded it to the server. By the time Georgina came padding into the living room at about 9 o'clock, over 500 people had already listened to the first part of our Asian adventure.

"How you feeling?" I said.

"Like the whole thing was some kind of hallucination," she said. "Did we really fly 6,000 miles to give a statue to a panda?"

"Listen for yourself!" I said, and I handed her a pair of headphones. It was the sound of Suzanne Gendron telling us about panda "posturing", just a couple of days before.

Bennsy rang me. "I've just listened to the Singapore show!" he said, "Sounds great!"

"Thanks," I said, "Fancy a pint in The Gay Legs?"

"I'll see you in there at seven," he said.

"By seven o'clock tonight, you'll be fast asleep," said Georgina. And she was right.

I awoke on our second morning back in London feeling slightly uneasy. As if I'd left something somewhere, or forgotten to do something important. I explained my feelings to Georgina, and she said she'd had a similar feeling the night before. As we sat in the living room eating breakfast, we both fell quiet as we tried to remember what it was we were supposed to try and remember. Georgina suddenly banged the table, sending my Squeezy Marmite flying.

"That's it!" she said.

"What?" I said.

"Carbon footprint!" she screamed. "We said we were going to work out our carbon footprint for all that travelling and plant some trees or something!"

MESSY EMISSIONS

I grabbed my coffee and jumped onto the laptop. True, if you travelled half way around the world to do something so seemingly pointless, the least you could do was repair the damage. After a bit of Googling I found an organisation who could "offset" our flights. Their site even had the government's "Act on CO2" calculator, so we could work out the emissions from our travel.

We began by calculating our carbon footprint for the return trip to New York, which turned out to be 2.54 tonnes. Then we totted up the emissions for the round trip from London to Hong Kong via Singapore.

"Wow, look at that!" I said to Georgina. "Six and a half tonnes of CO2."

We "offset our emissions", and our business credit card was charged exactly £157.15.

"Do you feel better now?" asked Georgina.
"I think so," I said. "What do they do with the money?"
"It says they buy Carbon Credits," she said. "Which are used to finance carbon reduction schemes."

Feeling very green indeed, Georgina immediately went out and bought one of the brand new, re-usable, Crouch End Shopping Bags. Meanwhile, I went into the studio and transferred all the photos from New York, Singapore and Hong Kong onto the PC. I spent the rest of Sunday afternoon fighting off jet lag and uploading the best snaps onto the Sowerby and Luff website.

HAPPY NEW YEAR

For the holiday season, we visited Georgina's parents and, after our recent travels, the long drive to North Yorkshire seemed faster and shorter than it had ever done before. Was the world actually shrinking around us, or were we just imagining it?

New Year's Eve was cold and frosty in Georgina's village. In front of a glowing log fire, at a minute to midnight, we joined hands to sing Auld Lang Syne, and Georgina whispered in my ear.
"So, when are we going to do it all again?" she said.
"I thought you didn't like flying," I replied.
"That was the *old* Georgina," she said.

They do say that it's "shared interests" that help to keep a relationship strong but, in the case of Georgina and myself, we've not only shared our passion for podcasting with each other, we've shared it with thousands of listeners around the world. The love and support those complete strangers have shown us has, without doubt, helped us get through some quite difficult periods in our relationship. In return, through our "talking bollocks", we hope we've been able to help a few of our listeners through equally challenging periods in their lives, and put a smile on their faces - if only for 40 minutes a week.

I think those three or four weeks in the autumn of 2007 changed both of us immeasurably. We discovered that there was life outside of the ordinary, that even the most ridiculous notions were achievable, and that the world was an infinitely more friendly and generous place than either of us had ever imagined. As far apart as New York and Hong Kong, our listeners had given up their time, their ingenuity, even their *beds* for us, in order to become part of our mad little podcasting club.

We simply cannot express our sheer wonderment at the generosity of strangers. Emails that turned into adventures. Ridiculous ideas that morphed into airline tickets. If you'd asked either of us at the beginning of 2007, "Will you be flying around the world this year?" the answer would have been laughter. But we did it. We followed our hearts and everything seemed to fall into place.

When Lord Kibble left us at Hong Kong Airport, Georgina cried. Not because she knew we'd made a friend for life, but because we'd made so many friends. It was as if a sudden realisation overwhelmed her. We'd shared the lives of so many who had emailed us to tell us their story, or to become a small part of ours. We'd shared with them our joys and sadnesses, and the long-distance friendship had been reciprocal, even though we'd made friends through the most random of connections.

Our daft little podcast had somehow become a symbol of optimism and friendship. All from a spare bedroom, 10 feet by 8 feet, in Crouch End.

As a direct result of our new-found podcasting celebrity, the following year was to see us embarking upon a whole lot of new activities. In the Summer of 2008 we were invited to present the live breakfast show at 96.3 Coast FM in North Wales, and our syndicated breakfast show "Brian and Georgina's Full English" found its way to local radio stations all over Europe. We also told the story of "Sex Tips for Pandas" as a nightly comedy show on the Edinburgh Fringe, and were able to meet up with many more of our regular listeners.

But, for the time being at least, that chilly New Year's Eve was the end of an adventure. After everyone had gone to bed, I poured myself a glass of whisky and checked our emails on the laptop.

From: "Charlie"
Subject: I haven't listened for months…

It's been hard dealing with school, work, football and the school musical. Not to mention, I've came out to my friends, and that has been really hard. My life has changed, but you have still been in my heart. I just want you to know that you guys get me through a lot, and your humour makes me feel like there are still people in this world that care about me. Your show doesn't just make people laugh, it makes their days better, and it makes them feel that they have something to hold on to.
From an old friend, Charlie.

I drowned the lump in my throat with a gulp of Famous Grouse, and took my iPod out of my pocket. I plugged in the headphones, and quietly listened once again to our podcast from Hong Kong. As the theme music played, I heard the lyrics of "Dreams of Piccadilly" as if for the very first time.

There is a place where dreams live…

Georgina appeared in the doorway, a blue toothbrush in her hand.
"Are you coming to bed?" she said.
"You know what?" I said. "With a bit of positive thinking, you really *can* discover a place where dreams live."
Georgina yawned. "Can't you come up with a better way to end a book than that?" she said.
"No," I replied.

Chapter 27
Three Years On

All of that happened three years ago. Wow, time flies. In this, the second edition of "Sex Tips for Pandas" we added a few photographs which weren't in the original edition. We also thought you might like to know what we've been up to since, so we've added this extra chapter.

Soon after returning from Hong Kong, we saw an advert in Media UK which said that a small community radio station called 102.8 Chorley FM were looking for presenters. I contacted them and they listened to a few of our podcasts.

We eventually agreed that we would record a weekly show for them, which would go out late at night during the week. We'd never done radio before so we had a lot of fun recording a series of shows for them. They then asked us to record some breakfast shows for them. which would be played out when their regular breakfast presenter was not on the air.

Around that time I went on one of my quiet little writing trips - this time to North Wales. I was staying in a small bed and breakfast near Penllech Bay, when my mobile phone rang. It was a chap called Steve Simms.

It turned out that Steve was the programme controller of a commercial radio station called Coast FM. He had been listening to a few of our podcasts and really liked what we did. He'd then visited our web site and seen that we were doing breakfast shows for Chorley FM.

"Would you like to come and cover the breakfast show at Coast FM next week?" he asked. "If it goes well I might have a permanent job for you. Between you and me, you're way better than some of the presenters I've got now!"

As you can imagine, this came as a bit of a shock. By a stagering coincidence, the Coast FM studios were only about 20 miles from where I was staying, so I said I'd jump in the car and drive up to meet Steve for dinner.

We sat in a Harvester restaurant and he practically offered myself and Georgina a job. We talked about money, we even talked about relocating from London to north Wales.

Georgina was very exited when I rang her and told her all about it.
"But do we really want to move out of London?" she asked.
"Do we want a breakfast show?" I replied.
"I suppose so," said Georgina. But not very convincingly.

We had about a week to prepare for the show. Steve told us that we could do all the same stuff on the radio as we normally did in the podcast, so "Things That are Nice To Say" and Dead Penguin were about to make their debut on local radio.

PLAYING WITH THE BIG BOYS

We arrived in Wales 24 hours before our first show, so that we could sit in with one of their DJs and I could learn how to drive the sound desk. They had already made a load of jingles for us, and Georgina set to work doing prep for the programme.

Because Coast FM were at that time a part of the Capital Radio Group, we had the same playlist and access to the same programme research as Johnny Vaughn had in London, so we were definitely now playing with the big boys.

Everything was going swimmingly until Steve asked me how many live shows we had done at Chorley FM.
"Oh, we don't do it live," I replied, "That show is recorded."
Steve looked a little worried, "So how many live radio shows have you done altogether?" he asked.
"None," I said.

The expression on Steve's face said it all. He had obviously believed that we had a whole lot more experience than we actually had. But it was too late for him to back out of his offer now. We were already in the studio.

"OK, I guess I'd better sit in with you, " he said.

The radio station booked us into a hotel opposite ths studios, and at four o'clock the following morning we crawled out of bed and staggered into work.

"Do you think we could do this every day?" I asked Georgina.

"I have no idea," she yawned.

I was absolutely terrified. Not of performing, I was used to that, but I had to press all the button as well. Records, jingles, news bulletins, weather updates, traffic reports - none of these things appear in a Sowerby & Luff podcast.

Steve insisted we call ourselves Brian & Georgina. "It's more friendly," he said.

The first show went OK. I only made a couple of mistakes, and Georgina was bright and lively despite the early hour. We went on the air at 6am and were live until 10am. It was the longest 4 hours of my life, but by far the most exciting.

After the show I had a bacon sandwich with Steve at the Burger Van outside the studio.

"How was it?" I asked.

"Not bad," he said. "Considering."

Our stint with Coast FM was very short. Too short, really. By the time we got the hang of it and were beginning to get pretty good at live radio it was over. Steve was very honest with us. He simply did not have the time to devote to training Sowerby & Luff to be radio personalities. He needed a breakfast presenter with way more experience, who could hit the ground running.

I disagree with him. I think that he had taken a punt on us we'd be on BBC radio by now. But it wasn't to be.

Soon afterwards, Coast FM were taken over by Heart FM and most of their local programmes became network shows. Then Steve left. So, our big radio break just sort of faded away.

Around the same time we were asked by a listener to produce a weekly podcast for a hedge fund company in the City of London. "Loz n Belly" features the Managing Director and the chief economist of GLC Limited. Every Monday they sit down together at Soho Studios and chat about the financial markets. Georgina directs the studio in the morning, and I edit the show in the afternoon.

The day before they recorded the first show, Lehman Brothers collapsed. So plenty to talk about there. The world economy has had a pretty tough ride ever since, but Loz n Belly has just recorded show 150, and is still going strong.

HI DI HI SEAS

One of the oddest jobs we've done since coming back from our Far East adventure involved getting on a ship and crossing the Atlantic.

One afternoon, while I was editing Loz n Belly, I got an email from an agent who booked acts for cruise ships. He said that he had been let down at the last minute by a man who gave talks about comedy on a Fred Olson ship called the Boudica. Would we like to do the job instead?

"What would we have to do?" I asked.
"Simple," he said. "You just have to give five 45 minute talks."
"How long do we have to spend on the ship?" I asked.
"Three weeks," he said.
"Where's the ship going?" I enquired.
"Barbados," he said.

"What???" screamed Georgina when I rang her and asked if she fancied three weeks in the Caribbean.
"How much do we have to pay?" she asked.
"They're paying us," I said.

So, we landed a dream job. But there's always a catch, isn't there? The catch on this job was that the passengers on the ship were mostly over seventy-five years old and not one of them had heard of podcasting. Neither had the ship's entertaiment manager, who looked and sounded exactly like Ted Bovis out of Hi Di Hi.
"What the hell is podcasting?" he asked me.
"It's what we're going to talk about in our act," I replied.
"You're going to crash and burn, son!" he said, and then he walked away smiling.

Ted was right. We crashed and burned during our first two lectures. I went into the ship's library and wrote three completely new talks. But it was too late. We turned up for our third talk, and we were the only ones there.

Luckily Fred Olson were not able to put us off at Barbados. They had to bring us home. So we still got a free three week holiday and a nice little fee. It was our most spectacular failure since the Svendborg Comedy Festival.

Then Georgina and I decided to do a show on the Edinburgh Fringe. Called "Sex Tips for Pandas" the idea was that we would perform the book on stage, while at the same time hosting a showcase of up and coming comedians.

We also planned to record every show and release a new podcast every single day of the 25 night Edinburgh run. Which was ambitious to say the least.

We booked ourselves into a Free Fringe venue called The Dragonfly and started to do warm up gigs on the London circuit. Richard Cray acted as our producer and began to book acts for the show.

Then, about two months before we were due to leave for Edinburgh, Georgina's dad died. We stayed in North Yorkshire for several weeks, and did our best to support Georgina's mum. It was an difficult and harrowing time for everyone. All thoughts of Edinburgh were forgotten.

About a week before the festival began, Georgina suddenly announced that we should go ahead and do the Edinburgh show. Since her dad had been a keen writer and actor himself, she was sure that he would have wanted us to go ahead and do it. I asked Georgina if she was absolutely sure, and she said yes.

The first couple of gigs in Edinburgh went really well. Then Georgina collapsed. Despite her determination to do the festival it was all too soon. She really hadn't yet recovered enough, either physically or mentally.

Georgina crawled into bed in our Edinburgh flat, and looked like she wouldn't be getting up for a very long time.

Richard had booked about 30 acts for the Edinburgh run, so we simply couldn't pull the plug on the show. We'd have been letting too many people down. I hosted the next three gigs on my own, and Richard Cray intrepidly manned the sound desk and continued to edit the daily podcasts.

Despite the way she was feeling, Georgina incredibly only missed five shows during that 25 night run. She slowly got back on top of performing again, and I think eventually it became good therapy for her, and helped her to cope with one of the most difficult and challenging times of her life.

Soon afterwards we started a new podcast series called Sowerby & Luff's Big Bang, which got a great response. It got nominated for a European Podcast Award, and was voted runner-up in the UK catagory. Inspired by this success we entered one of our specials "Brian & Georgina's Best Podcast Ever" for the Sony Radio Awards. But we didn't win.

The following year we were back in Edinburgh with another showcase called "Sowerby & Luff's All Stars". The plan was that we would compere the first week of the show then come back to London leaving the gig to be hosted by a variety of guest hosts.

This seemed like a good idea at the time, but turned out to be fairly disasterous. For a variety of reasons the producer Richard Cray fell out with the venue and with the guy who runs the Free Fringe - an old mate of mine called Peter Buckley Hill. It all ended in tears when Richard closed the show down with just two nights to go.

As well as specific security issues with the venue, Richard's complaint was that the Free Fringe was chaotic and badly run. I suppose I have to partly agree with him. It's not the slickest operation on the planet.

But two days later Peter Buckley Hill was presented with the prestigious Edinburgh Spirit of the Fringe Award. So he must have been doing something right. Richard Cray and I have not worked together since. Which is a pity.

We followed Big Bang with another series called Blah Blah Taxi, which I think we both reckoned to be our best podcast ever. It even had its own iPhone app, and all kinds of merchandise like T-shirts and baseball caps. The was even a Blah Blah Teddy Bear.

TAKING A BREAK

The following year we felt we needed a break from doing comedy podcasts, and instead embarked upon a series of more serious review shows. We reviewed travel, electronic goods, TV shows and apps.

It wasn't as much fun to record as Blah Blah Taxi, but we were asked to review numerous luxury hotels around the UK. So the summer of 2011 turned out to be a splendid one, with lots of four-poster beds and fine cuisine.

The listeners, however, never really took to The Review Programme, so after just 15 episodes we were persuaded to re-launch our comedy podcast. As a result, in September 2011 we brought out "Brian & Georgina's Fat Chance". And that just about brings us up to date.

We still keep in touch with Emily Gordon in the United States and Lord Kibble, who now runs a chicken farm in Australia. Maybe we'll go and visit him some time. I wonder if we can persuade a publisher to pay for the trip....

Appendix

1) Extract from *The Sowerby and Luff Show* [Ep21]

BRIAN: What's the next item on *Dead Penguin*, Georgina?

GEORGINA: On *Springwatch*, there was a brilliant clip of a swan being head-butted by a duck.

BRIAN: That was superb, wasn't it?

GEORGINA: I love that. "When Animals Attack!"

BRIAN: The duck was...

GEORGINA: Angry...

BRIAN: It was protecting its territory, wasn't it? 'Cause it had babies. And this swan was just innocently...

GEORGINA: Innocently meandering...

BRIAN: Swimming...

GEORGINA: Like swans do...

BRIAN: But it obviously wandered into the "No Fly Zone". Unwittingly. Like the Belgrano. It had sailed into this duck's territory, and before it knew what was happening, this fucking duck swooped down like a Stuka...

GEORGINA: Stuka?

BRIAN: Like a Luftwaffe Stuka...

GEORGINA: It was a Stuka Duck...

BRIAN: And from behind, it head-butted this swan…

GEORGINA: It was nasty…

BRIAN: On the back of the head…

GEORGINA: Yes.

BRIAN: It was one of the most sensational pieces of television I think I have ever seen! And as if to underline how spectacular it was…

GEORGINA: Yes…

BRIAN: They showed it again in slow motion.

GEORGINA: We watch too much TV. We should get out more.

BRIAN: We can't afford to get out more, Georgina. We're skint.

GEORGINA: Yes.

BRIAN: Georgina buys all her clothes from Cancer Research, you know. Never goes to a posh shop.

GEORGINA: I am the ultimate recycling machine. But I get designer clothes *from* the Cancer Research shop. You know the euphemism for second hand clothes?

BRIAN: No.

GEORGINA: Vintage. They even wear them to the Oscars now.

BRIAN: Ask me what I do with my old clothes.

GEORGINA: What do you do with your old clothes?

BRIAN: Wear them.

GEORGINA: He he.

BRIAN: This is an email from "Matt" – ooh, this is my favourite email ever...

GEORGINA: Your favourite email of all time?

BRIAN: If you remember, we were slagging off Harvester Restaurants recently, and Matt says "I *like* Harvester Restaurants, because if they didn't exist, then the restaurants I go to would be full of morons!"

GEORGINA: Excellent Matt, thank you.

BRIAN: Time for one more?

GEORGINA: OK, quick email from "Doctor Graham" – you know how he recently mentioned St Neot, and I said who's St Neot?

BRIAN: Mm.

GEORGINA: St Neot apparently "Began life as a soldier, but then renounced the marshal lifestyle to live in a monastery at Glastonbury".

BRIAN: OK.

GEORGINA: His bones were "housed in the priory, but were finally lost during the reign of Henry VIII."

BRIAN: That was very careless of them, wasn't it? How can you *lose* bones?

GEORGINA: I think you're related to Henry VIII, Brian, and are therefore, ultimately, responsible for the dissolution of the monasteries.

BRIAN: How can you *lose* bones???

GEORGINA: They'll have been in a little box...

BRIAN: So, at some point then, some monk was walking along the street and suddenly went "Aggghhh! Those bloody bones, I've left 'em on the tube!"

2) Extract from *Sowerby and Luff in New York*

BRIAN: We're in the Big Apple, and we've just been on the cruise haven't we?

GEORGINA: Yes, we cruised around Manhattan, and then we came back in a "semi-circular shape."

BRIAN: We did the "half-circular" tour, and it's the *only* way to see Manhattan. We were battling to try and get our photographs taken, because obviously we need *both* of us in a photograph. We were crammed onto the bow of this boat, going around the Brooklyn Bridge, and I said to this guy "Can you take our picture together?". And he took the camera, and he pointed it at us, and he said "Do you want Manhattan in the background?" There's no answer to that is there?

GEORGINA: "If you could pan around and just get sky please?"

BRIAN: We really liked the Health and Safety instructions that they gaved us. "When you get off the boat, get off on the side where the harbour is. Don't get off on the other side, and go into the river. During the tour, Manhattan will be on your left". So you think, hang on, are they telling people this because someone once went on that tour, and looked the wrong way...

GEORGINA: And missed Manhattan?

BRIAN: We also went to the Metropolitan Museum yesterday, didn't we?

GEORGINA: That was great.

BRIAN: It was top of your list of places to go.

GEORGINA: I like to be a bit of a culture vulture whatever city I'm in. That Temple Room was incredible.

BRIAN: Yes, the Americans really do it in style. If you go to the British Museum you get the occasional large sarcophagus. But the Americans took an *entire temple*. It's an amazing museum. But for some reason we couldn't find the Van Goghs….

GEORGINA: We couldn't…

BRIAN: But I liked the big black painting of nothing.

GEORGINA: What was it called Brian? What was the big black painting of nothing called?

BRIAN: It was called "Untitled". So, not only could the artist not be bothered to paint anything…

GEORGINA: He couldn't be bothered to title it either.

BRIAN: We walked up to the very end of Fifth Avenue, which has got a kind of small version of Marble Arch at the end of it. It's a great place to look out for "Crazies".

GEORGINA: Yes. There was a "Crazy" in the fountain.

BRIAN: A perfect example of a "New York Crazy". He was actually having his morning shower in the fountain. Almost naked.

GEORGINA: He kept his trousers on. His pants.

BRIAN: He dried himself off, then he spent about fifteen minutes randomly shouting at passers-by. No-one does "Crazies" better than New York.

GEORGINA: I know. They have it absolutely to a T don't they?

BRIAN: No-one does exhibitionism better than New Yorkers. There was also a girl with a hoop…

GEORGINA: A Hula Hoop. And she was just dancing, and a lot of people were watching.

BRIAN: As if to say, "Look at me, look at me! I'm dancing with a Hula Hoop!"

GEORGINA: I want to do something now. I want to buy a Hula Hoop now.

BRIAN: We walked up Fifth Avenue, and of course one of our missions while in New York was to buy a gift to take to the pandas.

GEORGINA: A fertility symbol...

BRIAN: For when we go to China in a couple of weeks time. And we stumbled across, in Greenwich Village, a great little thrift shop...

GEORGINA: A Salvation Army thrift shop.

BRIAN: So we had a little rummage around, and what should we stumble upon but a little fertility goddess.

GEORGINA: Isn't life wonderful that it gives you options like that.

BRIAN: It's about 20 centimetres tall, and it's an "Earth Fertility Goddess". A statue to the Rice Mother, which is an ancient Thai fertility symbol. So, we're going to take something from Thailand, to China....

GEORGINA: Right. Via New York...

BRIAN: And it will help the pandas to mate, I'm certain it will. It says that the Rice Mother becomes pregnant "when rice flowers bloom", and that she "delights in the scented powder received from the stamen" and she "swells of its fertilisation" – much like a pregnant woman.

GEORGINA: That's gotta help.

BRIAN: So that is what we're going to be taking to Hong Kong with us, and we'll be presenting that officially to the director of Ocean Park Zoo.

3) Extract from *Sowerby and Luff in Singapore*

BRIAN: We've just arrived at Swan Lake Gazebo, in the middle of the park in Singapore.

GEORGINA: There's a huge statue of swans in the middle of it. The famous Black Swans of the Botanical Gardens.

BRIAN: I'll bet you there's mosquitos. *[Reads from sign]* "This gazebo was built in the 1850's, and stood for many years in the grounds of old Admiralty house." That's going back to the days of the British Empire. "In 1969 it was dismantled and re-erected at the entrance to the rain forest." This is the *rain forest*?

GEORGINA: We're very near the Equator, Brian. In fact as close to the Equator as I've ever been in my life

BRIAN: We're virtually standing on the Equator, Georgina.

GEORGINA: Can we try that thing to see if the toilet bowl flushes clockwise or anti-clockwise?

BRIAN: I think on the Equator it just goes straight down. Email us, heading your email "I know which way the water goes down the toilet bowl..."

GEORGINA: ...on the Equator!

BRIAN: We got an email this morning from "Billy Boy" in France, who's actually sent us a picture of a Boeing 767 painted like a panda.

GEORGINA: Lovely. And it's Nippon Airways.

BRIAN: It seem that Nippon Airways, in order to celebrate their anniversary, have painted all their 767's like pandas.

GEORGINA: I think what they're actually doing is celebrating the fact that Sowerby and Luff are going to have breakfast with pandas in Hong Kong.

BRIAN: Had we known that there was such a thing as a panda jumbo jet, then I think we would have tried to fly to Hong Kong by Nippon Airways.

GEORGINA: I'd love to have been inside a Giant Panda.

BRIAN: Mm.

GEORGINA: On our aeroplane I had "Weird Elbow Man" next to me. He kept nudging me in the ribs with a very bony elbow. And you know me, I'm a tenacious little pit-bull. So I kept nudging him back. We had a "War of Elbows" for the entire twelve hour flight.

BRIAN: Last night at the hotel we were watching what has become our favourite Japanese game show…

GEORGINA: Yes, we went to bed at 10.30pm and at half past twelve we were still watching this mad programme…

BRIAN: We don't know what it was actually called, but we called it *Name That Fruit*, because it seemed to be just a whole load of contestants looking at pictures of fruit…

GEORGINA: Slices of fruit…

BRIAN: And trying to guess what they were.

GEORGINA: One was a tomato.

BRIAN: Japanese television's fantastic isn't it?

GEORGINA: And a big hands up to the people on Japanese television who were telling us at what temperature cats ate their food.

BRIAN: Oh yes..

GEORGINA: Apparently, if you put a really hot bowl of cat food in front of a cat it knows by instinct when to start eating it. It doesn't have to put its paw in. And do you know what the temperature is that cats will start eating hot food?

BRIAN: What?

GEORGINA: Sixty one degrees. You heard it here first on *The Sowerby and Luff Show*.

BRIAN: We had to come half way around the world to learn that a cat eats its food if its below sixty one degrees?

GEORGINA: Singapore's very clean isn't it?

BRIAN: They call this place the "Fine City", because you can get fined for everything. You can get fined $1000 for chucking litter.

GEORGINA: But there are so many cleaners that if you dropped a cigarette, I think there would be someone to catch it before it reached the ground.

BRIAN: Our favourite story about how clean they are over here is the "Pissing in the Lift Story."

GEORGINA: You're not allowed to urinate in lifts.

BRIAN: This was a huge problem here. And what they actually did in order to stop it was they hid a camera in a lift in a hotel...

GEORGINA: A heat-sensitive camera...

BRIAN: So that when people started pissing, the heat of their urine on the floor...

GEORGINA: Triggered a camera!

BRIAN: But they didn't just fine them. They took all of the pictures, and they put them on the front page of one of the Singapore newspapers.

GEORGINA: Yep. They did indeed.

BRIAN: So they were not only charged, but they were also humiliated as well.

GEORGINA: And I think quite a lot of things here are punishable by death.

BRIAN: We've just had lunch in a little Chinese restaurant, where I had jellyfish for the first time. Bit like octopus, but a bit more chewy. I wouldn't have it again.

GEORGINA: But its good to say you've had it once.

BRIAN: Yes. What did you have for breakfast this morning?

GEORGINA: I had beef burgers with curry soup, and I also had Duck Porridge.

BRIAN: Duck Porridge?

GEORGINA: I chose the Duck Porridge over the Frog Porridge.

BRIAN: I'm quite dull. Wherever I am in the world I tend to have scrambled eggs and bacon. But they seem to have a problem with getting hold of streaky bacon.

GEORGINA: Maybe there aren't any streaky pigs out here.

BRIAN: We got an email today from Roger O'Donnell in Massachusetts...

GEORGINA: How far is that?

BRIAN: 12,000 miles away, Georgina. Roger has actually sent us something about the pandas at Santiago Zoo.

GEORGINA: They're doing quite well aren't they?

BRIAN: Yes. The pandas names are Bei Yun and Gau Gau. They've only mated three times since 2003, but remarkably they've been successful on *every* occasion. Gau Gau has a 100% hit rate, and they've had three babies. At Santiago they call Gau Gau a "One Shot Guy." Maybe the luck from Santiago Zoo will rub off on us. And of course, we do have the Thai Fertility Goddess which we bought in that thrift shop…

GEORGINA: In New York.

BRIAN: And we'll be presenting that to the head of Hong Kong Zoo in just four days time.

GEORGINA: I can feel myself getting moist already.

4) From *Sowerby and Luff in Hong Kong*

BRIAN: Georgina and I are very excited because we've just arrived in the panda enclosure at Ocean Park in Hong Kong. We're here with Ocean Park's PR person Gillian Cheng, who's showing us around, and the pandas Le Le and Ying Ying are just arriving for their breakfast.

GEORGINA: Gillian, you were given two young pandas, and you already have two fully grown pandas. Have any of the pandas actually mated successfully in Ocean Park?

GILLIAN: Not yet. Those two big pandas are too old.

GEORGINA: Too old to mate?

GILLIAN: And these two here are too young. They are not mature enough to fertilize.

BRIAN: Did you notice on the roof of this building when we came in that there were two *giant*, Giant Pandas!

GEORGINA: Even more *giant* than the giants.

BRIAN: Fifty foot tall pandas. So huge that you could see them from space. So there's no doubting that this *is* the panda enclosure.

GEORGINA: Oh yes.

BRIAN: The pandas are now entering the enclosure. Here comes Le Le.

GEORGINA: It's French.

BRIAN: At the moment the pandas are at the back of the enclosure. They're looking towards us. They're looking towards the bamboo...

GEORGINA: Are they a bit shy do you think?

BRIAN: Gillian was saying that they're quite used to being looked at – to being on camera – so I don't think they're shy...

GEORGINA: They're just not hungry.

BRIAN: They're taking their time. Do you think they have to bring a "blue voucher" with them like we do at the hotel? A breakfast voucher?

GEORGINA: That's what they're doing now. They're very domesticated. They're very docile. They're chatting away with the keeper.

BRIAN: They are, yes. But they don't seem to want their breakfast for some reason. I wonder why that is. Because they've got a direct eyeline to the bamboo now.

GEORGINA: You know why don't you? Because they're going to have to walk all the way down here - at least a two foot high hill - in order to get the bamboo.

BRIAN: And also because we're here.

GEORGINA: He's going back to bed. He can't be bothered with the bamboo.

BRIAN: No.

GEORGINA: So Le Le is the panda equivalent of Brian Luff. He's gone back to sleep.

BRIAN: The bamboo can wait.

GEORGINA: Even when they're playing with the toys, they exert the *least* amount of energy possible, don't they?

BRIAN: Ying Ying has now come over and sat right in front of us. Georgina's only a few feet away taking some pictures. Gillian, how old are these ones?

GILLIAN: Two years.

GEORGINA: There's something very endearing about the way they loll. They sit a bit like Brian on the sofa when he's watching television.

BRIAN: Incredibly relaxed, aren't they.

GEORGINA: They are. Very chilled. Gillian, how many visitors do you get to see the pandas?

GILLIAN: We just got the total visitors for the park, and last year we got 4.92 million.

GEORGINA: Wow! That's a lot of people visiting pandas.

BRIAN: Ying Ying is now looking directly at Georgina. We have direct eye contact with the pandas.

GEORGINA: We have. It's winning me over. It's charming me with its come-hither eyes.

BRIAN: Yes. OK, we're going to leave the pandas to their breakfast now...

MUSIC STING

BRIAN: We're now here with Suzanne Gendron, who is the – let me get this right – you're the Director of Zoological Operations and Education?

SUZANNE: Well, I'm actually the *Executive* Director of Zoological Operations...

BRIAN: I was so close...

SUZANNE: Also the Conservation Foundation.

BRIAN: OK, well anyone who's been listening to *The Sowerby and Luff Show* for a long time will know about our obsession with pandas.

GEORGINA: It's become an obsession with me.

BRIAN: And we've spent a long time talking about them - particularly about their mating habits.

GEORGINA: And about our concern for them.

BRIAN: So we've come 6,000 miles, to the other side of the world, and we have just presented to Suzanne, our gift...

GEORGINA: A gift from the people of Great Britain...

BRIAN: The gift is for Ying Ying and Le Le. Suzanne, we're told they're too young to mate at the moment, how long before we can expect them to get "loved up"?

SUZANNE: It'll probably be about three more years.

BRIAN: OK.

SUZANNE: Typically they're over four years old, and their birthday is in August. And typically the breeding season is February and March. The very unusual habit of pandas is that there's only three days a year when each individual female is absolutely receptive. Therefore, they have to make sure that in the wild the males and the females can be in the same place.

BRIAN: Mm.

SUZANNE: And "habitat fragmentation" means that within the bamboo forest - where the pandas are - if its broken up by streets and villages and farms they may not be able to get to each other in that short window of time. It's usually a couple of weeks beforehand that they'll start announcing "Hey, times comin'!"

BRIAN: Mm.

SUZANNE: That is what one of the big challenges is for reproduction success in the wild. With pandas under human care, in Zoological facilities such as Ocean Park, the opportunities for the two pandas to be together is highly likely. But not all pandas are compatible with each other...

BRIAN: That was going to be my next question. How are these two getting on with each other?

SUZANNE: They're doing quite well. They were chosen because from birth they were compatible animals. They seemed to play together well. When we first met them in March of this year they even had "sexual play" as part of their repertoire.

BRIAN: Do they flirt?

SUZANNE: Ah, they *do* flirt!

GEORGINA: Brilliant!

BRIAN: That's amazing. Panda flirting.

GEORGINA: How can you tell when a panda is flirting?

SUZANNE: There's posturing by the female, that shows she's receptive, and there are behaviours that show that he is also interested. But these two are still too young to know "follow-through", or be mature.

BRIAN: If we hear in about two years time that these pandas have successfully mated, we will completely take the credit for that. The Chinese are very into luck aren't they?

GEORGINA: Everything here has a good luck charm. But three days of the year is a really fine line, isn't it? Is there something that we, as humans, can help them with?

SUZANNE: Well, there's a number of things. Good nutrition is probably the biggest success. The other key is… they're solitary animals, so they're not going to be living side by side in the same exhibit when they're sexually mature. They'll more than likely be in separate enclosures, which makes them more comfortable. So for us to know when to put them together, we'll be watching the urinary hormones – because they'll start to increase. We'll be watching her behaviour. She'll start scent marking. She'll start bleating, and making a noise like… [Suzanne makes a bleating noise like a female panda]

BRIAN: That's very good. Do that again.

SUZANNE: (Slightly flirtily): Maybe later. But I wouldn't want to get Le Le over-excited.

BRIAN: We must just ask you this, because it's something that one of our listeners spotted about a year ago. One of the zoos that have pandas actually said that they were showing the pandas videos of other pandas mating, in order to show them what to do. Is that true? Or is that just an urban myth?

SUZANNE: Actually that's true. At one point, about five to ten years ago, when success of panda breeding under human care was so low, they were trying *everything*. One of the thoughts was that because the cubs had been rescued from the wild – they'd lost they mothers – they had grown up without having any "learned behaviour" from watching mom and a male. That possibly that was what was causing this problem.

BRIAN: Mm.

SUZANNE: So, could we show them videos and have them learn that way? But videos also have sound, and that sound can also trigger… But really what appears to be the biggest trigger is if you have a receptive female – the hormones and the urine – and you have that on a piece of cloth. Then that is something that is going to be able to trigger the male.

BRIAN: Is it very competitive the panda breeding business? Are you now really gutted that Santiago Zoo are one step ahead of you? Is there a sense of competition here?

SUZANNE: We all have one goal. That is to ensure the pandas survive.

BRIAN: You're all on the same team.

SUZANNE: We work very, very closely with Santiago.

BRIAN: You're exchanging notes? You're helping each other as much as possible.

SUZANNE: But there is keen competition in panda breeding *between* the pandas themselves. And this is what's exciting. The female will do her bleating - she'll do her scent marking - and she'll start to get the males aroused and attracted from her region. They'll come and compete for her, and she will take the strongest.

BRIAN: How many of them are left now in the wild? Just how scary is it in terms of protecting them?

SUZANNE: The numbers are 1,700. But that is an improvement over 1,000 in the eighties.

BRIAN: I was intrigued to find out that your new panda house here has been partly funded by the Jockey Club. So, ironically, every time someone puts a bet on at Happy Valley, and loses, the pandas are getting the money. We think that's fantastic.

GEORGINA: We do. Gambling supports pandas.

BRIAN: We were there on Wednesday night...

GEORGINA: We lost...

BRIAN: And we probably contributed quite a lot.

GEORGINA: I think we probably paid for that bamboo we've just seen them eating.

BRIAN: So is that similar to the lottery funding we see in the UK, I suppose?

SUZANNE: That was a one-off gift to build this original building, and we are very grateful.

GEORGINA: In a 24 hour period, how many hours would a panda sleep?

SUZANNE: About twelve to twelve and a half hours. So slightly more than human.

GEORGINA: Not an awful lot more than you [Brian] though...

BRIAN: Maybe that's why the panda has become so popular on our programme, maybe it's because..

GEORGINA: You've turned into a panda?

BRIAN: So, Suzanne, thanks a million for taking the time to talk to us on *The Sowerby and Luff Show*. We are absolutely convinced that these two pandas are going to become the most successful breeding pandas on the planet, thanks to our Thai Fertility Goddess. This little statue comes from Thailand, but we actually bought it in New York…

GEORGINA: It's been around the world.

BRIAN: It's been all the way from Thailand to New York to Hong Kong, and we think that it's been gathering luck along the way.

SUZANNE: It'll be a very interesting study to see what happens next year in all those places you've passed through.

BRIAN: It could make a difference…

GEORGINA: With our little goddess…

BRIAN: And I think if we are successful we could be in great demand.

GEORGINA: As fertility symbol givers.

BRIAN: We could go to Santiago…

GEORGINA: They don't need our help.

BRIAN: Thanks Suzanne.

SUZANNE: It's been my pleasure.

BRIAN: This is Sowerby and Luff.

MUSIC STING

BRIAN: Have you had a good time in Hong Kong Georgina?

GEORGINA: I don't want to go home.

BRIAN: It's snowing in London, you know that don't you?

GEORGINA: It's 4 degrees in London, it's 25 degrees here. I want to stay.

BRIAN: Yes, we're sitting in the sunshine outside Ocean Park Zoo in Hong Kong, but we're heading off home tomorrow. Once again a huge, huge thank you to all the people who have made it possible for us to be here in Asia.

The Authors

Brian Luff and Georgina Sowerby have been writing and producing comedy together for 8 years, and they present one of the UK's most critically acclaimed podcasts. They have also presented breakfast shows at Sony Award-winning Coast 96.3 and for 102.8 Chorley FM, as well as syndicating their programmes to numerous radio stations around Europe and appearing live in Edinburgh.

Brian started his career as a journalist for ITV. He was a commissioned writer on Simon Pegg's first TV sketch show We Know Where You Live, and he co-wrote and produced the cult Channel 4 and MTV comedy series Pets. Brian's novel Sex On Legs scored a world first in 2006, when it became a premium download audiobook without first going into print. He has since edited the BBC comedy website and produced interactive content for The Mighty Boosh, The Peter Serafinowicz Show and Q.I.

A former actress and more recently an account manager for Saatchi and Saatchi, Georgina organizes regular comedy scriptwriting workshops for Bull Comedy, and has written sketches for the award-winning Mensch Markus Show in Germany, as well as contributing articles for North magazine and Podcast User. Since 2003 she has produced one of London's longest-running fringe comedy shows Sketch Club and in 2006 she co-created the chart-topping viral movie Mark Your Territory for Maverick Films. Georgina once worked as the press officer for Viagra, and has featured in a pop video with Blur. But she can't remember which one it was.

Sowerby and Luff Quotes

"Blazing a trail for the new medium" DAILY MAIL

"This very funny podcast has maintained a consistent presence in the iTunes podcast chart" TIME OUT

"One of the most popular podcasts on the planet!" LONDON LITE

"Best comedy podcast" METRO

"You two are very funny" TRACEY ULLMAN

"Georgina Sowerby and Brian Luff's weekly comedy podcast, live from a pub in North London, has apparently been downloaded over three million times. It's not a sketch show and it's not stand-up comedy - so what is it, and why is it so popular? Well, Georgina and Brian talk fluent twaddle. That's it. Like all the best kinds of reality radio, it's the fizz between the couple that provides the entertainment. In a recent webisode: "Hens who live on volcanoes, and 18,000 mummified cats..." RADIO TIMES

"Hilarious!" MAC FORMAT

"Brilliant!" PODCAST USER

"Brian Luff changed the face of publishing for ever this week when his novel, *Sex on Legs*, became the first to be published only as a podcast, the online audio sensation that has changed the face of listening for ever" THE GUARDIAN

"Big hitters on the scene" SUNDAY TIMES

"Very funny show" ABOUT: PODCASTING